STRATEGIZING AGAINST SWEATSHOPS

Matthew S. Williams

STRATEGIZING AGAINST SWEATSHOPS

The Global Economy, Student Activism, and Worker Empowerment

TEMPLE UNIVERSITY PRESS

Philadelphia • *Rome* • *Tokyo*

TEMPLE UNIVERSITY PRESS
Philadelphia, Pennsylvania 19122
tupress.temple.edu

Library of Congress Cataloging-in-Publication Data

Names: Williams, Matthew S., 1974– author.
Title: Strategizing against sweatshops : the global economy, student
   activism, and worker empowerment / Matthew S. Williams.
Description: Philadelphia : Temple University Press, [2020] | Includes
   bibliographical references and index. | Summary: "Tells the story of how
   the student anti-sweatshop movement on US college campuses was able to
   coordinate a massive change in strategy in response to new labor tactics
   undertaken by target garment industry corporations. Demonstrates
   that a decentralized movement can coordinate in response to changing
   opportunities."—Provided by publisher.
Identifiers: LCCN 2019011975 (print) | LCCN 2019980629 (ebook) |
   ISBN 9781439918210 (cloth : alk. paper) | ISBN 9781439918227
   (paperback : alk. paper) | ISBN 9781439918234 (ebook)
Subjects: LCSH: United Students Against Sweatshops. | Anti-sweatshop
   movement—United States. | Student movements—United States. | College
   students—Political activity—United States. | Sweatshops. | Clothing trade. |
   Employee rights. | Social justice.
Classification: LCC HD2337 .W55 2019 (print) | LCC HD2337 (ebook) | DDC
   331.25/6—dc23
LC record available at https://lccn.loc.gov/2019011975
LC ebook record available at https://lccn.loc.gov/2019980629

♾ The paper used in this publication meets the requirements of the American National
Standard for Information Sciences—Permanence of Paper for Printed Library Materials,
ANSI Z39.48-1992

Printed in the United States of America

9 8 7 6 5 4 3 2 1

To the members of MRAP for
helping me survive grad school

Contents

Preface: The Continuing Relevance of Progressive Student
Activism in an Age of Right-Wing Populism   ix

Acknowledgments   xxi

1   Introduction: Theorizing Social Movement Strategy   1

I   POLITICAL OPPORTUNITY STRUCTURES

2   Globalization, the Apparel Industry, and the Roots of
Sweatshops   35

3   Higher Education as a Political Opportunity Structure   45

II   AN ANATOMY OF UNITED STUDENTS AGAINST SWEATSHOPS (USAS)

4   The Origins of USAS   57

5   USAS's Campus-Level Strategy   66

6   USAS's Ideology of Worker Empowerment   77

7   The Organization of USAS   85

III CYCLES OF CONTENTION AND STRATEGIC INNOVATION

 8 The Brands Strike Back: Corporate Social Responsibility and
    the Creation of the Fair Labor Association   97

 9 The Creation of the Worker Rights Consortium (WRC)   115

10 Embedded Autonomy and the Fire Alarm Model:
    The Organization and Monitoring Practices of the WRC   130

11 Transnational Solidarity Campaigns   145

12 The Designated Suppliers Program   181

13 SweatFree Communities   203

14 Conclusion   223

    Appendix: Methods and Data   237

    References   241

    Index   257

Preface

The Continuing Relevance of
Progressive Student Activism in an Age
of Right-Wing Populism

In this book, I examine the evolution of the strategy of the U.S. anti-sweatshop movement, focusing on the period from the mid-1990s to 2007 (when I conducted my research), with special attention to three groups organized, supported, or inspired by U.S. college students: United Students Against Sweatshops (USAS), the Worker Rights Consortium (WRC), and SweatFree Communities. USAS in particular was a dynamic force, taking advantage of the particularities of the social environment on college campuses to effectively advance the cause of workers' rights in sweatshops around the world. In part, this book explores how the college campus facilitates such activism. While the vagaries of my life and career intervened between my research in 2007 and the publication of this book, my findings have much to tell us about activism today, particularly the continuing power and relevance of progressive student activism. This includes student activism on labor issues in a political climate in which right-wing populists seem to have co-opted much of the white working class in the United States. While I focus on USAS in this book, it is only one of the student activist groups that have leveraged the distinct features of college campuses to advance progressive causes. In fact, the college campus remains a crucial site for the advancement of social justice activism in response to the current resurgence of right-wing activism, even as conservative activists and political leaders work to make the campus a contested environment for progressives.

The case study of anti-sweatshop activism explored in this book is strik-ing because it took place in a context in which the labor movement in the United States and globally had weakened. Indeed, the decline of orga-nized labor has been intimately tied to the rise of sweatshops. The ability of business owners to move production from locations with strong labor unions, such as the northeastern United States, to sweatshops overseas, where unions were weak or nonexistent and labor laws were poor or un-enforced, played a major role in undermining organized labor. In many cases, business owners were able simply to move sites of operation away from strong unions. Even when they did not physically relocate produc-tion, the threat of doing so could extract significant concessions from once strong unions. Even when sunk costs would, in reality, prevent busi-ness owners from relocating production, the threat of moving was a pow-erful management tool, since workers were in no position to know for sure whether such threats were empty or real (Anner 2011; Luce 2014; Moody 1997).

Moreover, in many places, including the United States, organized labor contributed to its own decline. Many labor leaders clung to models of unionization that, problematic even in their heyday, now actively un-dermined the labor movement's ability to respond to these developments. In many cases, in the period following World War II and during the con-solidation of the welfare state, the labor movement had ceased to be a true movement, growing close to and comfortable with those in power, both in business and in government. In the United States, this took the form of what is known as "business unionism," where labor leaders saw the job of the unions not as challenging business and trying to alter the balance of class power in society, but as acting as its junior partner in a system of cross-class collaboration for the betterment of businesses and their em-ployees. Most U.S. unions focused on ensuring that their members re-ceived benefits, such as health care, pensions, and higher wages, rather than concerning themselves with the fate of nonunionized members of the working class—one of the contributing factors to the lack of national health care in the United States today (Fantasia and Voss 2004; Luce 2014; Moody 1997).

In many developing countries, labor unions had a clientelist relation-ship with those in power, providing labor support in return for material benefits for the unions—but again without an alteration in the balance of class power. Labor union leaders would subordinate the union's agenda to that of the state or an established political party, supporting their patrons by mobilizing people to vote for them in elections, rallying people behind their policies, and such. In return, the union would be rewarded with various benefits from the elites controlling the state. In the better cases, frequently under authoritarian populist regimes, such benefits extended to all members of those labor unions that remained loyal to state power holders and resulted in an increased standard of living for much of the working class, but at the long-term cost of its demobilization and disempowerment. In the most corrupt cases, the benefits extended to only those in control of the union, with the rank and file left out in the cold as union leaders lined their pockets with members' dues (Anner 2011; Moody 1997; Skidmore and Smith 2005).

Such accommodationist approaches, whether in the United States or the Global South, meant that, when business owners turned against organized labor, abandoning the old collaborative or clientelist relationships and attempting to undermine any power the unions held, old-guard labor leaders were unprepared to respond. Instead of developing new strategies, many old-guard union leaders further undermined the power of organized labor by clinging to models that no longer worked. In some cases, old-guard leaders were unable to grasp the scope of the situation, mistakenly believing that the assault by business on organized labor was a temporary phenomenon that would cease when the economy improved. In some cases, old-guard leaders may have feared that an innovative approach to unionism would result in loss of their power, with organizing drives bringing in new members who might vote in new leaders (Fantasia and Voss 2004; Luce 2014; Moody 1997).

There have been two responses to this crisis of organized labor. The first has consisted of various attempts from within to revitalize the labor movement, reform existing unions, start new unions, develop strategies that respond to the new circumstances labor finds itself in globally, and return organized labor to its roots as a social justice movement. The second has consisted of moves by right-wing populists to step into the void left by the decline of organized labor, co-opting elements of the working class by appealing to legitimate grievances and fears through scapegoating other vulnerable, marginalized social groups and empowering charismatic, authoritarian leaders—sometimes people drawn from the very class of business leaders actively undermining labor rights and the living standards of the working class. In the United States, this second trend is most obviously visible in the 2016 election of Donald Trump to the presidency with the support of large portions of the white working class, especially in the deindustrialized Rust Belt region. But Trump's election is best understood as symptomatic of a wider trend that goes back decades before Trump became engaged in politics.

The revitalization of segments of organized labor as a labor movement is often referred to as "social movement unionism" or "community unionism." In this conception of unions, labor leaders focus on aggressively organizing new constituencies—often groups that historically have been at the margins of both society and organized labor, such as women, people of color, and immigrants—while adopting new, more confrontational strategies to improve conditions for workers. To do so, labor unions increasingly partner with other progressive groups, including civil rights activists, progressive religious congregations, community organizing groups, and student activists. In such campaigns, the goal is not just to put in place policies that benefit union members but also to fight to protect members of the working class more broadly and build broad-based movements for social justice (Fantasia and Voss 2004; Luce 2014; Moody 1997). Although much of the discussion of social movement unionism has focused on the alliances built within the United States, for many segments of the labor movement, it has also included building new alliances globally, including supporting the anti-sweatshop movement and trying to raise labor standards for all workers globally (Luce 2014; Moody 1997). The activist groups that are the focus of this book—USAS, the WRC, and SweatFree Communities—are an important part of this global movement. The struggles of these groups and their allies to coordinate and strategize collectively must be understood as a central element of the growing movement to organize for workers' rights worldwide. The dynamics of coordination among these various groups of protestors are therefore essential to understanding the workings of not only the student anti-sweatshop movement but also student movements and workers' rights movements more broadly.

Even as labor activists and their allies seek to revitalize the labor movement, they must contend with the rise of right-wing populist movements that appropriate working-class grievances. This rise has been facilitated by the fact that many historically left-of-center parties—including the Democratic Party in the United States under the influence of the Democratic Leadership Council (the "New Democrats" such as Bill Clinton, Barack Obama, and Hillary Clinton)—have increasingly embraced the very neoliberal ("free market") policies that undermine the standard of living of their working-class base and unions' ability to exercise power, leaving many white working-class people disaffected and open to recruitment by the right. For instance, Democratic president Bill Clinton played a central role in the passage of the North American Free Trade Agreement, which facilitated the movement of production by U.S. businesses to sweatshops in Mexico. This turn to the right by its traditional political allies has significantly weakened the U.S. labor movement and increasingly alienated working-class voters from the Democratic Party (Frank 2004; Fraser 2017).

This situation has helped right-wing populists capture the loyalty of white working-class people. Populist rhetoric and movements have a long history in the United States, on both the left and the right. Populism involves championing an ill-defined group, "the people," who are characterized as producers—productive contributors to the economy—and pitting them against people who are characterized as nonproductive, parasitic members of society. While in left-wing populism activists defined large capitalists as nonproductive enemies of society, in right-wing populism capitalists are counted among the productive classes, as entrepreneurs and job creators. Right-wing populists have instead traditionally characterized socially marginalized groups such as poor people, people of color, and welfare recipients as idle and a drain on the nation's resources. In the period following the social upheavals of the 1960s, right-wing populists also increasingly targeted vaguely defined, out-of-touch, amoral liberal elites as controlling the government, the media, and higher education and seeking to impose their values on ordinary, traditional Americans (Kazin 1995). Thus, populism and the contestation of who can speak for "the people" have a long history in the United States. Since the 1960s, student activist groups on both the left and the right have participated in this conflict. Therefore, understanding the successful strategies that campus activists have developed over the decades is important to considering the future of political activism and movement building in the United States.

In the 1970s, U.S. conservative leaders began harnessing right-wing populism as a way to undermine white working-class support for liberal policies. U.S. conservatism comprises several distinct but interwoven ideological strands. What unites them is not, contrary to common rhetoric, support for small government. Instead, as Sara Diamond (1995) argues, conservative politics involve opposition to the use of the state as a means of redistributing resources but support for a strong, even repressive, state in maintaining social order. For the purposes of this brief overview, the two most important elements of contemporary U.S. conservatism are free market libertarianism and moral traditionalism. The free market strand of conservative thought sees ownership of private property as the foundation of individual liberty. Therefore, the state should act to protect private property. However, libertarians view any taxation that goes beyond what is needed to provide this level of order and security as an immoral theft of people's property. Thus, they oppose welfare programs and the like, which seek to foster some minimal redistribution of resources to the poor. Moral traditionalists add to this a belief that the state should act to uphold traditional morality by promoting the central public role of religion, particularly Christianity, and conservative norms around gender roles and sexuality, such as opposition to abortion and gay marriage (Diamond 1995; Horwitz 2013).

The paradox of right-wing populism is that it represents itself as opposing the establishment while it actually supports many aspects of the political establishment and the historical privileges of the dominant social groups in U.S. society—for example, Christians, whites, men, heterosexuals, and those who are well-to-do (Dietrich 2014; Horwitz 2013). While right-wing populism is often represented as primarily a white working-class phenomenon, much of its leadership, in fact, comes from the white middle class. Nonetheless, it holds strong appeal for many white working-class people, who historically supported the Democratic Party and the protections for labor unions and working-class people that it promoted (Hardisty 1999). As the leadership of the Democratic Party moved to the right on economic issues, working-class people increasingly found little reason to support it. At the same time, by moving to the left on issues of race relations, gender roles, and sexuality—supporting affirmative action, abortion rights, gay rights, and so on—the Democratic Party leadership alienated many socially conservative white working-class people (Fraser 2017; Hardisty 1999). The New Democrats foolishly assumed that white working-class people would have nowhere else to go (Frank 2004). But, of course, many members of the white working and middle classes simply stopped voting. And others were drawn to right-wing populism, as conservative leaders tapped into the resentments of white working-class and downwardly mobile white middle-class people about the changing social terrain by appropriating the language of social conflict and anti-elitism that traditionally had been the territory of the left. The conservative leadership did so by scapegoating poor welfare recipients, people of color, immigrants, feminists, secular humanists, and LGBTQ people as the sources of the nation's problems, including the economic hardships that downwardly mobile members of the working and middle classes increasingly faced (Fraser 2017; Hardisty 1999). Thus, right-wing leaders squared the circle of anti-establishment conservatism by falsely painting liberals and members of historically oppressed groups as the new establishment, threatening the rights and freedoms of socially conservative, Christian, heterosexual, white working- and middle-class people. They appealed to the sense of traditional morality among white working- and middle-class people—including respect for traditional, oppressive hierarchies of race, gender, religion, and the like—to secure their support for the very neoliberal economic policies that undermined their economic security and left them feeling vulnerable and exploited by the elite.

It is worth stressing that, although some right-wing populist groups and leaders engage in explicit hate mongering, others do not. Even as conservative leaders play on privileged groups' fears of the loss of their privileges, they often avoid the use of language that is explicitly bigoted and instead use language that is nominally inclusive. Instead of explicitly attacking people of color, for example, they use coded language that criticizes welfare recipients and urban crime, playing into negative stereotypes about blacks and Latinos. While they attack undocumented immigrants, they leave open the possibility that immigrants might become "real Americans" if they immigrated legally and assimilated culturally. This allows people in right-wing movements to view themselves as tolerant and inclusive, working for the common good (Dietrich 2014; Hardisty 1999). People who are drawn to right-wing populism typically feel as though liberal elites—people in federal government agencies, Hollywood, and academia—hold their adherence to conservative religious values on issues of gender and sexuality in contempt. In their view, having worked hard and played by the rules, they are entitled to a piece of the American dream of economic success. But, instead, even as the American dream becomes harder to achieve, they see liberal social policies as allowing other groups whom they view as not having worked as hard, such as immigrants and people of color, to cut in front of the line and leave white working- and middle-class people behind (Hochschild 2016b). While playing to this perception, right-wing populists in general, and President Trump in particular, set themselves up as saviors (Hochschild 2016a).

The solution to the growth of right-wing populism is progressive movement building, not only stressing issues of economic exploitation and class conflict but also incorporating broad-based considerations of how different forms of oppression interact and intersect. Activists need to emphasize that far from causing white working-class people's economic hardship, poor people, welfare recipients, people of color, immigrants, and LGBTQ people are facing the same struggles. Such coalition building is hard work, but those who promote social movement unionism are already actively undertaking it. Student groups are often important partners in such coalitions.

In this context, progressive student activism, including that of groups such as USAS, is crucial. Despite the general rightward shift of politics in the country as a whole and the growth of populist conservative activism on college campuses in particular, often with the intent of quashing progressive groups, the distinct characteristics of campuses facilitate progressive activism and progressive successes. On the one hand, college students have higher levels of "biographical availability" (McAdam 1986) than much of the population: because they are less likely to be constrained by family obligations and full-time jobs, they have more time for activism. On the other hand, college campuses in and of themselves help facilitate activism because they create a relatively self-contained social environment in which students can network with one another for the purpose of movement building. Strong norms of freedom of speech and association on college campuses also facilitate such activities. Finally, the relatively small scale of the campus and the tradition of open protest ease the way for college students to effectively pressure administrators to change campus policies. Many progressive movement organizations in addition to USAS and other labor rights groups are active on college campuses in the United States— for example, Black Lives Matter and other civil rights groups, the feminist movement against sexual harassment and assault, immigrant rights groups, activists who support environmentalism and oppose climate change, and Palestinian rights groups.

Just as there has been right-wing backlash against progressive gains in U.S. society as a whole, the same has been true on college campuses. Right-wing populist groups are increasingly active on campus, with encouragement from national right-wing media and with funding and training from national organizations such as Turning Point USA and Campus Reform (Kolowich 2018). At the same time, the right has increasingly sought to silence and demobilize the left on campus. Ironically, these actions often take place under the banner of defending freedom of speech. Progressive activists are accused of engaging in disruptive and disrespectful behavior and of failing to conduct themselves in a way that is consistent with college campus standards of open dialogue and inquiry. When they protest against right-wing speakers on campus, the right accuses the left of trying to silence them and refusing to listen to alternative viewpoints. More generally, the right tries to paint a picture of the left as intolerant and puritanical in the promotion of "political correctness." Palestinian rights activists in particular frequently face accusations of anti-Semitism. Increasingly, not only right-wing leaders but also members of the left-of-center establishment and college administrators demand that progressive student activists adhere to strict standards of civility. In some cases, college administrators seek to institutionalize these expectations in student codes of conduct. In practice, by depriving student groups of one of the main weapons of the weak—disruptive protest—these codes demobilize them, silence them, and undermine their ability to achieve their goals (Brulé 2015; Sculos and Walsh 2016).

In spite of the increasingly hostile climate for progressive student activism, however, college campuses remain sites of relative freedom for students to organize, mobilize, engage in consciousness-raising, educate people more broadly, and protest (Crossley 2008; Lewis, Marine, and Kenney 2018). The reasons, which are twofold, are explored particularly but not exclusively in Chapters 3–5. First, a college campus is a relatively self-contained social environment whose small scale facilitates the mobilization of people and access to the authorities. Second, despite the fact that college campuses are relatively self-contained environments, they and their administrations have numerous—though in many cases, not immediately visible—social ties with other organizations and institutions. These are pressure points through which students can leverage their power to effect change off campus. This book explores colleges' connections to the apparel industry through the licensing programs that give companies the right to produce garments that display a school's name and logo—ties that USAS has leveraged to put in place codes of conduct that mandate that the companies that produce such licensed apparel must be in compliance with labor standards. USAS is only one of the progressive movements on campus that have used the enclosed campus environment to leverage such ties.

Much student activism is an extension of campaigns in the wider society—for labor rights, against sexual harassment and assault, and for immigrants' rights. The relatively contained environment of the college campus facilitates experimentation with and institutionalization of new social practices. One example is USAS's fight for labor rights on campus, for both adjunct faculty and campus workers, such as cafeteria and security staff. Although USAS started with a focus on sweatshops overseas—the focus of this book—over time, adopting a more expansive understanding of sweatshops, the organization identified fighting on-campus labor abuses as within its mission. This fight has taken a variety of forms. For instance, USAS initiated a campaign to have colleges discontinue their contracts with Sodexo, a company that provides cafeteria services, which was cited for its union busting and abusive treatment of workers (Grasgreen 2011). Other actions include supporting on-campus unionization efforts and the Fight for 15 campaign by pushing for a $15-an-hour minimum wage on campus (United Students Against Sweatshops n.d.[a], n.d.[c]). In addition, USAS has worked with groups such as New Faculty Majority to pressure schools to give adjuncts greater job security and a living wage and has supported adjuncts' unionization drives (Flaherty 2013a, 2013b; Schmidt 2013; United Students Against Sweatshops n.d.[b]). All of these campaigns endeavor to raise labor standards within the contained environment of the college campus, not just for the sake of campus workers and adjunct faculty but also to raise standards nationally.

Another student activist attempt to use the contained social environment of college campuses to advance nationwide progressive goals is the effort to push administrators to declare their college campuses sanctuaries for undocumented immigrants. Creating a sanctuary campus involves putting in place policies to support undocumented students, ranging from offering financial assistance (since such students cannot receive federal financial aid) and providing legal counseling to barring Immigration and Customs Enforcement from entering campus without a warrant. Administrations at many schools have been responsive to activists' demands, even as some have refused to use the term "sanctuary campus" to prevent false expectations about the extent to which they can protect undocumented students (Kelderman 2017; Najmabadi 2016a, 2016b; Redden 2016a, 2016b, 2018). Whatever the limits of such protection may actually be, this movement is leveraging the well-defined administrative boundaries of the college campus to create a social environment where undocumented students enjoy a greater degree of support and protection than they have off campus. This effort, in turn, counters the increasing normalization of xenophobia in the wider society.

Another campaign that uses the college campus as a cultural incubator for more progressive social mores is the push for affirmative consent—"yes means yes"—to become the new norm for sexual interactions on campus, with students expected to obtain clear verbal or physical consent before engaging in sexual acts. These activists view the existing "no means no" standard as placing the burden on the victim of sexual assault to speak out at a time when fear or shock may hinder this response (New 2014; Wilson 2016). Despite some inconsistency in the way students, especially male students, interpret which signals mean "yes" (Flaherty 2017), this standard has become increasingly normalized at many colleges. The ground this standard has gained on college campuses and the rise of the national #MeToo movement against sexual harassment and assault have led legislatures in many states to consider making affirmative consent the legal standard for all adults (Beitsch 2018). This is another example of how changing norms on college campuses can serve as a beachhead for changing norms in the wider society.

Other examples of student activism more closely parallel the campaigns that are the focus of this book, the efforts by USAS to use colleges'

institutional ties with apparel companies to force them to respect workers' rights. Student activists championing a variety of causes have sought
to pressure administrators to use investment funds as a point of economic leverage—just as they used their licensing agreements with apparel
companies—by divesting from industries and businesses that contribute
to social ills, such as the private prison and gun industries (S. Brown
2015). One of the most prominent examples is environmental activists'
push to have colleges and universities (along with churches, city governments, foundations, and other organizations) divest from fossil fuel companies as part of a wider strategy in their fight against climate change.
Even if such divestment has only a modest financial impact on fossil fuel
companies, it helps to highlight expanding fossil fuel extraction and stig-
matize fossil fuel companies (Gitlin 2016; Marklein 2015). Another example is the campaign to push colleges to divest from companies that are
complicit in Israel's occupation of the Palestinian territories, such as Caterpillar, which sells equipment to the Israeli military that it uses to de-
stroy Palestinian civilians' homes (Horowitz and Weiss 2010; Kurwa
2015).

College campuses may be relatively self-contained social environments that facilitate student activism, but they are not socially isolated.
Student activists can use colleges' cultural and organizational connections to the wider society to push for broader social change, with the campus as a launching point for expanded social leverage. While student activism alone will not end the dominance of right-wing populism in U.S.
politics, college campuses provide important sites for activist battles that
can help expand the progressive movement in the United States. Labor
rights groups such as USAS can play an important role in rebuilding the
U.S. labor movement and U.S. labor unions. To challenge the appeal of
right-wing populism, progressive labor unions must challenge the power
of an increasingly reactionary capitalist class and its hold over the nation's
political leadership in both major parties. They must tap into people's dis-
content by presenting a progressive populist message and mobilize people
against the increasing economic and social inequalities. To do so, they
must build alliances with a broad range of groups through social movement unionism. USAS and other groups provide a vehicle for college students to take part in this coalition-building process. This study examines
some of the major mechanisms these students employ to organize and
strategize in coordination with other progressive groups.

Acknowledgments

First and foremost, I thank the many anti-sweatshop activists who took time out of their busy schedules to share with me both their experiences in the anti-sweatshop movement and their reflections on the process of trying to achieve justice for sweatshop workers. For guiding me through this research project, I thank both the members of my dissertation committee—Bill Gamson, Sarah Babb, Bob Ross, and Charlotte Ryan—and the participants in the dissertation seminar, led by Natasha Sarkisian. In addition, my various editors at Temple University Press and the anonymous reviewers gave me feedback that helped me further refine my work.

The Robert and Riza Lavizzo-Mourey Grant enabled me to travel to Washington, DC, to interview face-to-face many of the activists who are included in this book.

STRATEGIZING AGAINST
SWEATSHOPS

1

Introduction

Theorizing Social Movement Strategy

One of the major puzzles scholars of social movements seek to piece together today is how movements make strategic decisions and when and how they strategically innovate. While we may know a good deal about individual movements' strategies (including those of the anti-sweatshop movement), we know less about how movements arrive at those strategies. Research on the question of how movements interact with their sociopolitical environment—often referred to as the political opportunity structure (POS)—has a longer history, but most scholars agree there is much to be done in this area of study, as well, with both supporters and critics of the current paradigm noting its vague, ad hoc nature in practice. In this book, I examine the emergence and growth of the U.S. anti-sweatshop movement in its early phases (roughly 1997–2007), paying particular attention to three groups—United Students Against Sweatshops (USAS), the Worker Rights Consortium (WRC), and SweatFree Communities—and the processes of strategic innovations in which they are engaged.

The use of sweatshop labor has a long history, going back to the dawn of the industrial revolution, but made a worldwide resurgence beginning in the 1970s as firms from the United States and other industrialized nations increasingly outsourced much of their production overseas, pressuring contractors in developing countries to keep prices as low as possible. They generally accomplished this by shifting the burden of cost-cutting onto their workforce, creating highly exploitive conditions—in other words, sweatshops (Bonacich et al. 1994; Rosen 2002). Although conditions certainly vary from one factory to another, it is still possible to broadly describe the conditions that prevail in sweatshops. The workforce consists predominantly of young women, whom employers—seeing them through patriarchal eyes—view as more dexterous and docile (i.e., more skilled at sewing and less likely to rebel than men). A typical workweek is six days a week, twelve or more hours a day. Pay is minimal, sometimes not even meeting the legal minimum wage of the country in which the factory is located, let alone a living wage. Overtime is usually mandatory—again regardless of what the actual law says. At times, when workers must complete large orders, they are forced to take advantage of the few hours of sleep they are allowed by bedding down underneath their sewing machines. Factories are generally unsafe and unsanitary. Sexual harassment is typically pervasive. Women may be fired for being pregnant, so that their employers do not have to pay for maternity leave. Where racial differences exist, as with East Asian factory owners in Central America, there may be racial harassment as well. Armed guards may be present to keep workers in line, with the police available to back them up when the guards alone cannot bring sufficient force to bear to repress workers (Bonacich et al. 1994; Brooks 2007; Klein 1999; Pangsapa 2007; R. Ross 2004).

Some U.S. activists became aware of these issues relatively early on. For instance, activists engaging in solidarity with Central American progressive movements during the 1980s, particularly those also involved with the labor movement, became aware of the growth of sweatshops in these countries as they traveled to them to provide support for movements there resisting intervention by the U.S. government (Brooks 2007; Seidman 2007). Despite this, an anti-sweatshop movement as such did not begin to take off in the United States—and the issue did not begin to receive widespread media coverage—until the mid- to late 1990s.

In some ways, the origins of the U.S. anti-sweatshop movement and the series of innovations explored in this book began with a series of news stories. In 1995 and 1996, there were a series of major reports on the return of sweatshops in the apparel industry. This coverage was fueled in part by the sensational nature of the cases involved. On August 3, 1995, the *Los Angeles Times* broke the story of a factory in El Monte, California, where roughly seventy Thai immigrants were being held in conditions of virtual slavery. In 1996, Charles Kernaghan of the National Labor Committee (NLC) and the major U.S. apparel union UNITE revealed that Kathie Lee Gifford, a talk show host who had cultivated a maternal persona, was producing her personal line of clothes in sweatshops employing child laborers, both in Honduras and New York City. Although such sweatshop production had been common since the 1970s, the salacious nature of the scandals—modern-day slave labor in one case, a maternal celebrity profiting from child labor in another—gave these cases attention that more run-of-the-mill sweatshop cases did not. This was a blessing for groups like the NLC and UNITE who had been trying to call attention to the resurgence of sweatshops for some time, with relatively little success (R. Ross 2004).

While the El Monte and Gifford scandals called some attention to these facts, media coverage soon petered out. It was enough, however, to spark an interest in anti-sweatshop activism in some sectors, including among college students. Independently, over the course of the 1995–1996 school year, anti-sweatshop groups sprang up on a number of college campuses, fueled by concern that their schools were doing business with companies who profited from sweatshop labor. Eric Dirnbach (interview), referring to events when he was a graduate student at the University of Michigan, told me:

> There was really nothing going on around campus about that [issue], and there was some news coming out, the Kathie Lee scandal and some other things about some Nike problems with sweatshop factories in Indonesia and other Asian countries, so we decided we were going to try to do something about that. [. . .][1] We protested at football games and had some meetings with the administration, etc. Our demands were a little incoherent at that point—it basically was drop the Nike contract or get them to do the right thing. It was not quite clear to us at the time exactly what the right thing would be.

This lack of coherence appears to have been common among student anti-sweatshop activists at the time. In addition to being unsure of their exact demands, in many cases, they did not have a clear plan for pressuring the administrators of their school. They might organize a piece of street theater on campus to raise awareness of the issue of sweatshops, but they did not necessarily have a clear idea about how that might translate into a long-term plan for changing college policy.

Roughly ten years later, over the summer of 2005, a national student anti-sweatshop group, United Students Against Sweatshops, convened a meeting, which included not only people from other U.S. anti-sweatshop

---

1. Ellipsis points enclosed in square brackets indicate my omission of material from quoted text.

groups but also anti-sweatshop activists from across the globe. Their goal was to come up with a plan that would allow them to force major apparel companies to change their business practices, particularly the fashion in which they outsourced their manufacturing, something that lies at the root of the problem of sweatshops. Their goal, in other words, was to devise a plan that would bring about major structural changes in the industry. The product of this meeting was the Designated Suppliers Program (DSP), in which companies doing business with participating schools would be required to source an increasing percentage of their clothing for those schools to particular factories, which had been certified by the Worker Rights Consortium, an independent monitoring organization, as being generally respectful of workers' rights. While this was certainly ambitious—as it would turn out, perhaps too ambitious, since it was never implemented—there was no reason for USAS and its allies to think it was unrealistic. They had already pressured more than 150 colleges and universities into adopting codes of conduct meant to guarantee labor rights and then persuaded those schools to join the WRC, which would act as the monitor that saw that these codes were respected. Indeed, USAS and its allies had founded the WRC for this very purpose. And while the campaign for the DSP was unsuccessful, the cycle of innovation that designed the DSP itself nonetheless had a significant long-term impact, informing the creation of the Accord on Fire and Building Safety in Bangladesh, a binding agreement that started in 2013 in which large apparel firms would pay to upgrade safety conditions in Bangladeshi factories.

Clearly, the U.S. student anti-sweatshop movement had evolved significantly over ten years. It had gone from being a network of only loosely connected groups on various campuses to a national organization that many considered at the cutting edge of the U.S. anti-sweatshop movement as a whole. It had also gone from being unclear about how to effectively pressure the administrators of members' own colleges to designing a detailed plan to alter some of the basic business practices of the major firms of the apparel industry, behemoths of the corporate world such as Nike and Reebok. This book traces the successive cycles of innovation that USAS and allied organizations engaged in over this time period—the process of strategizing by which they charted their course from loosely connected student groups to a national movement and from tactical incoherence to a well-developed strategy that took advantage of the unique source of leverage the organization's members hold as college students. More specifically, I analyze three cycles of innovation in the anti-sweatshop movement in the 1997–2007 period: the creation of the WRC, the DSP, and the SweatFree Communities campaign/SweatFree Purchasing Consortium.

In some ways, I focus more on the process of strategic decision making itself than on the resulting strategy per se. We know quite a bit about what types of strategies generally work for movements, and which have worked for the anti-sweatshop movement in particular, but we know less about how movements arrive at these strategies—the process of strategizing—the puzzle I focus on here.

Recent research has established that successful social movements analyze their social environment and develop their course of action accordingly (Alimi 2007; McAdam 1983; McCammon 2003, 2012; McCammon et al. 2008; Shriver and Adams 2010). Furthermore, movements are most likely to do so when they have recently suffered a defeat that makes it clear that their current strategy is not working (McCammon 2003, 2012). Scholars have also shown that the form of organization a movement adopts is important, with more open, deliberative, democratic forms fostering strategic innovation and closed, hierarchical forms with decisions made by fiat from the top down stifling innovation (Ganz 2000, 2009; McCammon 2003, 2012; Staggenborg 1989).

What we do not know is the exact process by which movement organizations analyze their environment and engage in processes of strategic innovation in response to changes in the social environment. In other words, we know something about the inputs (the organization of movements, how they relate to their social environment) and the outputs (the strategy itself) but relatively little about the process of strategizing in which a movement uses the inputs to produce a coherent, successful strategy. Just because a movement needs to innovate strategically does not mean it will do so or do so well. Barbara Epstein (1991) examines the U.S. nonviolent direct action movement of the late 1970s and early 1980s, which, despite having a highly open, deliberative form of organization, proved unable to strategically innovate following failure. Over the course of this book, I look at the question of the strategic evolution of the U.S. anti-sweatshop movement, with a particular focus on USAS and the WRC, seeking to understand not simply what input factors allowed them to strategize successfully but also the decision-making process they used during both periods of strategic stability and periods of innovation.

I also develop a more robust model of political opportunity structure through looking at the anti-sweatshop movement's interactions with its social environment across multiple social institutions—particularly college campuses, transnational corporate production chains, and city governments—thus drawing out what elements of the social environment are most important in multiple institutional contexts. Doing so allows me to address a number of problems with the current model of POS that scholars have noted. First, the concept traditionally has been deployed in a way that is very state-centered (Armstrong and Bernstein 2008), while the anti-sweatshop movement's conflicts have been primarily with the major apparel corporations and, specifically in the case of USAS, with college and university administrations. Second, as both critics and proponents of the concept of POS have noted, the concept is a vague one, often used as an ad hoc heuristic device. Although a number of scholars have tried to develop universal models of political opportunity, most analyses of social movements develop their own, idiosyncratic set of factors that apply primarily to that case but are not always relevant for other cases (Gamson and Meyer 1996; Goodwin and Jasper [1999] 2004; Jasper 1997, 2012; McAdam 1996). In this book, I develop a multi-institutional model of POS that not only can be applied to such diverse social institutions as corporations and colleges but also takes into account how the opportunity structures of these different institutions interact with one another. Because this model was developed for multiple institutions simultaneously, I believe that it addresses much of the vague, ad hoc nature of current models by identifying elements that are consistently important, thereby creating a model of POS that is robust enough to also apply across multiple cases.

Strategy

The Current Literature

As I look at the question of strategy in this book, I focus just as much, if not more, on the process of how the anti-sweatshop movement made decisions that led it to arrive at its strategy as on the strategy itself. While I consider how the anti-sweatshop movement used consumer pressure and carried out transnational solidarity campaigns, analysis of these matters is secondary to my consideration of how the movement planned these campaigns and engaged in the process of strategic innovation. Thus, my purpose here in reviewing the literature on strategy is to look not at the extensive literatures on consumer activism (B. King 2008; Micheletti 2003; Micheletti, Follesdal, and Stolle 2004; Seidman 2007) or transnational campaigns (Armbruster-Sandoval 2005; Bandy and Smith 2005; Bob 2001; Keck and Sikkink 1998; Pallas 2017; Sikkink 2005; Stewart 2004) but at works that deal with how movements create and execute successful strategies—what we might call the literature on strategizing instead of strategy.

It is useful to start by defining some key terms. "Tactics" and "strategy" are two words often used in one breath, as if they were largely synonymous. However, I follow the definitions implicit in Aldon Morris's (1993) study of the Birmingham civil rights protests and distinguish between tactics and strategy to highlight how activists draw on the diverse range of actions that are familiar to them to craft a larger campaign or plan. A *tactic*, as I define it here, is a discrete action that a social movement organization can take that is modular (i.e., standardized and repeatable)—something such as a rally, a sit-in, street theater, or a strike (see also the literature on tactical repertoires, including McAdam, McCarthy, and Zald 1996; Tarrow 1998; Taylor and Van Dyke 2004; Tilly 1978). *Strategy*, by contrast, operates on a higher level, trying to connect the different pieces together. Strategy involves a set of interlinked practices, including how movements assess the opportunities and constraints in their larger social environment (Alimi 2007; Koopmans 2005; McAdam [1982] 1999; Tarrow 1998), recruit people into movement organizations (Morris 1984), form alliances with other groups (Bandy and Smith 2005; Bystydzienski and Schacht 2001), frame their ideas for a larger audience (Ferree et al. 2002; Ryan 1991; Snow and Benford 1988), and select a particular set of tactics to use to pressure authorities (McAdam 1983; McCammon et al. 2008; Tarrow 1998; Tilly 1978). In other words, strategy covers the range of actions a movement consciously takes to reach its goals, connected together into a holistic plan.

Among social movement theorists, there has been a fair amount of consensus about what makes a movement's choice of tactics effective—that they generate large-scale social disruption, which puts pressure on authorities to resolve the crisis to restore business as usual. The risk is that these authorities may respond with repression, but in the right circumstances (i.e., given the right political opportunities), they may instead make concessions to activists to restore social peace (Flacks 1988; Gamson [1975] 1990; McAdam 1983; Piven and Cloward 1977; Tarrow 1998). James Jasper (1997) has been a dissenting voice, arguing that social movements have their primary impact not through the pressure they put on authorities by means of the disruption they generate, but through the changes they bring about in the wider public discourse, putting on to the agenda previously neglected issues, such as animal rights. Other researchers have called into question the dichotomous nature of this debate. For instance, Mary Fainsod Katzenstein (1998) has argued that in certain contexts, such as feminist activism within the Roman Catholic Church, challenges to the dominant discourse can be disruptive in and of themselves. Kenneth Andrews (2001), in his study of the Civil Rights Movement's involvement in Mississippi in implementing programs that were part of President Lyndon Johnson's War on Poverty, argues that disruptive protest, changes in public discourse, and a movement's capacity to negotiate with authorities once it has brought sufficient pressure to bear are all important factors in a successful strategy (see also Dixon, Martin, and Nau 2016; Downey and Rohlinger 2008).

Implicit in much current analysis of tactics is that the development and deployment of tactics is largely an instrumental matter. Jasper (1997), however, emphasizes that movements do not use purely instrumental grounds to evaluate which tactics they use in any specific case from among the range with which they are familiar. Tactics have a symbolic as well as a strategic value, saying something about the collective identity of the group. Within the same broad movement, some individual groups may gravitate toward direct action and away from lobbying, or vice versa; doing so helps define them, respectively, as radicals and reformists. Jasper does not deny that the effectiveness of any given tactic does play a role in determining whether a group will adopt it but insists that the group's values and collective identity are equally, if not more, important (see also Taylor and Van Dyke 2004).

Some theorists (see, e.g., Downey 1986; Ferree 1992) have tried to take into account both the instrumentalist and the symbolic perspectives on strategy by arguing that when movements strategize, they take into account both instrumental and ideological or value-rational concerns, engaging in a tradeoff between the two. Francesca Polletta (2005), however, argues that this is a false dichotomy. Rather, what activists see as instrumentally effective involves a value-laden process of cultural interpretation. Rather than there being a tradeoff between ideological and instrumental concerns, they are two sides of one and the same process, as activists use their beliefs to make sense of what impact their tactics will have on the world—and therefore what will be effective.

A number of scholars (Alimi 2007; McAdam 1983; McCammon 2003, 2012; McCammon et al. 2008; Morris 1993; Nepstad and Vinthagen 2012; Ryan, Jeffreys, and Blozie 2012; Shriver and Adams 2010) have shown that social movement organizations are capable of actively analyzing their sociopolitical environment, looking at the opportunities and constraints, to decide when it is appropriate to mobilize and which tactics they should use. For instance, Eitan Alimi (2007) shows that the first intifada broke out in Palestine when the grassroots leadership in the Occupied Territories perceived, through following Israeli news reports, that there was a growing divide in Israeli society between those who supported and those who opposed the occupation. Further, while not renouncing armed struggle, the leaders of the intifada emphasized the use of nonviolent tactics (protests, strikes, boycotts) and tactics of limited, nondeadly violence (stone throwing), believing that deadly tactics would backfire and undermine those in Israel who supported an end to the occupation.

Such an assessment of the sociopolitical environment does not necessarily produce strategic innovation. Movements may observe particular political opportunities open but choose not to take advantage of them because they have different strategic priorities in terms of the goals they are seeking to achieve (Bernstein 2003). Or a movement may believe that the openings occurring mean that familiar strategies, which would have been dangerous to use before, will now be effective. The Czechoslovakian environmental movement engaged in actions of escalating degrees of confrontation as it sensed repression levels lessening with the collapse of communism (Shriver and Adams 2010), but it does not seem to have engaged in strategic innovation per se. It seems that strategic innovation is most likely to occur in periods of uncertainty, whether as the result of wider social upheavals (Armstrong 2002) or the movement's hitting roadblocks. Doug McAdam (1983) and Holly McCammon (2003, 2012) both argue that it is after a failure or series of failures that movements seem most likely to innovate, modifying their tactics in light of clear evidence that they are not having the impact on their social environment—that they are not affecting their opponents—as they wish. McCammon (2003), for instance, shows that the U.S. women's suffrage movement began to move from behind-the-scenes tactics such as lobbying legislators to public protest when the movement ceased making gains through the former set of tactics.

Organization is essential to the development of strategy. At the most basic level, social movement organizations train activists in the skills necessary to engage in strategic action (Van Dyke and Dixon 2013). But the type of organization matters: a number of scholars (Ganz 2000, 2009; McCammon 2003, 2012; Ryan, Jeffreys, and Blozie 2012; Staggenborg 1989) have found that particular types of organization and leadership give rise to good strategy. In contrasting the success of the small and newly formed United Farm Workers (UFW) with the failure of the efforts of the large and established American Federation of Labor–Congress of Industrial Organizations (AFL-CIO) to organize farmworkers in California during the 1960s, Marshall Ganz (2000, 2009) emphasizes the importance of how the UFW promoted deliberative decision making, how its leadership was accountable to the members, and how the leadership was drawn from a range of backgrounds, which brought a variety of social networks and activist knowledge to the process of strategizing. The AFL-CIO's Agricultural Workers Organizing Committee (AWOC), by contrast, was led by one person, who operated in a very top-down manner, had little firsthand knowledge of the people he was seeking to organize or how the agricultural sector worked, and did not consult with organizers familiar with the constituency or industry. Consequently, the UFW, despite having fewer resources, had a better base of knowledge and was therefore more strategically successful. Other scholars' findings are similar to Ganz's—that movement organizations that are more open and democratic and that have a more diverse membership are more likely to do a good job of assessing the political opportunities open to them and to respond creatively in the face of new challenges, producing strategic innovation.

But these factors that foster good strategy do not always lead to it. Epstein (1991) gives us the case of the U.S. nonviolent direct action movement of the early 1980s, which, according to the above findings, *should* have been innovative—it failed to achieve its goals (of shutting down nuclear power plants and research centers) and had a highly democratic, deliberative organization with a diverse membership. Yet following its failures, the movement did not strategically innovate, clinging to the sole tactic of nonviolent direct action even as it should have become clear that this tactic in isolation was not winning gains. Epstein argues that the problem was the movement's ideology—specifically, that the movement's groups became trapped in a form of "magical thinking," where nonviolent direct action had become so central to their collective identity that they were unable to see the possibility that this tactic might not be effective in some circumstances and in isolation from other tactics, especially more conventional ones such as lobbying. This shows that, depending on how dogmatic or flexible a group's ideology is, it may hinder as well as help it in the process of strategic innovation, signaling the crucial role ideology plays (see also Westby 2002).

What this tells us is that decentralized, democratic social movement organizations with a flexible, non-dogmatic ideology generally do a better job of analyzing the POS and developing strategies that are suited for such conditions. But while this tells us about the output (strategy), it does not tell us about the process of generating that output (strategizing). How do movement organizations and networks analyze their environment? How do they decide which tactics will work best? How do they combine those tactics into a larger plan? How do they alter their strategy when necessary—how do they decide when to do so and how does the process of innovation take place? Ganz (2009) gives us an inside look at the UFW that helps us understand why that organization produced a better strategy than AWOC, but while he shows us *why* organizationally the participants made better decisions, he does not show us *how*—or, more exactly, he does not provide a theory of the process. What goes on in a movement as the participants engage in the process of strategizing remains something of a black box to scholars, a box that I open in this book to examine its internal workings. To better understand movement strategy, we need to understand more of the details of the process of strategic decision making.

Strategic Models and Innovation

My research confirms much of the existing literature. The episodes of strategic innovation I examine here occurred in the face of, if not failures, situations that were clearly challenges to the movement. The open, democratic, deliberative organization of both USAS and the wider network of anti-sweatshop activists facilitated the process of creative thinking necessary for strategic innovation (Figure 1.1). And the movement's victories rest on a combination of disruptive protest, creating changes in public discourse that put sweatshops on the public agenda, and successful negotiations with authorities, with changes in public discourse being disruptive in certain contexts, particularly when challenging targets deeply invested in cultivating a good public image.

While the existing work on strategy provides an important starting point in the analysis of *strategy*, it still leaves much unexplored. In particular, the work does not look into the process of *strategizing*, as distinct from the plans that are the outcome of this process. Both Alimi (2007) and McCammon and her colleagues (2008) stress the importance of a movement taking the time to analyze the social environment, but they do not get into the details of the interpretive-analytic process by which movements do so. This is not a simple matter, and there are no guarantees that a movement's analysis of its environment will be either accurate or useful. Ganz (2000, 2009), McCammon (2003, 2012) and Suzanne Staggenborg (1989), however, present us with models of what types of social movement organization are most likely to strategize successfully. Epstein (1991) highlights the important role ideology plays. In this book, I begin by exploring the process behind formulating strategy in more depth, presenting a model of how movements strategize that I apply to the anti-sweatshop movement throughout this work. In particular, I look at the models USAS has developed to fight campaigns on campus to get college administrators to give into its demands and those that the U.S. anti-sweatshop movement as a whole has used to organize successful solidarity campaigns in support of workers on the ground in sweatshops across the world.

In examining how this process of innovation happened, I found that it involved a dialectic between experience and ideology. The process is an

▓ **Dialectic between experience and ideology**
  - Strategic models
    - *Consolidation of movement's collective experience*
    - *Standardized plans of action*
  - Ideology: Combination of values, a theory of how the social world works, and norms for action

▓ **During periods of non-innovative, routine activism, activists apply their existing strategic models, adapting them for use in their specific social context.**

▓ **Movements innovate when they face new challenges that their existing strategic models do not address.**
  - Ideology is used as a lens through which to view the social world in an analytic-interpretive process to clarify goals and interpret the social context (POS).
  - Existing strategic models are revised or new ones are created in light of this analysis.
  - Ideology may be modified: changes in movements' understanding of the social world or norms for action may be applied to better achieve goals/fulfill values.

▓ **New strategic model is deployed.**

Figure 1.1 The elements of strategy.

interactive model—looking at how social movements interact with their social environment to develop their strategies. The movement's collective experience was consolidated by activists in the form of *strategic models*, standardized plans of action that, on the basis of experience (both their own and that of past activist generations), they believed were effective, at least in particular social contexts. As with the cases that McAdam (1983) and McCammon (2003) examined, setbacks or new challenges caused the anti-sweatshop movement to reexamine both its social environment and its strategic models, modifying them or developing new, experimental ones. Crucial to this process of reexamination was the anti-sweatshop movement's *ideology*, a combination of values, a theory of how the social world works, and norms for action. The movement used its ideology both to clarify its goals and to interpret and analyze the political opportunity structure, particularly the causes of the movement's setbacks. On the basis of this analytic-interpretative process, it would modify existing strategic models or develop new ones. It then deployed these new strategies and, when faced with new challenges, engaged in another iteration of this process. Further, it is not only a group's strategic models that change in the process of strategic innovation. Its ideology may change, as well, as its examination of the social environment leads the group to reconsider elements or refine its analysis.

Strategic models form the basis for social movement strategy during non-innovative, relatively routine periods of social movement action. They involve linking together tactics, frames, mobilizing structures, and so on in relatively standardized (though not necessarily dogmatic or static) ways—models of strategic activity that can be passed from one movement to the next and from one generation of activists to the next. Most of the time, the anti-sweatshop movement engaged in strategizing in a rather routine fashion, applying existing strategic models to familiar political opportunity structures. This is not to say it did so blindly. USAS chapters, for instance, faced different constraints and opportunities on different college campuses and tweaked the strategic model for campus campaigns through a process of consensus-based deliberation to make it fit their particular campuses. But they did not have to engage in any deep debates about changing this strategic model in any way: it was flexible enough to apply to a wide range of college campuses without a need for major rethinking (see Chapter 5). Only during periods of strategic innovation are strategic models seriously questioned and revamped.

While movements rely on existing strategic models when things go smoothly, in moments of crisis or transition, when they must innovate, they need to reassess their strategies. In doing so, they reflect on their experiences in light of their ideology. Both William Gamson and David Meyer (1996) and Alimi (2007) stress that, in making strategic decisions, movements are engaging in an interpretive process in which they seek to understand their social environment—the POS—and take the wisest course of action in light of that interpretation. In discussing the beliefs movements hold and proclaim, scholars of social movements have leaned heavily on the concepts of frames and framing (McAdam, McCarthy, and Zald 1996; Tarrow 1998). A number of scholars (Ferree and Merrill [2000] 2004; Oliver and Johnston 2000; Westby 2002; Zald 2000), however, have expressed concern that, as a result, the concept of framing has been overextended and its analytic clarity reduced. As a remedy, they suggest that we should (re)introduce the concept of ideology to the study of movements, with several (Downey and Rohlinger 2008; L. King 2008; Maney 2012) specifically arguing for its importance in understanding strategy. Ideologies and frames, understood in this light, are different phenomena and play different roles in movements. An ideology is the underlying set of ideas that inspires and guides activists in their actions, while frames are sets of ideas strategically deployed to win support among nonactivist audiences (Gillan 2008; Oliver and Johnston 2000; Westby 2002). In other words, ideology contributes to the process of strategizing, while frames are a product of that same process. Movements' frames may, in fact, deviate from their ideology to some degree if the movement believes there is a strategic benefit in this (Westby 2002).

Here I wish to follow Pamela Oliver and Hank Johnston's (2000) definition of "ideology": a core set of values, a theory (not necessarily coherent) about how the social world works, and norms for taking action in the world in the light of these values and theory. Of the three elements of ideology, the most important, according to Oliver and Johnston, are the movement's values. While movements may change their values, this is relatively rare and a long, difficult process, involving much reflection and discussion. Although changing their theories and norms is also an involved process, movements are more likely to do so in light of their successes and failures, but in ways that are consistent with their values; theories and norms change as movements seek to better understand how to see their values realized.

The articulation of ideology and the learning and adaptation of strategic models are not things that happen spontaneously. The process of interpreting and analyzing the social environment and taking action occurs in the context of social movement organizations and the networks between them. Movement organizations and networks play two crucial roles in strategizing—creating a system of institutional memory, whereby the knowledge of strategic models and the relevant skills (Van Dyke and Dixon 2013) for implementing them are passed on to new generations of activists, and facilitating a process of deliberative decision making, in which activists actively interpret their social environment, decide how to apply their existing models, and determine what innovations to adopt. Over the course of this book, I look at how USAS has drawn on the strategic knowledge of older social movement organizations, such as UNITE HERE, the major U.S. apparel union, and the United States Student Association (USSA), a student organizing group. I also examine how USAS has passed on its knowledge to new members through annual conferences, something that is especially important for student groups such as USAS, which by their very nature have extremely high turnover rates as experienced members graduate and new students join. I also explore how activists made decisions at various key points in the evolution of the movement's strategic models, as well as somewhat more routinely in campus-based and international solidarity campaigns, and how these decision-making processes shaped the resulting strategies.

	First Cycle		Second Cycle		Third Cycle
Starting Strategic Model	Corporate campaign + campus direct action campaign	→	Corporate campaign + campus direct action campaign + independent monitoring	→	Corporate campaign + campus direct action campaign + independent monitoring certification with worker participation
New Challenge	Fair Labor Association		Unionized factories closing down		Applying the model to city and state government purchasing
Innovation	Worker Rights Consortium		Designated Suppliers Program		SweatFree Purchasing Consortium
New Strategic Model	Corporate campaign + campus direct action campaign + **independent monitoring**		Corporate campaign + campus direct action campaign + independent monitoring + **certification with worker participation**		Corporate campaign + **citywide lobbying campaign** + independent monitoring + certification with worker participation

Figure 1.2 Cycles of innovation in the U.S. anti-sweatshop movement.

In particular, I examine three successive cycles of strategic innovation by the anti-sweatshop movement (see Figure 1.2). In succession, I look at (1) how the difficulties enforcing codes of conduct for apparel producers and the industry's creation of a relatively toothless monitoring body, the Fair Labor Association (FLA), spurred activists to create one that they believed would be more effective, the WRC (see Chapters 8–9); (2) the ephemeral nature of the victories the movement won with the monitoring of the WRC and accompanying protest campaigns, which led it to create the DSP to institutionalize gains over the long term (Chapter 12); and (3) the movement's migration with the founding of SweatFree Communities into a new social context, from college campuses to city governments, which led it to modify its strategy to fit the new environment (Chapter 13).

We start before the first cycle of innovation by examining the movement's organization, ideology, and existing strategic models (Chapters 5–7) so we have some sense of the inputs that the movement processed when it needed to engage in such innovation. I explore in detail the new challenges listed above that spurred the movement on to innovation and examine the resulting new strategic models. And I examine the process by which the movements innovated, opening up the black box. The first

cycle—covered in Chapters 8 and 9—began when companies started promoting corporate social responsibility (CSR) programs such as the FLA as
a solution to the sweatshop problem, supposedly sidelining the need for
labor unions and other activist groups. In each such cycle, we see the movement engaging in deliberative, democratic decision making to apply its
ideology of worker empowerment to its past experiences, trying to better
understand how to overcome the obstacles it had encountered. The movement's activists use their ideology to interpret and analyze the political
opportunity structure, their own past successes and failures, and the limits
of what their current strategic model can achieve; then they formulate a
new strategic model, which they deploy in conflict with their opponents.
In the case of the rise of CSR, activists quickly concluded that allowing
companies to regulate themselves would result in failure due to the inherent conflicts of interest involved: the very practices that maximize companies' profits are among the major driving factors in sweatshops. On the
basis of this analysis, USAS and its allies developed an alternative model of
independent monitoring and designed the WRC to embody these principles. In this process of innovation, activists may well modify not only their
strategic models but their ideology, as well: as they analyze the world, they
may deepen their understanding of it and make their ideological models
more sophisticated. Analyzing the limitations of CSR made anti-sweatshop
activists realize the importance of empowering workers so they did not
have to rely on the paternalism of others—and therefore the importance
of the movement's supporting the right of workers to unionize. This cycle
begins again when activists come up against the limits of their new model.

Political Opportunity Structure

The Current Literature: Political Opportunity
Structure's Supporters

It would be a mistake to analyze the anti-sweatshop movement's strategy
in isolation. The movement's strategy was born out of both activists' analysis of their social environment and their attempts to alter that social
environment, particularly the conflicts they had with powerful foes, who
ranged from college administrators to transnational apparel corporations.
Given this, to understand how the anti-sweatshop movement has strategized, we must understand how its interaction with its social, political,
and economic environment influenced its choices—how that interaction
constrained the movement, where it found opportunities, what its analy-

sis was of the social forces it was up against. In other words, we need to understand what social movement scholars refer to as the POS of the anti-sweatshop movement.

Although not without its critics (Goodwin and Jasper [1999] 2004; Jasper 2012), the concept of *political opportunity structure* has become central to the way social movement scholars make sense of how movements interact with other social institutions in their environment. The primary focus has been on how movements interact with nation-states. McAdam (1996, 27) produced a synthesis of a wide variety of models of the POS, citing the following four factors as the crucial ones that repeatedly show up across multiple cases:

1. The relative openness or closure of the institutionalized political system
2. The stability or instability of that broad set of elite alignments that typically undergird a polity
3. The presence or absence of elite allies
4. The state's capacity and propensity for repression

Although other scholars have produced other syntheses (Gamson and Meyer 1996; Tarrow 1998), McAdam's synthesis is often seen as the classic one that has defined how scholars think about political opportunity structure (Goodwin and Jasper 2012).

Even among those who support the utility of the concept of POS, there have been a number of criticisms of how it has been used in practice. One major criticism is that the concept of POS remains vague, more of a sensitizing concept than anything else (Gamson and Meyer 1996; McAdam 1996). Gamson and Meyer (1996), for instance, argue that it is often "defined exclusively ad hoc and after the fact" (276) and that "it threatens to become an all-encompassing fudge factor" (275). Instead of developing a coherent definition of POS, too many scholars have simply identified what aspects of the social environment are most relevant to the success or failure of the movement they are studying and labeled those elements the political opportunity structure, leading to a bewildering variation of definitions from one scholar to the next (Meyer 2004). It was the very proliferation of such ad hoc, after-the-fact definitions of the POS that led McAdam to develop his synthesis of its major elements, but it is not clear that this has led in practice to any consensual focus on these elements in ensuing empirical studies.

Another major criticism of how the concept of POS has been used is that it has exclusively focused on movements' interactions with nation-states, something that can be clearly seen in McAdam's synthesis above. The implicit assumption in much of this work is that nation-states are the main opponent and target of movements. Elizabeth Armstrong and Mary Bernstein (2008), however, point to a growing body of literature that shows that movements have contentious interactions with many other social institutions. As an example, they point to the work of Katzenstein (1998), who documents that the primary target for many Roman Catholic feminists has been the church, which they seek to reform to make it more inclusive and egalitarian with regard to gender. The anti-sweatshop's activities analyzed in this book provide another good example: the movement's main conflicts have been with apparel corporations and college administrations, with the state remaining largely in the background. For these reasons, Armstrong and Bernstein call for the development of a multi-institutional theory of POS. They also critique most conceptions of POS for focusing primarily or exclusively on social structure while downplaying the significance of culture.

A number of scholars have begun to take steps to address these weaknesses. Most markedly, there have been a number of studies that seek to extend the concept of POS beyond a focus on the state. Both Myra Marx Ferree and her colleagues (2002) and Mattias Wahlström and Abby Peterson (2006) have proposed the idea of a discursive or cultural opportunity structure (DOS or COS). Ferree and her colleagues (2002) focus primarily on the structure of the mass media and which social actors and cultural frames for interpreting events have the most credence. Wahlström and Peterson's concept of COS is somewhat broader, including factors outside the mass media, such as public opinion. Joseph Luders (2006), Rachel Schurman (2004), Sarah Soule (2009), and Wahlström and Peterson (2006) have all developed concepts of an industry or economic opportunity structure (IOS or EOS), seeking to better understand how movements interact with corporations.

Many of these expanded models make room for culture as a central element of the POS. This is most obvious among those scholars who discuss the DOS or COS (Ferree et al. 2002; Wahlström and Peterson 2006). But other scholars have incorporated culture into discussions of state-centered opportunity structures and economic opportunity structures. Anthony Oberschall (1996; see also Gamson and Meyer 1996) has emphasized the centrality of legitimacy to the power of state authorities, while Schurman (2004) discusses the centrality of the culture of both the industry and individual firms in the industry opportunity structure.

Despite these advances, many of these models of the DOS/COS and IOS/EOS continue to be somewhat ad hoc, focusing on variables specific to the cases they study, without offering models that can easily be applied across multiple cases. The two major exceptions are Ferree and her colleagues' (2002) analysis of the DOS and Luders's (2006) analysis of the EOS.

Ferree and her colleagues (2002) argue that in public life, there are any number of *social arenas* in which social movements and other groups come into conflict. They focus on the fight over the framing of the issues the contestants are concerned with, each side struggling to ensure that its interpretation of social reality will prevail. The most important arena for such discursive conflicts in contemporary society is the mainstream mass media: which frame prevails in the mass media has consequences far beyond it, helping to define the larger public agenda. Unlike a real arena, the terrain in the mass media is uneven, with some groups having a structural advantage over others, features that help define the DOS. Journalists and editors do not act as neutral referees but are themselves active participants in the conflict. They act as gatekeepers, choosing which social actors and which frames will be admitted to their social arena and how much prominence or "standing" they will have, often actively promoting certain actors and frames over others.

Luders (2006) seeks to define the EOS in terms of the tradeoff in costs businesses face between those caused by the disruption to their businesses from movements (such as lost profits due to boycotts) versus those caused by making concessions (such having to pay workers higher wages or a political backlash from a countermovement). Different types of businesses have different vulnerabilities—for instance, businesses that sell consumer goods directly to the public are far more vulnerable to boycotts than those that deal mainly with other businesses. A business's place in the EOS may thus be assessed by looking at the disruption versus concession costs it faces. Luders notes that such costs and businesses' assessment of them may shift over time, leading to shifts in the EOS. Although he focuses on economic costs to businesses, Luders suggests that this model could be applied in other social spheres, such as the calculations political leaders must make about the costs and benefits of making concessions to movements.

The Current Literature: Political Opportunity Structure's Critics

Two major social movement theorists, Jeff Goodwin and James Jasper ([1999] 2004; see also Jasper 1997, 2012), while agreeing that it is important to look at the social environment in which movements operate, would have us dispose of the concept of the political opportunity structure entirely. It is not simply that they think it is applied in a vague and ad hoc way; they argue that the whole concept is misleading and confusing. They argue that when we speak of a political opportunity *structure*, the metaphor of social structure can sometimes obscure as much as it reveals. Although social scientists are, in principle, all perfectly well aware that social structures change over time, the metaphor of structure tends to make us focus on what is fixed in the social environment, not what is undergoing transformation. According to Goodwin and Jasper, this tends to obscure the fact that movements can, by their actions, change the political opportunities and constraints they face—something that should be a central focus of the study of social movements.

The metaphor of structure also tends to obscure the fact that the structures with which movements interact are not passive—they consist of elite social actors (Jasper 2012; Jasper and Poulsen 1993; McAdam [1999] 2004), such as corporations and governments, that respond to movements, sometimes in ways that harm movements (repression or countering their messages), sometimes in ways that help (whether through concessions or making strategic blunders). While classic definitions of political opportunity, such as McAdam's (1996), include elite actors as part of the POS, Goodwin and Jasper ([1999] 2004) argue that in too many analyses they are not treated as agents, and the POS is treated in a static—as well as ad hoc—fashion.

Because of this, Jasper (2004, 2006, 2012; see also Jasper and Poulsen 1993) suggests scrapping the concept of POS altogether and replacing it with a model of *strategic interaction*. Jasper also claims that most opportunities—those things that movements react to and take advantage of—are actually blunders on the part of the movement's opponents (see also Jasper and Poulsen 1993). He argues that what we should focus on is the "players"—the social actors—and the social arenas within which they operate, including the rules that constrain players acting in those arenas. In this conceptualization, Jasper argues that if anything suits the core concept of POS, it is the rules governing social behavior in any arena. But he also notes, "If the rules of arenas matter, it is because a player is interpreting, enforcing and creating them. There are other factors in a given environment, such as physical resources, cultural meanings, and rules, but they matter primarily when they are put into action—and play—by other players" (22, citations omitted). In terms of McAdam's (1996) classic four aspects of POS, Jasper says only the first—openness—is related to the rules of the arena. Elite alignments and potential allies, which are closely related, are about the actions of other players. Meanwhile, repression actually consists of two elements: the capacity and the propensity for repression. Because social actors must interpret their environment to take advantage of potential opportunities, they may make errors—blunders that then can become opportunities for their opponents. A social actor's knowledge about the environment is then crucial to her or his success or failure (Jasper 2012).

A Revised Model of Political Opportunity Structure

In this book, I develop a revised model of political opportunity structure that takes into account many of the criticisms raised by both Armstrong and Bernstein (2008) and Goodwin and Jasper ([1999] 2004). This model not only includes social structure but also culture and elite social actors, applies across multiple social institutions, and emphasizes the interactional nature of the opportunities and constraints that movements face— that elite social actors and their decisions in response to movements constitute an important element of the POS (Figure 1.3).

A few words here about my choice in terminology: Some may question why I chose to retain the term "political opportunity structure" when I am considerably expanding it beyond its traditional focus on government social structures. I chose this path in part to avoid a needless proliferation of jargon. As for the use of the term "political" opportunity, the "politics" in "political opportunity structure" can be defined either narrowly, as referring specifically to government, or more broadly, as referring to power relations in all spheres of society. Most of the authors discussed above who are developing models of opportunity structures beyond states implicitly follow the first, narrower definition, reserving the term "political opportunity structure" for movements' interactions with governments and referring to their interactions with other social institutions by alternative terms such as "discursive opportunity structure" and "economic opportunity structure." In this book, I follow Armstrong and Bernstein (2008), who explicitly criticize this approach, arguing that we need a broader conception of politics that recognizes that power relations pervade all social institutions. While the different choices in terminology may be partly rooted in differing theoretical conceptions of power, they may also partly be different choices in semantics. I find it more useful to use "politics" in the broader sense and would suggest using the term "government opportunity structure (GOS)" to refer to movements' interactions specifically with states (though that issue does not actually come up in this book).

While focusing on the mass media, Ferree and her colleagues (2002) note that it is only one of many social arenas. I suggest that we can conceptualize the POS as consisting of multiple social arenas, constituted by a wide range of social institutions that interact and interlock with one another in complex ways, depending on the structure of and relations among those social institutions and key social actors, especially authorities/elites/

- ▓ **Political opportunity structures**
  - Social structures
  - Cultural norms and beliefs
  - Social actors

- ▓ **Social arenas**
  - Social actors embedded in social arena
    - *–Authorities/elites: e.g., power holders, gatekeepers*
    - *–Subordinate social actors, who may become challengers/activists*
  - Degree of openness and accessibility of
    - *–Elites*
    - *–Decision-making processes*
    - *–Discursive conflict*
    - *–Mobilizing opportunities*

- ▓ **Mobilizing opportunities: a movement's ability to organize independently and recruit new members**
  - Both structural and interactive

- ▓ **Structural leverage: ways that activists can undermine the structural sources of elites' power to influence their decision-making processes**
  - Institutional: voting
  - More commonly, extra-institutional: strikes, boycotts, protests
  - Both structural and interactive

- ▓ **Legitimacy: Both elites and challengers need to justify their actions; otherwise, there is much greater social resistance to implementing those decisions.**
  - Usually a discursive conflict, in which elites have the upper hand.
  - Both cultural and interactive

- ▓ **Elite countermeasures: e.g., repression, counter-framing, countermovements, token concessions**
  - Structural, cultural, and interactive

- ▓ **All elements are relative to the social actors in question.**

Figure 1.3 The elements of political opportunity structures.

gatekeepers, within them. Among the key connections examined below are the business partnerships that colleges and universities have with the apparel industry. This allowed student anti-sweatshop groups such as USAS to use the openings that exist in the POS of colleges and universities to exercise leverage over corporate targets over which they otherwise would have much less influence.

Each social arena is structured in distinct ways, with different social actors occupying positions of power, whether as authorities who control the decision-making process, gatekeepers who decide which other social actors are allowed access to the arena, or other roles that fit broadly within or are roughly equivalent to the elite of McAdam's (1996) state-centered model of POS. In addition to such power holders, other social actors occupy other, often subordinate roles within the social arena and may take action in the hope of changing the balance of power or, at least, shaping some of the decisions authorities make. The question, again posed by McAdam in the context of nation-states, becomes this: How open and accessible are those authorities to popular influence, and what opportunities do nonelites have to wield that influence?

"Openness or closure" is a key element in McAdam's (1996) formulation of political opportunity, but these terms are a bit vague and could potentially mean many things. Openness may be signaled by a more democratic social structure, but this does not have to be the case. Indeed, one of the paradoxes of the anti-sweatshop movement is that activists have concluded that government authorities, even in nominally democratic polities, are so committed to neoliberal policies that there are more openings to successfully pressure corporations at this historical juncture than there are in the government. The manifestation of the openness of authorities thus can come in many forms. As Chapter 3 shows, for student activists, colleges and universities are relatively open as social arenas. Although the governance structures of colleges are undemocratic relative to students, with administrators making most major decisions and student governments having only an advisory role, if that, the norms of colleges allow students to organize freely and express their views and require administrators to give some hearing to those views, however much administrators may disagree with them. In contrast, the workers in sweatshops whom USAS seeks to support operate in an extremely closed POS: not only are they formally excluded from decision making by the institution's authorities (management), but when they seek to influence management's decisions through the medium of a labor union, they usually face severe repression, ranging from the firing and blacklisting of union leaders to attacks by death squads and assassinations.

David Meyer (2004) argues that one way to bring order to this potential multiplicity of factors is to make a basic distinction between mobilizing opportunities and influence opportunities. *Mobilizing opportunities* refer to a movement's ability to organize independently and expand its membership through recruitment, a basic precondition to a movement's very existence. *Influence opportunities* refer to those social mechanisms that exist for movements to exert pressure on their targets, directly or indirectly, to alter their policies to accomplish the movement's goals. One set of opportunities may exist without the other: movements may be relatively free to organize but have little way to pressure authorities to change their actions.

I want to break down influence opportunities further, into two primary categories: leverage and legitimacy. One form of influence opportunities is what I call structural *leverage*—some way that activists can undermine the structural sources of elites' power. It is not enough for activists to have the opportunity to air their grievances to decision makers. They must have the means to influence the actual decisions. Luders (2006) defines this in terms of the sanctions or costs that movements can impose on decision makers. This could conceivably take institutional forms, such as mobilizing people to vote against elected leaders in a democratic polity, but more often for movements it takes an extra-institutional form, such as boycotts, labor strikes, or a general disruption of public order through unruly street protests. While such leverage is not usually defined in terms of being part of the POS, this is nonetheless consistent with a large body of research on social movements. These studies stress that while the power of elites rests on the normal routines of social institutions, because movements almost by definition lack large degrees of institutionalized power, they must exert leverage through the opposite means—finding ways to disrupt the normal functioning of social institutions that raise the costs for elites (Andrews 2001; Flacks 1988; Gamson [1975] 1990; Piven and Cloward 1977; Tarrow 1998). When such disruption is sufficient that elites feel their interests are threatened, they will respond—one hopes with concessions, but also possibly with repression and countermobilization. The anti-sweatshop movement has attempted to exert leverage both in the factory, with the workers striking at individual sites of production, and in sites of consumption, such as college campuses. It is noteworthy that often, for their campaigns to be successful, they must exert leverage from multiple sites at once to bring sufficient pressure to bear on their opponents.

The literature on discursive opportunity structures implicitly suggests a second way that movements can impose sanctions on powerful social actors: by undermining their *legitimacy*. Along with the work on the DOS, other work on social movements indicates that legitimacy or winning discursive contests is an important factor in the outcome of a conflict (Andrews 2001; Jasper 1997; Ryan 1991), with some counting it as part of the POS (Gamson and Meyer 1996; Oberschall 1996). Without legitimacy, those in positions of power have difficulty justifying their actions and encounter broadening social resistance to their action. This undermines their ability to achieve their goals in ways that are perhaps subtler than the disruption of the social order that comes from exercise of leverage by movements, but they are still quite real.

These elements of the POS are not static things that exist independently of movements and their opponents but are interactive in nature. The "arena" aspect of a social arena is a metaphor: the arena is constituted not so much by the physical space in which the action takes place, though this can be important, but by the very interactions of the individuals within the social arena. Without students, administrators, faculty, and staff, a college campus would amount to no more than a group of empty buildings—it is the interactions of people in these various social roles that constitute the arena. Similarly, leverage is a product of both social structure and how different social actors strategically interact with one another, and the capacity for delegitimation is both cultural and produced by strategic interaction. While leverage is rooted in social structure, it exists only potentially until activists find a strategy through which to exert it within the social arena in which they are acting. The fact that activists might be able to harm a targeted company through a boycott is unlikely to have any impact on the company in question until the activists actually initiate such a boycott—or, at the very least, threaten to. It will also not always be immediately evident to activists where they have leverage or what framing they might engage in to delegitimate their opponents. It may require some experimentation and innovation on their part as they try different tactics and strategies, looking for one that applies sufficient structural or cultural sanctions to elites that the elites are forced to respond.

The flip side of these dynamics of leverage and delegitimation is that a social arena's elite actors—the opponents of the movement—can respond in kind, taking a broad range of *countermeasures* to undermine the movement. This includes not only the framing battles just discussed and the repressive measures that are part of McAdam's (1996) model of POS but potentially a range of other actions, as well. Elsewhere, for instance, McAdam (1983) discusses measures that southern authorities took to undermine the Civil Rights Movement, such as making token concessions and inviting civil rights activists to participate in committees that were ostensibly designed to deal with the major issues but were, in fact, meant as little more than a bureaucratic delaying tactic. In the case of the anti-sweatshop movement, the authorities' first line of defense has been repression—firing and attacking workers when they attempt to unionize. But USAS has had to deal with administration committees meant as delaying tactics, as well as companies' creation of corporate social responsibility programs, which have proved to be more an elaborate tool for winning framing battles than an actual means of addressing the problems the movement raised (see Chapter 8).

These countermeasures taken by a movement's opponents are simultaneously structural, cultural, and interactive. Repression, for instance, involves the structural capacity of the authorities to use such coercion—having the soldiers, police, security guards, or paramilitary forces available to violently attack activists; the prevailing cultural norms, among both elites and broader publics, around the use of such coercion; and the strategic decision by elites to use such repression. Elites may have the structural capacity to repress their opponents but choose not to use it because it genuinely violates their own normative sensibilities; because they fear it will backfire by violating broader cultural norms and increase support for activists; or because they believe less blunt tools will do a better job of undermining the movement.

In conceptualizing all these elements of the POS, we need to think about them in relation to specific social actors. Differences in social location give social movement actors access to different social institutions—that is, different social arenas—and different forms of leverage and thus widely varying political opportunities (Piven and Cloward 1977). Sweatshop workers and student anti-sweatshop activists, despite belonging to a common transnational movement, have very different relationships to apparel companies. The workers are at the bottom of this social structure, interacting with their employers, contractors to whom the major apparel firms have outsourced production and who consequently have relatively little power in the larger picture. Students, by contrast, are consumers—and a particularly valued set of consumers at that, at which a great deal of marketing is targeted. The profits of the brand-name corporations depend on their reputation with consumers such as college students. Given this fact, the brands worry far more about the attitudes and actions of students than of workers, giving students openings that workers do not have, a point explored in depth throughout the book. Therefore, we must conceive of the POS always in relation to particular social actors, never simply in generic form (although in some cases it is certainly possible to make generalizations).

The Anti-sweatshop Movement: Contributions to the Literature

In addition to the broader contributions to the social movements literature this book makes, it aims to deepen our understanding of the anti-sweatshop movement in particular. Most of the existing research on the anti-sweatshop movement has focused primarily on the political economy of sweatshops, addressing the movement within that context (see, e.g., R. Ross 2004). A few works (Armbruster-Sandoval 2005; Brooks 2007; Esbenshade 2004b; Garwood 2011; A. Ross 1997) have focused primarily on the movement itself; still, given the number of academics who work closely with the organization, surprisingly little has been written on United Students Against Sweatshops in particular. Andrew Ross's (1997) edited volume was published in 1997, just as the movement was taking off and before USAS was formed. Ralph Armbruster-Sandoval (2005), Ethel Brooks (2007), and Shae Garwood (2011) look primarily at the transnational dimensions of the movement, while Jill Esbenshade (2004b) focuses on its monitoring programs.

Two books that deal with the anti-sweatshop movement describe USAS in more depth. The first is a brief, journalistic account by Liza Featherstone (2002), with some contributions by USAS members. While it provides useful history of USAS and an analysis of its ideals, it does not examine closely the strategic evolution of the organization or the wider movement. In addition, Featherstone's account was published in 2002, and this book considers two of the important developments that occurred between then and my own research in 2007: (1) the creation of the DSP by USAS and (2) the adaptation of USAS's strategy to the social arena of city and state governments by SweatFree Communities. The other main work on USAS is by Garwood (2011), who looks at USAS as one of four case studies of anti-sweatshop groups, along with the Central American STITCH, the European Clean Clothes Campaign, and the Australian FairWear. Garwood takes a comparative perspective on USAS that is very useful in contextualizing the organization in the larger transnational anti-sweatshop movement. Her book, however, does not go into the same depth in USAS and the WRC's history as this one. In addition, while Garwood does examine questions of movement strategy, she does not look at the process by which anti-sweatshop activists developed these strategies; nor does she look at the ins and outs of USAS's strategy in the same depth.

In addition, this book takes an in-depth look at USAS's strategy not only in transnational campaigns but also on college campuses, a subject to which other accounts of the anti-sweatshop movement typically give little attention. While its campus strategy may seem of marginal interest to those interested in issues of global scope, USAS would not have a successful transnational strategy without a successful campus strategy. USAS's leverage in transnational campaigns rests on its ability to persuade or coerce college administrations into upholding pro-labor codes of conduct for the companies that make clothes carrying a school's logo, something the companies must receive a license from the school to do (as discussed in more depth in Chapter 3). What we are seeing here is an interesting manifestation of local-global connections as they apply to movement strategy. USAS's strategy is successful because it operates at two different levels that at first glance are not closely connected—college campuses and the global apparel industry—but that are, in fact, articulated with each other in a way that has allowed USAS to exercise more leverage than one might expect.

I also look at the question of CSR, particularly in the apparel industry, from a new angle. Corporate social responsibility is closely tied to the dynamics of the interactions between movements and their corporate opponents, since major companies often seek to defuse activist campaigns by appearing to take the high ground by putting in place CSR programs or joining multi-stakeholder CSR organizations. In this case, the apparel industry helped create the FLA in response to anti-sweatshop activism, as discussed in Chapter 8. What my review of the literature in that chapter shows is that most analyses of CSR programs focus on their effectiveness, and they generally find such effectiveness sadly lacking. My argument is that CSR programs are effective—just not at their stated purpose. What they do allow major firms to do, with some degree of success, is counter the movement's framing by creating the appearance of doing something while not actually addressing the root problem of the need to change the production practices that have led to both the firm's high profits and workers' poor working conditions. Looking at CSR programs such as the FLA from this angle deepens our understanding of them and the role they play as a strategic countermeasure by firms to movements.

I also take a close look at the Worker Rights Consortium as an organization autonomous from USAS. The WRC is often treated as an extension of USAS, which is understandable since USAS drove the process of the creation of the WRC, and the two organizations continue to work closely together, with USAS members making up a third of the consortium's board of directors. However, a closer examination of how the WRC operates in Chapter 10 shows that there is a distinct division of labor between USAS and the WRC: USAS engages in protests and other confrontational actions, while the WRC monitors for violations of labor codes of conduct, conducts inspections of factories where such violations are alleged to have occurred, and issues reports on the findings. This division of labor heightens the effectiveness of each group: if the WRC finds violations that companies refuse to address, USAS can mobilize to pressure those companies to change course; when USAS mobilizes in such cases, the WRC's reports help bolster its legitimacy. But this division of labor works only because the WRC has established itself as an organization that is *not* an extension of USAS but one that operates autonomously from the student group and other anti-sweatshop organizations. For instance, the WRC seeks to cultivate a less confrontational relationship with the FLA—sometimes partnering with that group to do inspections—than USAS, which has called for the FLA's abolition. Being seen by all actors, including the movement's opponents, as an organization autonomous from both USAS and labor unions increases the WRC's credibility as an independent monitor and thereby increases the credibility of its inspection reports and the ability of groups such as USAS to use these reports to boost the legitimacy of their own campaigns.

The Road Ahead

The remainder of this book analyzes these matters in more depth. Chapter 2 provides an overview of the structure of the international apparel industry. This is important to understand for a number of reasons. One the major causes of sweatshops is this structure—major U.S. and European apparel firms contract out production to other, smaller firms in the Global South (and some places in the Global North, as well). These smaller firms are in competition with one another for these contracts, putting them in a bidding war against one another in which they offer to produce the goods for the lowest price possible—something that, for all practical purposes, forces them to run sweatshops. The anti-sweatshop movement is very much aware of these structural problems—it is central to the movement's ideological understanding of sweatshops—and its strategy is aimed at ultimately changing the structure of the apparel industry and thereby shifting the balance of power within it toward workers.

Chapter 3 considers another crucial set of social structures: those of the college campus. Here I look at how colleges' ties to large corporations, including major apparel firms such as Nike and Reebok, create the potential for students to exercise leverage over the apparel firms. I also look at how the structure, culture, and other social actors in colleges form the political opportunity structure within which student activists must operate. In some ways, it is quite open, for students may organize and spread their ideas freely. In some ways, it is relatively closed, because students do not have any democratic control over the officials who operate schools and because the culture of college campuses, among both administrators and students, is increasingly oriented toward consumerism and job training rather than toward being an active citizen.

Chapter 4 examines the origins of the anti-sweatshop movement, with a strong focus on United Students Against Sweatshops. In particular, I look at how USAS's origins are tied to the extension of an existing strategic model—the corporate campaign—by looking for new points of leverage. The corporate campaign involves looking for corporations' vulnerabilities, including points of connection with other organizations, and attacking these potential points of leverage from multiple angles. Organizers at the apparel union UNITE identified the licensing agreements colleges have with companies such as Nike to produce clothing with the school's name and logo on it as one such potential vulnerability. They helped student activists form the national network that became USAS in the hope of exerting leverage at this point—something that turned out to be far more effective than they ever expected.

Chapter 5 looks at the foundation of USAS's ability to exert leverage over apparel companies—its ability to exert leverage over the administrations of its activists' own schools, allowing USAS to make use of the licensing agreements as a point of vulnerability. Its campus campaigns present a particularly clear illustration of how a strategic model works in action. The student group has a clear model involving a gradual escalation of tactics over the course of the school year, starting by building up USAS's legitimacy on campus and then taking more confrontational actions, such as hunger strikes and sit-ins, to pressure the administration. It is not simply the combination but the sequencing of tactics that makes the strategic model distinct—and effective. Without gaining legitimacy first through petitions and rallies, a more highly contentious action such as a sit-in would likely fail, for the administration could counter it without damaging its own legitimacy. However, when USAS has high legitimacy, school officials can undermine their own legitimacy by taking action against the movement. Since USAS's global strategy to support sweatshop workers depends on being able to use colleges' institutional consumer power as a point of leverage over apparel companies, it is essential that the movement's campus strategy be effective.

Chapters 6 and 7 are an anatomy of USAS. Chapter 6 looks at the ideology of USAS and the wider U.S. anti-sweatshop movement, which emphasizes worker empowerment through independent labor unions. This focus has important consequences for the movement's strategy, since it is not trying simply to abolish sweatshops but to abolish them by creating conditions that foster strong labor unions. Chapter 7 looks at how USAS's organization fosters effective strategy. In part, this is for reasons explored already in the literature: USAS's consensus-based, democratic decision-making process fosters good strategizing. In addition to that, however, USAS has a national staff, including paid organizers, and annual conferences that facilitate the transmission of its strategic models and ideology to new generations of activists, which is particularly important for college students, where a generation is four years.

Chapters 8 and 9 explore the first cycle of strategic innovation—the creation of the Worker Rights Consortium. Chapter 8 looks at the instigating events—actions taken by the apparel industry in response to USAS's initial success in getting colleges to implement pro-labor codes of conduct for the apparel companies with college licensing agreements. Specifically, the industry created CSR programs—both its own, internal social compliance departments and the multi-stakeholder FLA—which it presented as an effective means to address the sweatshop problem. In doing so, the industry attempted to portray itself as having the situation well in hand and thus to define student anti-sweatshop activism as well-meaning but misguided and unnecessary. Extensive research by many scholars shows that CSR programs do not address the root structural causes of sweatshops and therefore are generally ineffective. I argue that what they do perform effectively is bolstering the legitimacy of the apparel industry in its conflict with the movement by creating the appearance of taking action—something many journalists and college officials buy into. The threat posed by CSR to the movement was exacerbated when many schools began joining the FLA as a way to monitor whether their new codes of conduct were being followed.

Chapter 9 looks at USAS and the wider anti-sweatshop movement's response to these developments: to develop the WRC as an alternative to the FLA and other CSR programs, with the intention of creating a genuinely independent and effective monitoring organization. This involved a creative process of looking at the weaknesses of the FLA through the lens of the movement's ideology—how it did not address the structural causes of sweatshops and how it failed to empower workers—and then creating an alternative that, they hoped, would be able to do these things. I also give a brief overview of the campaign to get schools to join the WRC.

Chapter 10 takes a closer look at the actual workings of the WRC, particularly at its approach to independent monitoring, what it calls the "fire alarm" model. Rather than regularly inspecting and certifying factories, as the FLA does, it responds to complaints by factory workers or groups, such as labor unions and human rights nongovernmental organizations allied with workers. This model of independent monitoring does much to bolster the legitimacy of the WRC and its reports—which USAS and other anti-sweatshop groups can use in their transnational campaigns in support of factory workers whose rights have been violated.

I look at these campaigns in Chapter 11, including the POS constituted by the global apparel industry, the strategic model used by the activists, and the transnational networks that work together to implement that strategic model in particular cases. Such campaigns are the real test for the various strategic models, such as using corporate campaigns and the WRC's monitoring programs, developed by USAS and its allies—and in a number of cases, the anti-sweatshop movement has scored important victories to help workers in specific factories around the world gain the right to unionize and collectively bargain with management.

These victories unfortunately proved ephemeral. In Chapter 12, I look at how USAS responded to this challenge with a second cycle of strategic innovation, producing the Designated Suppliers Program. The problem anti-sweatshop activists faced was that when workers at a factory successfully unionized, the cost of doing business with that factory would inevitably go up, as better working conditions raise costs. The major apparel firms, looking at only the bottom line, would take their business elsewhere, effectively putting the unionized factory out of business. The DSP was the result of the round of innovation in which anti-sweatshop activists from around the world considered how to take this structural problem on directly. The goal of the DSP was to alter the structure of at least that part of the apparel industry that produced college licensed goods by giving them financial incentives to stay with factories that treated their workers well instead of punishing them by taking their business, as well. This was obviously an ambitious goal—and, partly as a result of successful delaying tactics by the apparel industry, the campaign for the DSP eventually fizzled out. However, the principles and lessons behind the DSP live on, and we can see them being implemented in the Accord on Fire and Building Safety in Bangladesh, discussed in the epilogue to Chapter 12.

Chapter 13 looks at a somewhat different episode of strategic innovation. Rather than being the result of a setback, as the WRC and DSP were, SweatFree Communities was created as the result of an initiative taken by anti-sweatshop activists. Its members sought to take the model they had developed in designing the WRC and DSP and expand it by getting city and state governments to adopt pro-labor codes of conduct for the companies producing uniforms for government employees. Activists had to change their strategy for pressuring authorities significantly, given the very different political opportunity structure of college campuses versus city governments. But they also had to deal with the fact that they could not simply use the tried and proven WRC as an independent monitor. The reality of city politics and expectations of even sympathetic government officials required them to create a body with important organizational differences from the WRC that would weaken activists' influence even as it was supposed to play a parallel role to that of the WRC.

In Chapter 14, I make observations on the possible future of the movement, revisit my major theoretical arguments, and raise questions for future research.

I

POLITICAL OPPORTUNITY
STRUCTURES

Globalization, the Apparel Industry,
and the Roots of Sweatshops

Sweatshops and the Case of the Camisas Modernas Factory

In some ways, the Camisas Modernas factory in Guatemala, owned by Phillips–Van Heusen (PVH), a major producer of men's shirts, was a model factory. According to a report by Human Rights Watch:

> The company's employee welfare programs [. . .] were widely viewed by independent observers as exceeding the norm and arguably at the forefront of the maquila [production for export] sector. Managers expressed pride to Human Rights Watch in the company's support for a lunch room, at which the PVH subsidized hot lunches; a store, at which workers could make subsidized purchases; a clinic providing free medical attention on the plant's premises (which we were told is to include dentistry in the near future); a provision for interest-free loans; and generous provisions for ad hoc payments to be made to staff members or their families in the case of deaths and other family emergencies. (Human Rights Watch 1997)

Despite these perks, there were serious issues at the factory. The wages, at roughly 75–90 cents an hour (pay was actually based on a piece-rate system, where workers were paid by how much they produced rather than how many hours they worked), came to only half the amount required to put a family of five over the poverty line (Armbruster-Sandoval 2005; Bounds 1997). There was also a long history of union busting by management.

PVH opened up two Camisas Modernas factories in 1988, merging them in January 1997. The first organizing campaign began in 1989, after management lowered the piece-rate payments, meaning that workers would have to work longer or faster—producing more garments—to make the same pay as before. There was also a general atmosphere of disrespectful treatment by management, such as restrictions on access to bathrooms. It was in response to this organizing campaign that management began to put in place the socially responsible policies listed above at the same time that they fired union supporters, hoping to undermine the union. In 1991, the organizing campaign took off again, leading to the formation of the Sindicato de Trabajadores de Camisas Modernas (Camisas Modernas Workers' Union [STECAMOSA]). The union made contact with several U.S. labor rights groups, including the U.S./Guatemala Labor Education Project (US/GLEP), now the U.S. Labor Education in the Americas Project (USLEAP). The company responded by essentially bribing the union's leaders to resign, offering them extremely generous severance packages if they did so; at the same time, they put them on poorly working machines, thereby dramatically lowering the money they could make through the piece-rate system if they remained employed. The result was a 34 percent turnover rate for union members, compared with 2–5 percent for the workforce as a whole (Armbruster-Sandoval 2005; Human Rights Watch 1997).

In August 1996, STECAMOSA responded to these union-busting tactics by undertaking a clandestine organizing campaign, visiting workers at their homes. On September 2, in a surprise move, the union officially let management know that it had signed up 25 percent of the workforce, the legally necessary level at which the company would be required to bargain with the union. Rather than bargain, management refused to recognize that the union had gained the necessary number of employees. It also hired armed security guards—an extremely intimidating move in the context of the pervasive political violence in Guatemala.[1] Union members were again forced to work at broken machines, a move that pushed twenty of them to quit so they could find jobs elsewhere (Armbruster-Sandoval 2005; Human Rights Watch 1997).

---

1. Note that, according to the Human Rights Watch report, managers claimed that they hired the armed guards because of telephoned death threats they received (Human Rights Watch 1997).

The irony in all this is that Bruce Klatsky, the chief executive of PVH, considered himself a human rights advocate. He sat on the board of Human Rights Watch and was involved in the Clinton administration's efforts to create a coalition of apparel companies committed to socially responsible labor practices. Jeff Hermanson (interview, 2007), a board member of USLEAP, told me:

> During a board meeting of USLEAP in New York City, it came to our attention that Klatsky was scheduled to give a keynote speech at a fundraiser for Human Rights Watch. [. . .] So we actually told Human Rights Watch that we were going to picket their fundraiser. And [PVH] called us [. . .] and said, "What can we do to avoid this?" So we said, "Well, you can agree to send a Human Rights Watch investigation team to Guatemala, and we'll rely on their findings. If they find that Phillips–Van Heusen has violated Guatemalan labor law and international worker rights, we would call upon you to recognize the union and bargain." And they said, "OK, we'll do that." And they did that. And, lo and behold, the investigation disclosed that rights had been violated.

Klatsky reluctantly agreed to bargain with the union.

Fifteen months later, in December 1998, PVH closed the plant. It claimed to be doing so for economic reasons unrelated to the presence of a union—specifically, the loss of a major client for the goods produced at Camisas Modernas. Many labor activists, however, regarded this claim with suspicion, seeing the closure as a move to eliminate the only factory in the Guatemalan maquila sector that had successfully unionized (Armbruster-Sandoval 2005; Greenhouse 1999d; Hermanson interview). "Upon examining PVH's 1998 Annual Report, [US/GLEP] found that its profits on men's dress shirts, which were produced at *Camisas Modernas, increased* from $45 million to $50 million" (Armbruster-Sandoval 2005, 52–53). In addition, the work that workers had been doing at Camisas Modernas was now being outsourced to four other factories, with far worse conditions, including lower pay, longer hours, and none of the perks that Camisas Modernas had had (Armbruster-Sandoval 2005).

It is entirely possible that the decision was a strictly economic one and, at the same time, inspired by the presence of the union. The situation with Camisas Modernas was unusual in not only the benefits the workers received from the company but also the very fact that PVH actually owned the factory. Most apparel companies actually manufacture very little of the goods they market and sell. Instead, outsourcing to contractors, often small companies barely scraping by, is the norm in the industry. In closing down Camisas Modernas and switching to outsourcing, PVH was simply following this established pattern. One of the reasons that most companies prefer outsourcing is that it is cheaper. One of the reasons it is cheaper is that contractors generally do not have a unionized workforce, and therefore do not have to pay high wages, provide benefits, or respect health and safety standards. Indeed, when contractors do recognize unions, they—like Camisas Modernas—are usually forced to shut down in a year or two. This is not because the major apparel companies are punishing the contractors in some knee-jerk anti-union response. In fact, under pressure from the anti-sweatshop movement, the major apparel companies have sometimes played a role in pushing their contractors to recognize the union in the first place. It is simply that, once the contractor recognizes the union, its costs of doing business go up, and the major companies take their business elsewhere—that is, to contractors who can produce for less by ignoring workers' rights.

In reporting on the PVH–Camisas Modernas case, the *Wall Street Journal* reporter Wendy Bounds (1997, B1) notes, "The controversy cuts to the heart of a central question for U.S. manufacturers competing in the global economy: Can they keep labor costs low and still respect human rights?" In short, the answer seems to be no.

The Structure of the U.S. Apparel Industry

To understand why the answer is no and why outsourcing is so prevalent, we need to understand the structure and history of the apparel industry. The apparel industry is organized around what Gary Gereffi (1994, 2001) calls buyer-driven commodity chains, where the industry is dominated not by manufacturers, but by retailers, marketers, and merchandisers. This arrangement is typical of most labor-intensive consumer-goods industries, such as apparel, footwear, and toys. The greatest profits are to be made not in actually producing the goods, but in designing and marketing them. Thus, these firms maintain control of advertising and retail while farming out production. They are also driven to constantly innovate—producing new styles of clothing, for instance—because their products are so easily imitated by competitors (Green 1997; Korzeniewicz 1994; Rabach and Kim 1994). As a result of this, for many lead firms in buyer-driven commodity chains, the major asset is their brand image and identity, which is best understood as a nonmaterial form of capital. Much of the brand-name firms' work becomes not about managing labor, but about managing consumers, shaping how they use products and attempting to colonize ever more spheres of social life in a quest to increase the value of their brands (Arvidsson 2006; Klein 1999).

It is this low profitability of actual manufacturing that leads the major apparel firms to outsource most, if not all, of the production to smaller companies (Gereffi 1994; R. Ross 2004). When a firm outsources production, it hires another firm—the contractor or supplier—to produce the goods for it. Contractors may, in turn, hire subcontractors do some of the production they have been hired to do. In the eyes of the lead firms—that is, the companies that do the outsourcing—this system has two virtues. If a contractor's production costs grow too high, they can simply switch to a cheaper firm, without any financial loss resulting from giving up their own factories. As fashions change, they may switch suppliers, finding ones better suited to produce the new goods (Green 1997; R. Ross 2004). While the resulting production process is highly decentralized, power remains concentrated in the retailers, marketing, and merchandisers who control the most profitable part of the production process (Moody 1997). Retailers may charge as much as a 55–60 percent markup from what they pay the manufacturers/contractors (Appelbaum and Gereffi 1994). Some of the contractors who do the actual production are themselves large, transnational firms, based in Taiwan and South Korea, although they may do much of their production in other, lower-cost countries (Gereffi and Pan 1994). Most contractors, however, are small operations, often owning a single factory. In seeking to manufacture goods for the brand-name companies, these contractors are essentially in a bidding war with one another: whoever can produce the goods for the lowest cost while maintaining a certain quality will get the contract. Most contractors operate at very slim profit margins, often just getting by (Bonacich et al. 1994; R. Ross 2004).

This relationship between the lead firms and their contractors in turn defines the relationship between the owners of the contracting firms and their workers (Dolan 2004) and thus the sort of decisions management is likely to make within these arenas. Because the contractors operate at such slim profit margins, they in turn must shift the burdens of the drive to cut costs onto their workers, thus producing sweatshops. These asymmetries of power between the lead firms and their contractors and between the contractors and their workers have important consequences for the anti-sweatshop movement. When suppliers have been successfully pushed to recognize unions, raise their wages, and improve working conditions, these victories have proved short-lived. Typically, we see the same pattern as in the Camisas Modernas factory: the factories that make such deals shut down within a year or two because they can no longer afford to stay open. When contractors improve conditions for their employees, they raise their own costs of production—and, consequently, lose out in the bidding war to do business with the lead firms. The suppliers simply are not in a structural position to change the way business is done and how labor is treated. That power lies with the big apparel companies that dominate the production process even as they outsource most production, which therefore have become the focus of the anti-sweatshop movement's campaigns (Armbruster-Sandoval 2005; Esbenshade 2004b).

The U.S. apparel industry was one of the pioneers in pursuing global outsourcing as a way to avoid labor unions and cut costs. In many ways, the model for other companies was Nike, which has *never* manufactured anything itself but got its start importing running shoes from Japan. It then began giving orders on the design of the shoes as its profits increased in the United States (Korzeniewicz 1994). As early as the 1950s, however, well before the rise of Nike, many lead apparel companies were outsourcing production to companies in Japan, South Korea, and Taiwan, where labor costs were considerably cheaper than in the United States. In the 1970s, overseas outsourcing increased dramatically as a cost-cutting response to the economic downturn of that era. Not only U.S.-based firms followed this pattern; many of the Japanese, Korean, and Taiwanese suppliers also began moving their production to other countries in the Pacific Rim, both in Asia and in Mexico and Central America, seeking to escape the growing power of labor unions, which had successfully raised wages in Japan, South Korea, and Taiwan. While the contractors might directly set up their own factories in these new countries, they often subcontracted out production to new, local manufacturers in turn (Bonacich et al. 1994; Rosen 2002).

One of the main driving forces behind such outsourcing and movement overseas was the class conflict between the companies' owners and the unions representing (however problematically at times) apparel industry workers (Ross and Trachte 1990). The lead U.S. apparel firms wished to escape the marginal improvements the U.S. labor movement had won for garment workers, and the easiest way to do this was to go to locales where the labor movement was weak and in no position to challenge apparel manufacturers. Third World countries, particularly nondemocratic ones where governments had no qualms about violently repressing the labor movement, were a natural next step. This trend continues today, with contractors increasingly setting up shop in China and Vietnam, two countries where independent labor unions are totally illegal and only those controlled by and serving the interests of the nominally communist governments are allowed. It should be noted that some production remains in the United States—primarily in the traditional centers of New

York City and Los Angeles—but it is hardly free from exploitation. U.S. apparel contractors tend to rely heavily on easily exploited immigrant labor and operate outside the law, resulting in highly exploitive conditions similar to production sites overseas, driven by the same need to keep down costs (Bonacich et al. 1994; Esbenshade 2004b; R. Ross 2004).

Beginning in the late 1970s and accelerating in the 1980s, a dramatic shift happened in the policies of the United States and other First World countries that, among other things, facilitated the ability of U.S. and European firms to follow this pattern of outsourcing anywhere in the world. This was the rise of neoliberalism, which, though marked by a rhetoric of "free markets" and deregulation, is characterized more by a reorientation of the economic regulatory system, both domestic and international, in ways that undermine what collective power labor and other vulnerable social groups had built up in favor of transnational corporations. Because a full exploration of these trends is beyond the scope of this book, I highlight here only those aspects that are most relevant for understanding the rise of outsourcing. It is important to stress that the picture painted of neoliberalism by many writers, especially those sympathetic to it (see, e.g., Castells 2001; Friedman 2000)—that it is the natural result of the growth of global markets and advances in telecommunications technology, a rising tide governments cannot control or hope to turn back—is grossly misleading. Neoliberalism, rather, is the result of policies deliberately pursued by corporations and governments, particularly U.S. corporations and the U.S. government (Harvey 2005). Different countries took different paths toward neoliberalism, with some more ideological and some viewing it as a matter of pragmatic adaptation to the global economy (Fourcade-Gourinchas and Babb 2002), but it involved deliberate policy decisions by elites across the globe.

Some of the competitive pressures to produce overseas can be seen in the experience of Levi Strauss. In 1990, the company—which was committed to keeping production in the United States—dominated the jeans market, controlling a 48.2 percent share. As its competitors moved production abroad and were able to produce similar goods for less, Levi Strauss saw its market share shrink. Finally, in 1998, now with only 25 percent of the market, Levi Strauss felt compelled to move production to Mexico, resulting in mass layoffs in the United States (Rosen 2002). Thus, it would be difficult for any one company to buck the trend by trying to be socially responsible—it simply would not be profitable enough. In other words, the problem is a structural one. It is, however, a structural one of the apparel companies' own making. They pushed for the neoliberal policy reforms that facilitate outsourcing and have actively resisted any changes to these policies that would limit the potential for the abuse of labor rights. The apparel industry remains, therefore, collectively morally culpable for the prevalence of sweatshops.

Implications for Activists

The neoliberal restructuring of the global economy in general, and the rise of outsourcing in the apparel industry in particular, have major implications for activists: the ease with which they can gain access to different social arenas, what forms of leverage they have, what grievances and demands are seen as legitimate, the degree to which their frames are considered credible. With the rise of neoliberalism, many elite actors have become openly hostile to labor unions and other economic justice advocates. Even mainstream left-of-center parties, while maintaining their ties with the labor movement, have embraced neoliberal policies that actively erode unions' power and workers' security.

In general, economic justice activists have the sense that they have less access to the major social arenas where decisions about global governance are made. Anti-sweatshop activists have thus tried to develop strategies that bypass government enforcement. According to Jessica Rutter (interview, 2007), a USAS organizer from Duke University:

> I would say a lot the anti-sweatshop stuff that has been done has been because of a lack of government regulation or any kind of framework to look at labor standards in terms of free trade stuff. [. . .] Generally, the governments, both the U.S. government and national governments of places where a lot of this stuff is being produced, were actually pretty much working against improved labor standards. So this was definitely a campaign that looked at companies as the decision makers and was done because we thought it would be easier than using government as a target in terms of legislation, especially because it was so global. I would say the campaign itself really didn't address any kind of government regulation and did that on purpose because of the ineffectiveness of government to regulate this kind of stuff.

Most of the anti-sweatshop activists I spoke with wanted to see governments take a more pro-labor stance in their regulations, whether at the national level or through international agreements. They concluded, however, that, given the dominance of neoliberal strategies on the part of governments, such regulation would not come about any time soon. They also concluded that they actually have more leverage over private, for-profit corporations than over nominally democratic governments—a striking sign of the shallowness of democracy under neoliberalism.

Concurring with these activists, Marc Dixon, Andrew Martin, and Michael Nau (2016, 66) also suggest that such business targets—despite their lack of democratic openings—may, in fact, be more vulnerable than nation-states:

> Corporations, unlike the democratic nation state, are closed to most routine forms of claims making but lack the state's ability to channel protest into more acceptable mediums. At the same time, they are more vulnerable to delegitimation than the nation state. Indeed, a corporation's brand visibility to consumers and its reputation within the business community can be quickly tarnished by the revelation of malfeasance or other socially irresponsible behavior.

As we will see, much of the anti-sweatshop movement's strategy has involved delegitimating the corporate targets. Dixon, Martin, and Nau argue that such delegitimation is not usually enough on its own and that, in most cases, movements must also employ disruptive tactics targeting the corporation, something the anti-sweatshop movement does by holding the threat of the cancellation of lucrative licensing contracts with colleges over the heads of the firms.

Which social arenas activists have access to or leverage over is important, because not all social arenas are created equal. Thus, activists have to find ways to influence not only decision makers' choices but also the choices of those decision makers who occupy the most powerful arenas. The workers are at the bottom of this social structure, interacting with their employers, contractors who themselves have relatively little power in the larger picture. Both the workers and contractors are, essentially, disposable; the lead firms can always find others to do their work. Consumers, however, have some potential leverage over the brand-name firms; the profits of these corporations depend on their reputation with consumers. And some groups of consumers, such as college students, are particularly valued. Given this, the brands worry far more about the attitudes and actions of students and other consumers than they do workers, giving students leverage that workers do not have.

This structure, in turn, has consequences for both workers' and students' ability to form independent organizations—that is, how much they have in the way of mobilizing opportunities. Workers in Third World sweatshops typically have very little space to organize, facing repression—ranging from the firing of leaders to death squads—when they try to do so (Armbruster-Sandoval 2005). As already noted, the contractors who employ the workers are not really in a position to collectively bargain with the workers, even if they wanted to. Thus, contractors, due to their structural location, have many incentives to repress unions and few to tolerate them. U.S. activists are far freer to organize without fear of unpleasant consequences, even in the case of students, who are subject to school administrations that are antidemocratic in their organization. Student activists may be arrested if they are conducting sit-ins or the like, but they do not have to fear that the college administration will blacklist or assassinate them. United Students Against Sweatshops has used this relative freedom to act in solidarity with workers, bringing pressure on companies to recognize workers' independent unions and thereby altering the political opportunity structure and creating greater mobilizing opportunities for workers.

3

Higher Education as a
Political Opportunity Structure

The Corporatization of Higher Education

During and following its formation as a national organization over the course of the 1997–1999 school years, United Students Against Sweatshops (USAS) proved to be a dynamic force, dramatically changing the landscape of anti-sweatshop activism by putting apparel companies on the defensive. Before exploring the strategy USAS pursued, however, we first need to understand the power structure and the political opportunity structure on college campuses. Just as it is necessary to understand how the structure of the apparel industry shapes the options open to workers and their allies, we must understand how the structure, culture, and social actors in higher education shape the possibilities for student activism.

As part of this, we need to examine the increasing corporatization of higher education. This process, involving the penetration of neoliberal ideology and practices into the academy, is a significant part of the context in which student activists must operate. On the one hand, it creates an atmosphere on campus that is not conducive to activism, as administrators focus on maximizing revenues and students focus on training for jobs after graduation and the enticements of consumer culture. On the other hand, this very corporatization is what has given students a potential point of leverage over the apparel industry, for it is the very ties that apparel companies have formed with colleges and universities that students are turning against the lead firms to pressure them.

Corporatization refers to the fact that school administrators have increasingly adopted both the values and the techniques of big business in managing their campuses, students, faculty, and other employees, such as janitorial and food-service staff. In many ways, schools are increasingly operating as if they were for-profit organizations while maintaining their formal nonprofit status (Rhoades and Slaughter 1997; Slaughter and Rhoades 2004; White 2000).

The ongoing corporatization of higher education has taken place in the context of the rise of neoliberalism, described briefly in Chapter 2. Part of the reason for the shift lies simply in the shift in the larger ideological climate of the country (Aronowitz 2000). There also has been an increasing flow of ideas from the businesspeople sitting on schools' boards to school administrators. As the norms of the business world increasingly became the norms of society as a whole, and ties between higher education and big business tightened, the corporate executives who had long sat on school boards were increasingly able to implement policies at their schools that came from the for-profit world (Rhoades and Slaughter 1997; Slaughter and Rhoades 2004).

It should be emphasized that corporatization is an uneven process, the depth of which varies considerably from school to school. Some have become more deeply committed to it, while others retain more of an affinity for older ideals of academic autonomy and the pursuit of knowledge for the common good. Even at schools that are deeply corporatized, many members of the faculty may still adhere to older ideas, resisting the new imperatives the administration tries to impose of them. Administrators themselves may often be ambivalent and try to reconcile the two contradictory ideals (Slaughter and Rhoades 2004).

The corporatization of higher education is evident in a number of ways. It can be seen in changing patterns of employment of faculty. Administrators on many campuses have made moves to reduce the number of tenure-track positions, instead hiring adjunct instructors, who are little better than academic temps. This follows the increasingly corporate practice of replacing full-time employees with various forms of contingent labor. The use of adjuncts allows administrators to save a great deal of money, because adjuncts are paid far less than full-time faculty for the same work, and they do not get benefits. School administrators have also increasingly chosen to outsource such things as janitorial and food services. Again, this follows the practices of the corporate world and is a means of cutting costs. The companies to which such services are outsourced typically pay lower wages, provide fewer benefits, and engage in union-busting activities (Slaughter and Rhoades 2004; White 2000).

The most significant part of corporatization for this study is in the procurement contracts that most schools now have with corporations in a wide number of industries. As of 2000, Barnes and Noble operated roughly 350 campus bookstores, often displacing independent bookstores that had run them previously. Food services have long been outsourced, but while they were once outsourced to low-profile companies such as Aramark and Sodexho Marriott, high-profile brands such as Taco Bell, Pizza Hut, and Starbucks are increasingly taking over the campus. The Coca-Cola and Pepsi soda companies now compete with each other for exclusive contracts on campus. All of these companies have tremendous labor problems in one form or another. And they all see students as a captive audience for marketing, among whom they can build brand loyalty (Klein 1999; Kniffin 2000b). Colleges have also built such relationships with apparel corporations. Since it is these relationships that the anti-sweatshop movement has focused on, we look at them in more depth here.

Anyone who has set foot in a college bookstore has probably noticed the numerous items for sale, including T-shirts, baseball hats, and other forms of apparel with the school's logo imprinted on them. The schools do not produce these goods themselves. Instead, they typically sign a contract with an apparel company to produce these goods for them, giving them a license to use the school's logo; as with normal apparel production, the lead firms then outsource the production of the licensed goods to contractors throughout the world. Such licensed apparel constitutes a $2.5 billion market, one that is highly lucrative for both the colleges and universities and the apparel firms involved. The company pays the schools 7.5–8 percent of the revenue from the sales of the licensed goods, providing additional income for the schools (R. Ross 2004). Some licensees are less visible companies, such as Champion and Russell, while others are high-profile brand-names, such as Adidas, Nike, and Reebok (Benjamin 2000; Kniffin 2000b; Slaughter and Rhoades 2004).

In total, school-licensed apparel constitutes only 1–2 percent of the apparel market (R. Ross 2004). Because of the advertising and branding potential of this market, however, the lead apparel companies value it highly—well beyond any revenues they may bring in—and are loath to simply give it up. Having a license with a college essentially gives these companies a captive audience to which to advertise, an audience whose long-term brand loyalty they hope to build. Licenses with big-name sports schools are particularly sought after, because this gives the brands an opportunity to create synergy with the sports teams' brand, boosting their cachet further. In addition, when the games are broadcast, the television audience will see the brand's logo alongside the school's on the players' uniforms, giving them free advertising of the most sought-after sort (Slaughter and Rhoades 2004; Dirnbach, Nova, and Rutter interviews). As discussed briefly in Chapter 2, for companies such as Nike and Reebok, their brand is their most valuable asset, so their ability to build their brand image through relationships to schools is particularly important to them. It also gives them an opportunity to manage consumers' preferences, something that is as central (if not more so) to their operations as managing their employees (Arvidsson 2006; Klein 1999).

The licensed goods are not produced in specific factories. As with any other product produced by contractors for apparel firms, the production of such goods is scattered over the world in numerous factories, alongside nonlicensed goods, by both the same brand and others. Given this fact, anti-sweatshop movement members have sought to use this licensing relationship as a point of leverage to pressure licensees to change how they produce not only licensed goods but also their apparel as a whole. Specifically, the movement seeks to force the licensees to abide by codes of conduct when producing licensed goods, which, given the dispersed sites of production, could affect working conditions in the apparel industry beyond the narrow 1–2 percent over which schools have direct influence. As Jessica Rutter (interview), a USAS organizer at Duke University, noted:

> It's definitely a niche market, but it's also a market that universities have almost total control over, because they can say yes or no [to the licensing agreement]. The stuff is made or it's not made. So that's a very powerful relationship, one that doesn't necessarily exist in regular purchasing.

As I explore in Chapter 4, colleges' and universities' status as institutional consumers gives them leverage far greater than that of any individual consumers, even if consumers pool their efforts into a boycott.

Campus Governance and Student Activism

Perhaps the most obvious challenge students face in influencing decision making on campus is the authoritarian, antidemocratic nature of campus governance, where power is centered in the hands of administrators, who are not formally accountable to students. Traditionally, however, because administrators were mostly former faculty members, there was a good deal of accountability on the part of administrators to the faculty. As the campus becomes corporatized, though, this limited accountability has also grown weaker, as school administrators become increasingly accountable mainly to the nation's business elite, as represented on their boards (Waugh 2003). The boards of trustees of private schools and the boards of regents of public schools (the people who get to appoint school administrators) are not composed primarily of those with the most obvious connection to higher education—"educators, alumni, and local community stakeholders" (Kniffin 2000a, 158). Instead, they are—and long have been—dominated by corporate executives. College and university presidents themselves frequently sit on corporate boards; when they do not do so to avoid any semblance of impropriety, less visible administrators may sit on corporate boards instead. School presidents may also form ties with the corporate world by acting as consultants and sitting on the boards of nonprofits alongside corporate executives (Kniffin 2000a; Rhoades and Slaughter 1997).

Corporatization has produced significant changes in the structure and culture of school administrations. An increasing number of school administrators come not from within the ranks of the faculty, as is traditional, but from outside academia, often the business world. As a result, they have little understanding of academic values or culture, imposing in their place the technocratic norms of the business world—norms that such administrators tend to see as value-neutral, not an ideology in their own right. Such administrators, in addition to applying for-profit standards to academic work—valuing departments on the basis of how much revenue they bring in, for instance—have little patience with faculty's expectation that they should be able to participate in school governance. The norms of the business world are highly authoritarian, with administrators from business backgrounds used to imposing their decisions from the top down and having little patience for opposition (Steck 2003; Waugh 2003). And if such administrators have little patience with faculty's traditional prerogative to play a role in campus decision making, one may imagine they have even less patience for students' demands for such a role. In other words, as schools grow more corporatized, college and university presidents—particularly those at the upper-echelon schools—are increasingly seeing their primary loyalty as being to the business world and not the academy.

William Waugh (2003) concludes that, given this trend of school presidents becoming increasingly accountable to outside constituencies, particularly business, they have to worry less and less about their on-campus legitimacy. He worries what this may mean for the future of higher education and campus life. As shown below, the experience of USAS indicates that things may not be so cut and dried as Waugh fears. There are a number of factors that provide a counterweight to corporatization. One is the legacy of the student movement of the 1960s. Many of the current administrators came of age in that era, and some even participated in protests, giving them somewhat more comprehension of student activists than a previous generation of administrators might have had (Greenhouse 1999a; Zernike 1999). Student activism has also simply become a normative part of campus life: it is widely accepted that students have the right to protest. As such, campus administrators cannot simply afford to brush student activists off but must make at least some gestures toward listening to them and engaging with them (Robert J. S. Ross, personal communication, 2008).[1] As later demonstrated, administrators often try to get away with empty gestures, such as creating committees to study the issue raised by campus activists, but nonetheless they cannot simply ignore them altogether, and they often have to make substantial concessions.

This points to a broader phenomenon: administrators are still part of a relatively small campus community and must maintain some legitimacy in the eyes of that community, no matter how corporatized their campus. As Rutter (interview) put it:

> A campus is a closed environment, and it's easy to get access to the press, at least the campus press. There's also an enclosed decision-making process. As students, you have access to the college president, the person who makes the decisions, something a lot of other groups don't have.

Three things are at work here. One is the simple question of scale: the college or university as a social arena is so small that this, in and of itself, gives activists influence they might not have in another setting. The second is that the mobilizing opportunities for students on campus are wide open; student groups with a fair amount of autonomy are one of the norms of campus life, and administrators would be hard-pressed to justify restricting them. The campus environment is one where, even in the face of hostile forces, it is relatively easy to organize and mobilize around progressive issues (Crossley 2008; Lewis, Marine, and Kenney 2018). The third factor is that, while formal decision-making power may be monopolized by the administration, the discursive process on college campuses is wide open for students and faculty to join in (though nonfaculty employees usually have

---

1. Ross was one of the founders of Students for a Democratic Society in 1960. He is now a professor at Clark University and an adviser to USAS at the national level, positioning him to witness the changes in how campus administrators have dealt with student activists over several decades.

far less freedom to speak out). Most schools have at least one student newspaper, in addition to other student publications; students can organize a wide variety of their own events; and sympathetic professors can speak out in their support. This gives student activists multiple venues to make their case to the wider student body and build up their legitimacy. As Steven Lukes (2005) argues, while there is power in controlling the levers of decision making, there is also power in being able to set the public agenda. And student activists can build up enough legitimacy that they can help set the public agenda at their schools, forcing administrators to deal with questions such as sweatshops they might prefer to ignore. Getting something on the public agenda and getting the decisions about that issue made the way you want are certainly two different things, but even putting the issue of sweatshops on the agenda in the first place changes the nature of the playing field.

And administrators do have to worry about their legitimacy. According to Thomas Wheatley (interview), a USAS member at the University of Wisconsin (UW), Madison, "Even though they're not elected, university presidents are public figures." Eric Brakken (interview), also a USAS member at UW Madison, told the story of how the school's chancellor, David Ward, was forced to resign after mishandling a student protest. On February 21, 2000, Ward not only ordered the arrest of fifty-four student anti-sweatshop activists conducting a sit-in in his office but also sent in the riot police to do the job. Brakken noted that Ward

> took a lot of heat from the community and the campus for arresting fifty-four students and for profiteering from workers at sweatshops. Within three days of those arrests happening, he took a vacation for two or three weeks; when he came back from his vacation, he resigned.

Ward's resignation was effective January 1 of the following year. Many college and university presidents today hope to make a career of heading schools, moving from the leadership of one to the leadership of another. Discrediting oneself, as Ward did, can damage a long-term career (McSpedon interview). Thus, administrators, even when unsympathetic, must handle student activists with care.

This is not to minimize the impact of corporatization. It is to point out that, because administrations' priorities often conflict with those of progressive student activists, attempts to persuade administrations to adopt anti-sweatshop policies can be difficult and highly confrontational. But corporatization has not been total. As already noted, it is an uneven process. In the experience of Brent Wood* (interview),[2] a national organizer who has had dealings with many college officials, "most administrators [. . .] are torn. On the one hand, they want to accommodate students, and they want to do the right thing. On the other hand, they are very concerned about maintaining good relationships with the business community."

The degree of corporatization also varies considerably from school to school. The USAS member Amanda Plumb (interview) contrasted her experience with the relatively progressive, responsive administrators at Duke University, in North Carolina, where she was an undergraduate, with those of the University of Massachusetts (UMass), Amherst, where she was a graduate student. The administrators at Duke shared a concern with social justice issues with USAS. Jim Wilkerson (interview), the director of trademark licensing and store operations (and now a member of the WRC's board of directors), had independently taken an interest in the issue in the summer of 1997 after watching a show on the History Channel on the history of sweatshops. He also notes, "In those days, Nan Keohane was the president of Duke, and she had a very personal interest [in] and commitment to these types of social justice issues, something very rare among university presidents." Beyond the individual beliefs of the administrators, the administration as a whole sought to cultivate an image of an enlightened, liberal school, with a culture more akin to that of the Northeast than that of the conservative South (Plumb interview). As a result, they were open to the students, willing to negotiate with them and to implement a pro-labor code of conduct for their licensees. At UMass, Amherst, in contrast, Plumb met far greater resistance from the administration while working on the Killer Coke campaign, targeting Coca-Cola for its complicity in the use of death squads against union leaders at its bottling plants in Colombia:

> We met with the chancellor, and he said, "My job is to get the most money for your eyeballs," meaning, "My job is to make money for the school, and if that means selling ad space to Coca-Cola all around the university, that's my job—and I'm not going to cancel Coke's contract because they kill union activists. It is my job to make sure that the school is financially solvent."

Clearly, the chancellor saw his responsibilities entirely within corporatized terms—as maximizing school revenues—a far cry from the Duke

---

2. Pseudonyms used for particular statements at the interviewees' request are marked with an asterisk the first time they appear.

administrators, who sought to balance such concerns with more humanitarian ones.

The type of school can also make a difference. Zack Knorr (interview), a national organizer for USAS, said:

> Sometimes these smaller schools or even some of the bigger public schools, they may actually want to portray an image that they really encourage student activism—and some of them may somewhat mean it. The big universities, I think, are just more run like businesses.

Catholic schools have also been more responsive to students' demands, given the influence of the church's teachings on the importance of economic justice (Krupa 1999). It should also be noted that the issue itself may make a difference in many cases. Knorr noted that the last thing many administrators want to deal with is their own employees unionizing, since this represents a direct challenge to their power on campus. Thus, administrators who are willing to support monitoring their licensees to ensure that they do not use sweatshop labor may fight tooth and nail against organizing by workers on their own campuses, essentially supporting sweatshop practices at home while opposing them abroad.

Having examined the political opportunity structure within which it takes place, we can now turn to the rise of student anti-sweatshop activism.

II

AN ANATOMY OF
UNITED STUDENTS AGAINST
SWEATSHOPS (USAS)

The Origins of USAS

The Rise of Anti-sweatshop Activism

The rise of U.S. student anti-sweatshop activism is linked to a burst of media coverage of the issue of sweatshops in the mass media in the mid-1990s, which in turn is linked to the rise of anti-sweatshop activism among U.S. labor and religious groups. The roots of this activism lie in the involvement of labor activists in the Central American solidarity movement of the 1980s. This primarily church-based movement opposed the Reagan administration's proxy wars in the region, pushing for the United States to cease supporting repressive military governments in El Salvador and Guatemala and, in Nicaragua, the Contras fighting against the socialist Sandinista government. Among other things, the churches involved sent missions to Central American countries to see the effects of the war firsthand. Some of the church members who joined such delegations were also labor activists. They observed how the Guatemalan and Salvadoran governments repressed progressive labor unions, created export-processing zones (EPZs), and generally fostered a climate in which labor laws were weak or unenforced to encourage foreign investment, leading to widespread sweatshop conditions. These religious and labor activists became instrumental in forming some of the first U.S. anti-sweatshop organizations, such as U.S. Labor Education in the Americas Project and the National Labor Committee (NLC) (see Brooks 2007; Seidman 2007).

In 1995 the NLC, as part of a campaign against The Gap, produced a movie on EPZs and child labor titled *Zoned for Slavery: The Children behind the Label* and organized a speaking tour by some of the young women who worked at the Mandarin International factory in El Salvador producing goods for The Gap (Armbruster-Sandoval 2005; Brooks 2007). These events coincided with a raid by the U.S. Department of Labor on a garment factory in El Monte, California, where Thai immigrants were being held in what was essentially slavery. All this resulted in a wave of media coverage of sweatshops that put The Gap on the defensive. As a result, it suspended its orders with Mandarin International and pressured the contractor to improve working conditions, leading to some concessions to the union, including the first system of independent monitoring in the garment industry (Armbruster-Sandoval 2005; Brooks 2007).

Another important media event was the Kathie Lee Gifford scandal. As mentioned briefly in Chapter 1, Gifford was a prominent talk show host who had cultivated a wholesome, maternal image; she sponsored her own line of clothing sold through Walmart, from which half of the proceeds would go to charities that benefited children. In 1996, while visiting Honduras, Charles Kernaghan of the NLC learned that workers at the Global Fashions factory were producing goods for Gifford's line—and working under sweatshop conditions. Kernaghan brought this information back to the United States, where he publicized it. A few months later, the apparel union UNITE revealed that workers in a New York City sweatshop had contacted them for help—and that they, too, were producing for the Gifford line. Given the contrast between Gifford's image and the charges against her—including use of child labor—the media had a field day with the case, running a number of salacious stories (Brooks 2007; R. Ross 2004).

Many of the activists I spoke with saw this burst of media coverage as essential to the rise of the movement. Eric Dirnbach (interview), a researcher and campaign coordinator for UNITE HERE (the successor to UNITE), noted:

> The media played a vital and essential role from '96 up through the next five years. [. . .] There were a few early scandals in the mid- to late '90s that got a lot of media attention. I've seen studies that looked at the mention of the word "sweatshop" in media reports, and there were hundreds, if not thousands, of hits a year in various news articles.[1] [. . .] Without the media really propagating that, we wouldn't have had the success that we had.

---

1. For statistics on the rise in media coverage of sweatshops, see R. Ross 2004.

We can see here the importance of the national mass media as a social arena in which framing battles are fought. The anti-sweatshop movement won its initial skirmishes with the apparel industry, putting it on the defensive and undermining its legitimacy. This created the momentum for the anti-sweatshop movement to expand beyond its former bounds, including onto college campuses, as new social actors besides religious and labor groups took up the cause. As Chapter 8 shows, the apparel industry eventually found an effective means of countering the anti-sweatshop movement in the national mass media, using corporate social responsibility programs as a means of bolstering its legitimacy. This made the expansion of the anti-sweatshop movement to college campuses, where it had much more influence and success in discursive conflicts, all the more important.

The Start of Student Anti-sweatshop Activism

While events such as the Kathie Lee Gifford scandal prompted college students to take up the banner of anti-sweatshop activism, their initial efforts were diffuse and nonstrategic. While student anti-sweatshop activists were adept at engaging in creative guerrilla theater and other, similar actions, they initially had relatively little impact on either the national debate around sweatshops or the policies of the leading apparel firms. This began to change dramatically in the 1997–1998 school year, as the national network that would become USAS took shape. The students soon found themselves at the cutting edge of the U.S. anti-sweatshop movement as a result of a combination of creativity and the leverage the college licensing agreements (discussed in the previous chapter) gave them. Their actions expanded well beyond guerrilla theater to include not only participating in administration building sit-ins but also crafting an independent monitoring organization—the Worker Rights Consortium—which they then pressed their colleges and universities to join (see Chapters 8–10). This development gave the anti-sweatshop movement real teeth, since these schools had the power to penalize companies that failed to live up to their codes of conduct.

What happened to so dramatically change the nature of the student anti-sweatshop movement? There were several important developments, which I explore in this and the coming chapters. A number of national anti-sweatshop organizations—most importantly, the apparel union UNITE—took the student movement under their wing. They trained a new generation of student leaders, helping them to move from taking actions that were simply *tactical*, such as guerrilla theater, to developing coherent *strategies*, both for campaigns on campus and on the global stage. As part of this, they conveyed an ideology emphasizing worker empowerment through independent labor unions (as opposed to paternalism on the part of affluent, First World consumers) as central to the success of any campaign to abolish sweatshops. They also fostered the founding of USAS, a national organization that could coordinate actions across campuses and train successive generations of student activists in the organization's ideology and strategic models.

Many narratives of the student anti-sweatshop movement represent USAS as having originated solely with a group of students who interned with UNITE in the summer of 1997. While these students certainly played a crucial role, it is important to note that anti-sweatshop activism sprang up independently on a number of campuses following the media scandals discussed above. Some of these groups grew out of those that had been working on international solidarity issues for a while, as at the University of California (UC), Berkeley (Abrams* interview); some grew out of student groups in support of labor, such as the Student Labor Action Coalition at UW Madison (McSpedon interview); and others were set up for the specific purpose of addressing the issue of sweatshops, such as the Just Don't Do It Campaign (playing on Nike's slogan "Just Do It") at the University of Michigan (Dirnbach interview). There was, however, little, if any, coordination or sharing of ideas among campuses.

The actions students took consisted mainly of guerrilla art and theater. Eric Brakken (interview), who would become USAS's first staff person, recalled:

> At the University of Wisconsin [Madison], we protested when UW signed its contract with Reebok. We made T-shirts that said, "Free Bucky," the badger mascot of UW. A lot of guerrilla art, guerrilla theater. At the University of North Carolina, they painted tires to say "UNC Sweatshop." The basketball coach had a relationship with Nike.

Dirnbach recalled of his days as a student activist at the University of Michigan, "Our demands were a little incoherent at that point—it basically was drop the Nike contract or get them to do the right thing. It was not quite clear to us at the time exactly what the right thing would be." What the students had noticed, though, was that many schools had lucrative licensing contracts with major apparel companies. While they may not initially have been sure how to take advantage of this to exert real leverage over these corporations, making this connection would later prove crucial to USAS's strategy.

Despite this preexisting student activism, UNITE played a crucial role in helping students shape their actions into what would become the cutting edge of the anti-sweatshop movement. This help was twofold: they helped the students develop a national organization, and they provided them with the basic elements of a more strategic approach.

It does not appear, however, that UNITE initially expected student anti-sweatshop activism to become the dynamic force it did. The eleven students who interned at UNITE's New York City office in the summer of 1997 did so as part of a larger program of the AFL-CIO, Union Summer. This program sought to raise awareness among college students of the importance of unions in securing economic justice for workers, with the hope that some of them would go on to become professional organizers in the labor movement (Levin 1996; Van Dyke, Dixon, and Carlon 2007). At the time the students were interning with UNITE, the union was uncertain about how to go forward. Its traditional membership base of textile and apparel workers was rapidly eroding as the lead apparel firms outsourced production overseas. Those workers who remained were often in small sweatshops that were difficult to organize. Ginny Coughlin, the UNITE organizer who supervised the student interns, had them working on any number of issues, of which the connection between colleges and sweatshops was initially only one.

In this, they were following a strategic model known as the corporate campaign. This involves looking at the ties between corporations and other organizations, such as which other companies they were dependent on for finances, for component parts, or as customers who bought their products. In particular, they were looking for vulnerable ties that could be used as points of leverage by activists, as well as ways to delegitimize (or "name and shame") their opponents (Manheim 2001). Tom Juravich and Kate Bronfenbrenner (1999) document in detail one such campaign, by striking members of the United Steelworkers against Ravenswood Aluminum Corporation in West Virginia, in a conflict that lasted nearly two years, from October 1990 through June 1992. Lawyers working for the union hunted down legal documents showing that, through a series of shell corporations, Ravenswood was actually in large part owned by Marc Rich, a financier wanted for crimes such as tax fraud in the United States who was living in self-imposed exile in Switzerland. Organizers used this information to harm Ravenswood's image, while union members traveled to Switzerland and, with the help of Swiss unions, publicly shamed Rich, damaging the image he had established in Switzerland as a philanthropist. Meanwhile, rank-and-file members of the unions followed trucks from Ravenswood (which was still operating through the labor of strikebreakers) and photographed their deliveries (sometimes with the help of tip-offs by sympathetic drivers), documenting the companies to which Ravenswood sold aluminum. Under the threat of secondary boycotts, beer companies such as Budweiser and Stroh's stopped using Ravenswood aluminum in their cans, cutting into the targeted company's profits. We can see in the Ravenswood campaign the classic elements of a corporate campaign, looking for multiple points of attack on the company both to delegitimize it (by exposing its ties to Rich) and to exercise leverage over it (directly through a strike and indirectly through pressuring its customers to sever ties).

Thus, when the students interned with UNITE, they were looking for any and all apparel company ties that they might be able to use as leverage over the lead firms (McSpedon and Plumb interviews). Laura McSpedon, a student intern from Georgetown University, recalled:

> Ginny Coughlin [. . .] came to our Union Summer site and did a presentation on the garment industry and the structure of the industry and how it's set up to screw over workers pretty much. [She] said, "We think students have a role to play in solving this problem," and kind of posed the idea of students getting involved.

While UNITE was aware of the issue of college licensed apparel, it originally encouraged students to get involved with a campaign targeting Guess, which had little direct connection to campus life (McSpedon interview).

Only as the students researched the issue of colleges' and universities' ties with the apparel industry did it become clear that they had a potentially significant point of leverage there. Amanda Plumb (interview, 2007), a student intern from Duke University, noted:

> They gave us basic information about sweatshops and how the garment industry works, but a lot of the research on licensing and procurement, we did. It was a new tactic in corporate campaigns to look at these connections to universities. They knew there was a connection; they knew there were these contracts. But I just remember that we did the original research on our own schools, and that hadn't been done yet. It's not hard to do. It's literally picking up the phone and calling and looking up some websites. It didn't take a professional researcher to figure this stuff out.

At the time, college and university officials were willing to talk freely about these issues. Plumb doubts this would be the case today, after years of anti-sweatshop activism, but at the time the information did not strike most of the people the interns called as particularly sensitive.

Having gathered the details on these relationships for a number of schools, the interns began to put together an organizing manual and, when they returned to classes in the fall of 1997, began organizing on their own campuses while contacting students at other schools. This networking led to conferences in New York City in July 1998 and in Washington, DC, in July 1999, the latter of which saw the official founding of USAS (United Students Against Sweatshops 2009b). Even before USAS's official beginning, however, campaigns to get college and university administrations to adopt codes of conduct began to take off in 1997, with students coordinating their campaigns with one another nationally. Starting with Duke University, students at a number of other campuses—also including Georgetown, UW Madison, Notre Dame, the UNC Chapel Hill, and the University of Arizona—undertook sit-ins (Featherstone 2002). Eric Brakken (interview) recalled:

> We were egging each other on—if they're going to do it, then we're going to do it. [. . .] We had this wave of sit-ins; [. . .] there were like five or six schools. This was something new, and some campuses had gotten media. We began to get a lot of phone calls from students or e-mails from students that had heard about this. They wanted to figure out how to do this themselves.

Not only did all the sit-ins succeed; at other schools, students won concessions from their administrations without resorting to sit-ins, though in many cases at least the implicit threat of a sit-in loomed in the background (Featherstone 2002).

What precisely were the students trying to achieve with these sit-ins and other protests? They were attempting to apply the corporate campaign strategic model in a social arena where they felt like they had the most leverage. Specifically, they wanted the administrators of their colleges and universities to use the licensing agreements to put pressure on their corporate partners to follow college-designed (or, more exactly, student-designed) pro-labor codes of conduct. The more uncontroversial elements of such codes included measures such as a prohibition of child labor, health and safety standards, and the requirement that factories follow local laws on minimum wages and overtime hours and pay. More contentious elements included a recognition of workers' right to collective bargaining (i.e., to join a labor union), disclosure of the factory locations to the university, independent monitoring, and a living wage (i.e., a wage sufficient to support a family at some minimal level of decency). I explore some of these controversies more deeply in Chapters 8 and 9. In brief, though, apparel firms argued that disclosure would result in their competitors' getting access to their trade secrets. But there are rarely significant trade secrets involved in producing T-shirts, and many competitors, in fact, outsource production to the same factories. They claimed that unions and independent monitoring were unnecessary because the apparel firms themselves had an interest in improving conditions. And, finally, they claimed that it is impossible to properly measure what would, in fact, constitute a living wage. Student activists replied that companies could not be relied on to monitor themselves because of the conflict of interest involved. Instead, unions and outside monitors were necessary. And without disclosure of factory locations, independent monitoring could not take place.

In pursuing the organizational ties between their schools and apparel companies as a potential point of leverage, student activists were trying to exercise indirect leverage over the apparel companies, an approach central to the strategic model of the corporate campaign. USAS members continually emphasized to me that boycotts by individual consumers were of limited value and that students' real potential power lay in using their schools' position as institutional consumers to affect apparel firms. Trina Tocco (interview), a USAS member at Western Michigan University, put it this way: "If the goal is to impact the most amount of purchasing possible, how do you do that one consumer at a time and make it worthwhile?" Thus, USAS focuses its efforts on changing the purchasing and licensing practices of schools, not those of individual consumers on college campuses.

USAS members are well aware that in targeting the apparel made under contract with colleges and universities, they are directly targeting only 1–2 percent of the apparel market. They believe, however, that they can have a wider impact nonetheless. Marion Traub-Werner (interview), a USAS member at UNC Chapel Hill, put it this way:

> There was this particular segment of the U.S. clothing market, the university market, that you could actually push things through that would maybe set the standard for the larger industry also. If you were going to raise the standard in any way, universities were the right place to start. [. . .] First universities and then the rest of the industry, right? That's what happened with disclosure, right?

Universities were the first to demand disclosure [of factory locations], and now disclosure is quite normal for the brands.

With the success of the wave of protests that pushed administrators to adopt stringent codes of conduct containing provisions, such as disclosure, with which their corporate partners were unhappy, USAS—or, more properly, the network of student activists that would become USAS—had thus won its first round of victories. As these events unfolded, an approach that had started off as something based on the model of the corporate campaign entered into a period of substantial strategic innovation. As the students contended with successive challenges, their strategy morphed from a campaign that might exercise leverage over one corporation into something substantially different, targeting and monitoring not simply one, lone firm but a significant sector of the apparel industry. I explore this process in Chapters 8 and 9, after looking more closely at USAS and its campus campaigns in the next chapters.

USAS's Campus-Level Strategy

While USAS's ultimate goal may be empowering workers through victories that strengthen independent unions, many of its actions have focused on pressuring college and university administrators and taken place in the social arena of the college campus. This seemingly odd choice was made because, as discussed in Chapter 4, USAS has discovered that colleges' and universities' role as institutional consumers gives them a key point of leverage over the apparel industry that has been difficult to find elsewhere. USAS's strategy is thus a multilayered one, with both the campus-based campaigns I explore in this chapter and the transnational campaigns in support of sweatshop workers at particular factories I explore in Chapter 11 fitting together as elements in a larger strategic model. It is in many ways USAS's ability to organize successful campus campaigns that makes it possible for the organization also to organize successful transnational campaigns, a strategic marriage of the local and the global.

If they are to use colleges' institutional consumer power as a transnational point of leverage, USAS activists also need to find ways to exert more direct leverage over their schools' administrators. Campaigns to do this follow the same strategic model across different college campuses, though they do not play out in precisely the same way at each school, and students adapt the model to peculiarities of each campus. Much of this variation is due to the political opportunity structure on any particular campus, with some being more open to students' influence than others. For example, at

Haverford College, students not only were dealing with a progressive administration but also had an existing institutionalized voice in the form of the Committee on Investment and Social Responsibility, a legacy of anti-apartheid struggles in the 1980s. As a result, the administration agreed to join the Worker Rights Consortium (WRC) without a great deal of contention on campus (Grigo 2000; Caine* interview). In many other cases, students had to resort to such highly confrontational measures as sit-ins and hunger strikes to successfully pressure the administration. At yet other schools, officials agreed to students' demands without such measures, but it was the implicit threat of disruption that worked: knowing that a sit-in was a distinct possibility, administrators sometimes gave in to avoid actually having to deal with one.

Despite these variations, there is a clear strategic model that campus campaigns followed and that the USAS members I interviewed could talk about in abstract, generalized terms. Here I want to explore what the strategic model for a campus campaign looks like as an ideal type, drawing on USAS's experience at multiple schools and with multiple campaigns—not only the initial 1997–1999 campaign for codes of conduct but also the 1999–2000 campaign to press schools to join the WRC and the campaign from 2005 on in support of the Designated Suppliers Program (DSP).

The importance of looking at how practices such as organizing, framing, and choosing from among one's tactical repertoire are interlinked into a larger strategy can be seen in the ways that USAS runs campaigns on campus. On the face of it, USAS's experience at many other schools would seem simply to confirm the argument that disruptive tactics are what work as leverage. Whether in the initial campaign for codes of conduct or in later ones, USAS has had to use a sit-in—or, at least, the threat of one, whether explicit or implicit—at most schools to achieve its ends. Looking more closely at things, however, reveals a more complicated picture.

Although USAS activists were well aware of the possible necessity of engaging in a sit-in, they almost never started their campaigns with this tactic, for the very simple reason that it was likely to backfire. Instead, they engaged over the course of one or two school years in a campaign of gradually escalating tactics. They would start with moderate tactics that allowed them to build popular support on campus; only once they had this support were they in a position to engage in more confrontational actions, such as sit-ins, with any significant hope of success. The USAS national organizer Zack Knorr (interview) summed up the process this way:

> We start out doing more educational events, bringing people in, getting more people, and then once you've really made a name for

yourself on campus, once people know what you're doing, once you've developed stronger leadership within your group and gotten more members, and also once you've given the administration time to look at this so you can, in a sense, justify moving to more serious protests, then we started to really turn out those numbers in bigger and more aggressive form.

This gradual escalation had to be fit into a specific schedule—that of the school year, with its beginning in September and its end in May. According to USAS member Liana Dalton (interview), student activists

have to look at a campus organizing timeline and try to think about what can be won, realistically, in a semester or a year-long time frame. You have to take into account student turnover and the fact that you have to constantly be doing leadership development in your group because people are graduating and whatnot.

This somewhat limits the flexibility of student activists in deciding when to take which actions. They need to hit the ground running in September, working on educational programs from the start of the school year. At least, they must do so if they wish to be in a position where they can begin escalating tactics in the spring semester and possibly resort to a sit-in toward the end of the school year while retaining broad support for their demands and actions in the campus community.

Phase One: Education

USAS activists generally started their campus campaigns with meetings with the administration and various relatively low-key public actions. Speaking about his involvement with the campaign for the DSP in the University of California system, Knorr (interview) said:

The events we had in the first quarter—we did an initial rally and delegation to the chancellor just to present our demands. We did a teach-in, we did a fashion show, we did a mock sweatshop, a street theater kind of event, and we ended all of them with a little rally and some marching, just so that people would gain the experience of organizing those kinds of events. But we never tried that much for a huge turnout or to shut anything down, just because we were using that time mostly to educate the campus and to develop our group.

These sorts of actions were important opportunities for student activists to frame their message and thus gain legitimacy, convincing the campus community that sweatshops are a significant issue in which the school has some stake and about which the administration can do something. Through educational events and articles in the campus newspaper, they were able to convey their frame to a wider campus audience. The openness of the campus as a discursive arena and the many means students can use to convey their message—teach-ins, op-eds, rallies, and so on—greatly facilitated this. The preliminary educational work also served a valuable organizing purpose, increasing the number of active supporters (people who would turn out to protests or even engage in sit-ins) and the number of passive supporters (students who were generally sympathetic to USAS's demands that their clothes be sweat-free).

Popular stereotypes of students as left-leaning notwithstanding, organizing students in support of anti-sweatshop measures on campus is not necessarily easy, given the impact of the corporatization of higher education. Students have increasingly come to see themselves as consumers and as being in job training, not as being there to learn how to become active citizens. USAS thus faces a challenge in simply convincing students that they should care about these issues. Referring to USAS's campus organizing, Amanda Plumb (interview, 2007) said:

> We weren't telling students not to wear Nikes or "You're bad if you wear Nike" or "Don't shop at The Gap," because we would have really alienated most of the students. But people could understand, "Don't let Duke's name . . . be put on this stuff [made in sweatshops]" and "We're asking Duke to set up some standards."

Many students have a strong identification with their school's image. By pointing out the gap between the school's positive image and its practices that facilitate the existence of sweatshops, anti-sweatshop activists were able to foster a sense of betrayal (cf. Klein 1999). Many students, including not particularly political ones, become upset when they realize that the clothing bearing the logo of the schools with which they identify so emotionally are made in sweatshops (Featherstone 2002). It is this basic reaction that USAS harnessed and used to educate members of the campus community about the realities of the global economy and the necessity of codes of conduct and independent monitoring as a way to fight labor exploitation—and thus the legitimacy of their protest actions. Without that legitimacy, the administration would have had a much easier time simply arresting the students if they engaged in something like a sit-in.

At this early stage of the game, USAS activists were educating not only other students but also school presidents and other top administrators. By meeting with college officials, they also gained some legitimacy in the eyes of the administration, as they made clear, cogent arguments for their demands and established their willingness to start with institutional procedures. One point that they particularly needed to counter was the misconception, promoted by the apparel industry, that USAS members were dupes of UNITE HERE and simply being used to promote the union's protectionist agenda, which would harm, not help, Third World workers (Featherstone 2002; McSpedon interview). This effort to establish some legitimacy in the eyes of the administration was important in being able to conduct negotiations over the long run, even when the campus USAS chapter's actions grew more confrontational:

> I felt like being able to write professional letters to the administration and have good meetings with them would make it easier to get stuff out of them, because when push came to shove, they felt like we were reasonable people—and I don't think it limits at all how radical you can be in your tactics. (Reville interview)

Phase Two: Escalation

But as the USAS member Laura McSpedon (interview) argues:

> Ultimately I'm not sure it was arguments that won anybody over. [. . .] You have to have all that stuff in place and know your facts and be able to respond to each of those charges and have the literature you need to back it up. But ultimately we could have talked until we were blue in the face. It was really about the power we developed on campuses to embarrass the universities into doing the right thing.

In a sense, the first stage of any campaign was building that power; the second stage was exercising it through a series of more and more contentious tactics that gave USAS leverage over the administration while simultaneously delegitimating the latter.

For many students, however, part of the process of learning how to organize on campus was learning the necessity of exercising such power. Particularly among well-to-do students at elite schools, there was initially often a belief that they could win over the administration through rational arguments. According to Jess Champagne (interview), a USAS member at Yale:

Kids who go to Ivy League schools [. . .] are much more prone to
this idea, that if you just have the right argument and make the
right point and explain how workers are exploited, university administrators and others in power, they'll be like, "Oh, OK, let's do
that." And I think we're really kind of trained to do that. [. . .] Part
of my freshman and all of my sophomore year we spent primarily
negotiating with administrators, doing education on campus, and
just having these meetings. And clearly things were not changing,
and they [the administrators] lied to us and clearly didn't care.
That was when we realized [. . .], "Oh, they just don't care, and the
only way they are going to care is power."

It was at this point that Yale's USAS chapter began to focus on building a
broad coalition of supporters on campus and resorting to increasingly
confrontational tactics.

However, only over the course of a school year or two, when they had
shown that institutional procedures were leading nowhere, were student
activists able to establish such contentious tactics as a sit-in as legitimate in the eyes of the wider campus community. It was a matter of
preparing not only the campus community as a whole but also the student activists themselves to engage in an action as confrontational and
disruptive as a sit-in. Knorr (interview) describes the escalation of actions from the University of California system campaign for the DSP in
this light:

By the start of the second quarter, we were in a position where we
had the group members organize bigger, more aggressive actions.
We started out with an eighty-person rally where we marched inside the administration building and shut down the lower level for
only a short period of time. Then we did the same thing with our
bookstore. Then, at that point, it was really clear that we were going
to have to do a sit-in, so we started trying to slowly train people and
get them used to doing more kinds of aggressive and confrontational actions. So we tried to take a small step each time, instead of
jumping from a teach-in to a sit-in, where people have no experience with anything in the middle. So we tried for those rallies to get
more and more confrontational. Then we did a dance-in in our
chancellor's office once. We issued her an ultimatum, and she
missed it, so twenty of us went in with boom boxes and just had a
dance party in her office for about a half-hour. [. . .] When the next
quarter came around, that's when we did a sit-in.

Some confrontational tactics such as hunger strikes work specifically by shaming the administration, calling into question its legitimacy. At many schools, such attempts to embarrass the administration played a significant role in the escalation of the campaign, even when it culminated in a sit-in. McSpedon (interview) recounted a story in which she and other USAS members handed out leaflets before a large fundraiser at which students' parents would get to meet Georgetown's president, Father Leo O'Donovan. The leaflets urged parents to ask O'Donovan why he did not support sweatshop workers. "Probably, no one said anything to the president of the university," McSpedon said, "but it really freaked them out, just because we were trying to embarrass them—and I think we accomplished that."

A sit-in played a dual role in terms of strategy. First, it was both potentially disruptive of the workings of the college or university, thereby giving the students leverage over the administration—if administrators wanted to go back to business as usual, they needed to make some concessions to the activists. Second, with sufficient press coverage it became an embarrassment that damaged the administration's legitimacy, both on campus and nationally. Speaking of his experience with the sit-in at UW Madison during the initial campaign for the code of conduct, USAS member Thomas Wheatley (interview) said:

> There's two kinds of power you have [in a sit-in]. You have the power to interrupt work. If you can physically shut down the university's administration office, then you're interrupting the basic function of the university. In Wisconsin, that didn't happen. You'd have to have five thousand students sitting in to actually shut down the building. To a certain degree it was disruptive to the work, though. People were less productive in the administration office. The other thing is "Boy, there's a sit-in at the university— that hasn't happened since '68." So the local papers and local radio are going wild.

My interviewees differed with one another to some degree on the reasons for the effectiveness of sit-ins, some emphasizing the disruptive effect they had on the workings of the school and others the way the tactic worked to delegitimate administrators. The difference may in part be a product of the schools at which they were sitting in: it is easier to disrupt a small school than a large one through a sit-in, because such disruption requires fewer people when aimed at a small target. It may also be easier to embarrass better-known, large schools, because they are more likely to become the subjects of widespread media attention. In most cases, there is probably a mix of the two at work. Even in the case of UW, Wheatley (interview) said the students found a way to intensify the sit-in to the point where it was truly disruptive. Not only did the number of students joining the sit-in increase steadily over the course of three or four days— "It was forty students to start with, and then it was fifty-five, and then it was sixty-seven, and then it was one hundred"—but "on the final day, students decided to escalate and started banging on the walls in the middle of the day so that the administration staff could not complete their work." After an hour of this, the university president agreed to negotiate with the students and conceded to most of their demands. By disrupting the ability of his support staff to do their work, the activists were able to exercise leverage over the president.

In some cases, administrators gave in to students' demands to avert such high-pressure, high-profile actions. McSpedon (interview) tells such a tale from when USAS was campaigning to press Georgetown to leave the FLA and join the WRC the year after a successful campaign involving a sit-in had gotten Georgetown to agree to a code of conduct:

> To our total shock and amazement, about a week before we were planning on doing the sit-in, they gave in on all of our demands. [. . .] I was sitting next to the president of the university as he delivered his speech to us, and I was floored. I actually was looking at his notes in front of him, and they said nothing about agreeing to get out of the FLA and into the WRC, but he was saying it.

While the student activists had not publicized that they were going to do a sit-in, "it's certainly possible," McSpedon said, "that [the administration] got wind of it [and] remembered what happened the year before. We were building up our rhetoric and escalating our tactics."

Administration Countermeasures

Most school administrators would prefer to head off such highly confrontational tactics without conceding anything. One danger USAS activists faced in their campus campaigns was getting entangled in the countermeasures favored by college officials, who sought to sidetrack students by having them deal with people who actually had very little decision-making power or tying the students up in committees. McSpedon (interview) noted that, in the early days of USAS, "the university's first reaction as we were raising this stuff was to send us to the licensing department in the schools, which are usually part of the athletic department." This was a diversion because the licensing directors do not actually have the power to make decisions, particularly given schools' close relationship with the big apparel companies and those companies' opposition to enforceable codes of conduct and disclosure. Only by becoming sidetracked in this way at a number of campuses did the members of USAS learn that they had to refuse to deal with low-level officials and insist on interacting directly with school presidents.

The other sidetrack college and university administrators often sent students down was setting up committees whose stated purpose was to consider the issue in more depth and create an opportunity for dialogue among different members of the campus community. On the face of it, such committees sound reasonable, and in some cases—notably, at Duke University, where school administrators were sincerely interested in finding a solution—they could lead somewhere. By the nature of their jobs, administrators tend to be cautious and want to examine any new policy, even one they may in principle support, carefully before implementing it. In many cases, though, school administrators were not interested in actually coming up with a mutually agreeable policy. Instead, committees were intended to tie student activists up indefinitely in bureaucratic procedures that led nowhere.

According to Knorr (interview):

> The committee will be made up of one or two students, a couple faculty, and they'll ensure that there's enough administration members on the committee that the committee would never decide to do anything unless the administration wanted to. And then they'll take six to seven months to meet occasionally and have meetings that don't go anywhere. And their hope is that throughout this time they can appear that they're taking every step they possibly could, but they're basically trying to wait out the students until either they get tired of the issue, until key people graduate, or until it just kind of goes away.

USAS is now wise to this danger, but, as with being sent to deal with minor officials, this did not happen without activists at a number of schools falling into administrators' traps first.

In some cases, such committees have been made to work, even when the administration did not want them to. But for this to happen, students needed to step outside the protocols of the committee process and continue taking confrontational actions. McSpedon (interview) told me the story of the committee that was set up at Georgetown in the wake of the 1999 sit-in there:

> We actually had a number of the committee meetings where thirty or forty students sat outside waiting to hear what happened and made it clear we were not just four students sitting on this committee agreeing to things on behalf of everyone else. There was still actually a movement that cared about what was happening behind those closed doors.

The administration eventually gave in to the students' demands and created a code of conduct. McSpedon says she cannot be entirely sure why they did so, but she suspects it was "the fear of us disrupting things on campus again."

At other times, USAS decided it essentially needed to pull the plug on the committee process and start escalating its tactics again. The USAS member Molly McGrath (interview) told me about the campaign for the WRC at UW Madison:

> David Alvarado and I sat on this committee, and we went to a lot of meetings and did a lot of paperwork, but then eventually we decided that the only way to get the committee to agree to join this idea of the WRC would be create this crisis of legitimacy. [. . .] We withdrew publicly from the committee [. . . ,] and that made big news in the campus papers. I think we started giving deadlines to the chancellor—decide by this date to join the WRC or else.

The "or else" was a sit-in, which USAS managed to build such support for that the campus was struck by what McGrath described as "sit-in fever. [. . . A] lot of the activists in Madison had heard about the sit-in the year before, and they wanted to do another sit-in."

Conclusion

What all this shows is that for success, it was necessary for activists to fit together a broad range of tactics, from the relatively routine, such as lobbying the administration, to the disruptive, such as sit-ins; develop and spread a particular frame to the campus community, building up the legitimacy of not only their cause but also themselves as social actors, while delegitimating the administration; mobilize sympathetic students around the issue, all in a particular way that follows a strategic progression; and put themselves in a position to negotiate successfully with administrators, part of which entails giving the impression of being reasonable while participating in highly contentious actions. Looking at these elements in isolation reveals much less about the dynamics of social movements than looking at how these pieces fit together into an overall strategy. At least in the context of the social arena of the college campus, Andrews's (2001) model that emphasizes a combination of disruptive action, discursive change, and negotiating with authorities is clearly on target. USAS's success depended on building up its standing on campus, allowing it to shame and embarrass the administration. Then, with its own legitimacy strengthened and the administration's weakened, it had to take highly confrontational actions that could coerce the administration into agreeing to at least some of the students' demands, a process that involved negotiation once administrators had been coerced or shamed into coming to the table. This strategy interacted with the particular political opportunity structure of the college campus, where students could work within very open mobilizing opportunities and discursive processes. This, in turn, allowed them to mobilize so that they often delegitimated and then exerted a great deal of leverage over school officials, despite the antidemocratic structure of the formal decision-making process in higher education.

We can also see that both scholars who emphasize the importance of social structures (Gamson and Meyer 1996; McAdam 1996; Tarrow 1998) and those who emphasize a process of interaction among different social actors (Goodwin and Jasper [1999] 2004; Jasper 1997, 2012) are correct. The school administrators and the student activists are embedded in the social structure of the college campus, but in very different locations, giving them very different ways of exercising power. If students want to exercise power over school officials, they must shame them and disrupt their ability to work. If school officials want to exercise power over students, frequently all they need to do is delay by setting up committees and tying students up in them. Both the formal structure of the college campus and the specific strategic actions chosen by administrators for when they strategically interact with USAS constitute the political opportunity structure within which student activists must maneuver.

USAS's Ideology of
Worker Empowerment

The Role of Ideology

USAS's campaigns, both on campus and internationally, were shaped by a number of factors. In this chapter I look more closely at one element: USAS's ideology, or the set of ideas through which it makes sense of the world, including the political opportunities and constraints created by its environment and which strategies it makes sense to use in that context. USAS's ideology was very heavily shaped by its early ties with UNITE, resulting in a strong emphasis on worker empowerment and independent labor unions as the main means to such empowerment. It would, however, be a mistake to assume that USAS's ideology emerged fully formed as soon as the students began coordinating campaigns for codes of conduct at schools across the nation in the fall of 1997. As USAS members struggled with both their own administrations and the transnational apparel corporations, they reflected on those struggles and deepened the development of their ideology. I examine some of the crucial turning points in the evolution of USAS's ideology in Chapters 9 and 12 as I look at the reasons USAS began to develop, first, the Worker Rights Consortium (WRC) and then the Designated Suppliers Program (DSP). Here I present more of an ideal-typical overview of the movement's ideology. It should also be noted that this discussion of ideology is based on interviews with USAS's leaders, particularly national leaders who were part of coordinating actions across campuses. It is possible, even likely, that newer members and activists focusing on just their own campuses did not fully grasp the importance of worker empowerment and were more likely to be animated by an ill-defined, humanitarian opposition to sweatshops. However, this ideology was shared not just by USAS's leaders but also by people throughout the anti-sweatshop movement, including the broad network of groups involved in transnational solidarity campaigns discussed in Chapter 11 and those that helped formulate the DSP (see Chapter 12) and the independent organization SweatFree Communities (Chapter 13).

As discussed in Chapter 1, Oliver and Johnston (2000) define an ideology as consisting of a set of values, an analysis of the workings of society, and a set of norms for action by which activists hope to alter the workings of society to better realize their values. While many movements include groups and individuals with quite different ideologies who must find ways to work together (Ghaziani 2008; Maney 2012), in my interviews, despite probing for areas of disagreement with my questions, I found (rather to my surprise) that there was a strong consensus among anti-sweatshop activists (across the entire movement, not just those in USAS) about their core ideology. The core value of anti-sweatshop groups such as USAS was that of worker empowerment: that workers should be able to control their own lives and exercise their own power without needing to rely on the goodwill of others to guarantee their well-being. The anti-sweatshop movement's theories consisted of a sophisticated analysis of the international apparel industry and how it consistently fosters the disempowerment of workers and encourages the abuse of their rights. In particular, this theory emphasized that the problems are structural and not a matter of a few bad apples or misguided policies that can be corrected through corporate goodwill. The norms of the movement involved supporting independent unions for workers; fighting for concrete, incremental victories, such as the unionization of a particular factory; and fostering solidarity between students and labor, emphasizing working for a relationship founded on equality instead of paternalism.

Some may question whether this set of beliefs and norms truly constitutes an ideology, as the word is often used, referring to such systems of thought as anarchism, conservatism, fascism, feminism, liberalism, libertarianism, social democracy, or socialism. While the anti-sweatshop movement's beliefs are not a grand ideology in this sense, they nonetheless constitute a coherent set of beliefs about the social and political world, one that had a profound impact on how the movement acted. Further, the anti-sweatshop movement's beliefs have all the elements that Oliver and Johnston (2000) identify as composing an ideology. For these reasons, it seems useful to me to refer to the movement's beliefs as an ideology while acknowledging that this ideology of worker empowerment does not fall into exactly the same category as such "grand" ideologies as socialism or conservatism. It is also worth noting that, in addition to the ideology of worker empowerment that members of USAS and the larger movement held, individual members generally held to beliefs from one of the grand ideologies of the left—anarchism, socialism, progressivism, feminism, or liberalism. Other than adhering to broadly leftist or left-of-center beliefs, though, there was no consensus within the movement on anything larger than the ideology of worker empowerment. Nevertheless, this has given activists quite enough common ground to work together effectively, consistent with Donatella della Porta's (2005) work on the growth of "tolerant identities" in progressive movements, where activists focus on common goals and set aside differences in grand ideologies.

Values: Worker Empowerment

If USAS had one core value above all others, it was that of worker empowerment. The USAS member Laura McSpedon (interview) summed up the organization's perspective:

> The long-term goal for me was to create a structure and to create systems that opened up space for workers to organize unions in a way that it was closed when we started. And so then, within that, creating the codes of conduct, creating a monitoring system, all of that was really toward that end of workers having the power in their workplace to organize and have a voice and these structures are just meant to facilitate and support that.

What is worth noting here is that McSpedon—and most of the other antisweatshop activists I interviewed—defined their goals not simply as eliminating sweatshops, but specifically as empowering workers by creating the conditions for strong labor unions in factories across the globe.

There is an obvious tension here. The USAS members I spoke with were well aware that, at this stage of the game, only pressure from U.S. activists—particularly the college students affiliated with USAS—gave these workers the power to organize (an issue I explore in more depth in Chapters 11–12). Liana Dalton (interview, 2007), a former USAS member at UW Madison, told me:

Ultimately, we want to transcend this whole idea of brand [corporate] power over workers. The idea is that through engagement within these power structures, we will challenge these power structures. If what we're doing isn't working to build the capacity of the workers themselves to enforce [their demands] and ultimately looking to our own phase-out in the process, if it's requiring more and more monitoring and more and more involvement on our part, then that isn't really a sustainable alternative and that isn't really the direction we want to be heading.

USAS members understood that there are structural conditions that preclude worker empowerment and it is these structural conditions they sought to change. In addition, they adhered to norms of solidarity, where they sought, as far as possible, to put the workers, and not themselves, at the front and center of their organizing efforts. I look at both these points in more depth below.

Such an emphasis on worker empowerment may seem surprising in a student organization. McSpedon (interview) noted that this value was "definitely fostered by folks at UNITE and by the students who had originally thought through what this campaign could look like." Indeed, it was not immediately obvious to the first students involved in getting USAS's organizing efforts off the ground. The USAS member Amanda Plumb (interview), who came from a middle-class household, noted:

I think in the very beginning I don't remember that much of a focus on the right to unionize. It was more about living wages [and] disclosure. [. . .] I also grew up in [the anti-union state of] South Carolina, so this was all relatively new to me. I think a lot of us learned a lot about unions and their importance by doing this.

It was not simply contact with UNITE that fostered this awareness. Specific USAS members worked to foster this consciousness, as well. Marion Traub-Werner (interview, 2007), a USAS member at UNC Chapel Hill, said, "My big thing with USAS from the beginning was trying to do education among students to make it more around labor rights and specifically union rights, than around the National Labor Committee–type victimhood stuff."

The actual process of hammering out what an ideal code of conduct and monitoring system might look like (see Chapter 9) also served to heighten students' consciousness around these issues. And as USAS grew, the students started having more contact with the sweatshop workers themselves, both by participating in delegations to inspect the factories where licensed apparel was being made and through internships with unions and labor rights nongovernmental organizations in the Global South (see Chapter 11). Thus, while the seeds of a strong commitment to worker empowerment were planted by USAS's initial ties to UNITE, they really bloomed as the students explored these issues in more depth through the process of struggling to accomplish their goals.

The significance of worker empowerment can be seen in the fairly critical way in which a number of my interviewees spontaneously contrasted USAS and its allies' approach with that of the fair trade movement, which they regarded (whether fairly or not) as paternalistic instead of empowering. The USAS member Jessica Rutter (interview) said:

> Fair trade is very, very consumer-based. It's about having consumers take action; it's about making certain certifications, which sometimes end up being kind of problematic, because they don't always have to do with worker voice. And worker voice is the key part of the anti-sweatshop movement.

It is important to understand that, in addition to being a matter of values, these principles were instrumental. As noted in Chapter 1, Polletta (2005) argues that the ideology-instrumental distinction is a false dichotomy. Thus, anti-sweatshop activists argued that empowering workers was not only ethically desirable in and of itself but also, based on their social theory, the only way to effectively fight sweatshops over the long term. It was not simply that anti-sweatshop activists rejected paternalistic, consumer-centered forms of fair trade because they were inconsistent with their values; it was also that, on the basis of their values and social analysis, they did not think such fair trade could possibly end sweatshops, at least over the long term. If workers are not in a position to enforce their own rights, it is all too easy for those rights to be abused, if, say, consumer interest in fair trade drops off.

Social Analysis: A Structural Problem

USAS's social analysis consisted of a sophisticated sociological understanding of sweatshops as a structural problem requiring structural change. They understood that sweatshops are a normal part of the working of the global economy and that, to really tackle the problem, the rules of the global economy need to be changed. For example, Eric Dirnbach of UNITE HERE (interview) summarized the problem this way:

> The entire business model is a model that creates sweatshops. There's tremendous price pressure on the contracting factories to lower the prices that will charge for the apparel, which means wages have to be lowered. There's tremendous pressure on factories to deliver huge orders at the end of the month, which means you've got to work your workers a hundred hours a week. It's a buying model that creates sweatshop conditions, no matter what the companies say.

This analysis closely follows the one laid out in Chapter 2. Given that a number of academic experts on sweatshops, including Richard Appelbaum, Edna Bonacich, and Robert J. S. Ross, are allies of USAS and the anti-sweatshop movement, it is not surprising that activists have such an analysis.

As part of this analysis, the USAS activists were keenly aware of where they, as students, fit into the larger power structure, principally as consumers. Although consumers are important to apparel producers—indeed, many spend a great deal of time cultivating consumers with expensive ad campaigns—they have little real power within the industry because they are a diffuse, unorganized group. On the basis of its experience with the limited impact of boycotts by individual consumers, USAS emphasized using its schools' power as institutional consumers within the apparel production system. According to Rutter (interview, 2007):

> In terms of actually affecting Nike as a company, there's not really so much that you can do as an individual consumer. But if you bring in the university as a consumer, as an institutional buyer, [it helps] because the college market is extremely important [to the brand-name firms]. We could very much more easily influence our universities than the brands themselves, so the campaigns are structured in ways that we're kind of going up against the brands, but we're more going up against our universities to make them demand that the brands do certain things, which is just a much more effective strategy.

This strategy is more effective for the simple reason that it is in the relatively contained social arena of the college campus that students can most easily exert power, not in the more diffuse networks that make up the transnational apparel industry as a whole.

Norms: Solidarity in Support of Unionization

Rooted in these values and this social analysis, USAS developed a number of norms of action, the most significant of which were support for unionization, solidarity with workers, and a focus on concrete goals. In the eyes of USAS members, independent unions were the best organizational vehicles through which workers can become empowered. According to Ken Abrams (interview), a USAS activist at UC Berkeley, central to the work of USAS is

> the belief that if workers are able to exercise their right to organize without management interference, then the chance of seeing other rights respected is much greater because they can advocate for themselves in the factory, dealing with management directly when an independent monitor is not there—and most of the time monitors are not there.

In other words, it is workers' right to organize that serves as the guarantor of all other rights. This belief was reinforced by the relationships the students gradually built with groups in the Global South. Recalling the end of an internship she did with a Hong Kong labor rights groups, Dalton (interview) said:

> Basically, what my director in Hong Kong told me when I was going back to the United States was "If you do nothing more, at least go back and tell students over and over again, promote the right to organize, promote freedom of association." That's the heart of it because only when workers have collective power in their workplaces can sweatshops truly be eliminated.

The norm of solidarity is one in which USAS tried to avoid the sort of paternalistic relationship that it saw as a danger of the fair trade movement in favor of a relationship in which workers' concerns are put front and center. This meant USAS tried to consult with unions representing sweatshop workers and other grassroots labor rights organizations as it developed its strategy—a fact that becomes evident in Chapters 9 and 12, when I look at the development of the WRC and DSP. According to Rutter (interview, 2007), "Overall, what we do is about student-worker solidarity and using the power of the university to support worker demands—that's the very core of it." As with the value of worker empowerment, USAS members saw this not simply as a matter of principle but also as a matter of sound strategy: without the centrality of the input of workers, a campaign is unlikely to have the information it needs to be effective.

Reflecting on a campaign (not directly involving USAS) that had targeted The Gap, which had not only failed to correct the labor rights violations but also resulted in the firing of the workers involved, Plumb (interview) said:

> I remember for me it was, like, "Whoa—" I wanted to make sure that we are connected to what is going on in other places. I think well-meaning people can do damage by acting on principles but not really being connected to what's going on on the ground. I think the way USAS dealt with that was they started having students go on trips to maquiladoras [Mexican sweatshops] or doing research abroad and actually work[ing] with workers. There was also this effort to make sure there were organizations of workers involved with USAS and it wasn't just well-meaning students trying to save the world and in the process kind of being oblivious to some things.

Here again we see that important elements of USAS's ideology developed not simply as a result of the influence of UNITE but as a result of USAS members reflecting on their own experiences and the experiences of others' campaigns.

USAS also emphasized helping workers win concrete victories—specifically, being able to unionize and gain concessions from management in specific plants. Many of my interviewees emphasized that this was what drew them to USAS: the possibility of seeing concrete gains, which is not always something easily realized in other movements. For instance, the USAS national organizer Zack Knorr (interview) said:

> It was the first time where I really saw that activism had a real, concrete, achievable goal, and there was a real power analysis— that these are the institutions that have power; this is how we can leverage our universities to have power over these brands like Nike. Then seeing the supply chain map—how we can see that if we do that, it has an effect on what workers are doing here on the ground. Seeing that was really, really powerful for me, and just seeing that students could really make a difference.

Having analyzed USAS's ideology, we now turn to its organization.

The Organization of USAS

Sustaining the Organization

The development of the strategies discussed in Chapter 5 and the so-cialization into the ideology discussed in Chapter 6 did not happen spontaneously but were fostered by social movement organizations such as USAS and its allies. USAS does not exist in isolation. It forms part of a network of anti-sweatshop organizations that includes UNITE HERE, Global Exchange, and the National Labor Committee. This network, in turn, is part of a larger network of progressive activist organizations. Such movement organizations and the networks they form play two crucial roles: (1) they create a system of institutional memory, whereby the knowledge of ideology and strategic models and relevant activist skills are passed on to new generations of activists and the movement is sustained over the long term, and (2) they facilitate communication and a process of delibera-tive decision making in which activists actively interpret their social envi-ronment in light of their ideology, deciding how to apply their existing strategic models and what innovations they need to adopt.

Nella Van Dyke and Marc Dixon (2013) note that social ties with ex-perienced activists and activist organizations who already have valuable skills are crucial to helping newer activists acquire the skills necessary to organize and strategize successfully. Especially in its early days, the larger social movement network in which USAS was embedded was particularly important for fostering the student group's ability to develop into a stra-tegically effective organization. In a sense, these other social movement organizations acted as collective mentors for the newly formed student organization. UNITE obviously was central for the role it played in nurturing the strategic skills of the students who interned with the union. Under the supervision of UNITE staff member Ginny Coughlin, they developed an organizing manual that was crucial to student activists' early campus campaigns. UNITE continued to work with USAS, giving the student activists not only advice but also resources they could use to build up USAS as an organization. As noted in Chapter 6, one lasting legacy of this relationship is USAS's labor-inspired ideology of worker empowerment.

Other anti-sweatshop organizations that played a crucial role included the National Labor Committee (NLC), Global Exchange, Sweatshop Watch, and the U.S. Labor and Education in the Americas Project (USLEAP). Different campus groups tended to form close relationships with different organizations, depending in large part on geographical proximity: East Coast chapters tended to work more with UNITE and the NLC and West Coast chapters with Global Exchange and Sweatshop Watch (Brakken and Champagne interviews). All of these organizations had extensive knowledge of the issue of sweatshops that they shared with USAS, helping the first generation of student organizers develop their own expertise on these issues. According to the USAS member Eric Brakken (interview), these organizations were all eager to work with USAS. "By this point [USAS's 1999 founding convention], the student movement was the hot thing, and a lot of people tried to advise us," he said, coming to its conference and seeking to speak to and form closer ties with the student organization. This was true both because USAS represented a potentially large pool of grassroots members to mobilize in the various campaigns on which different organizations were working and because USAS's successes in pushing colleges to adopt codes of conduct put it at the cutting edge of the movement.

In addition, the NLC and Global Exchange had a long history of taking U.S. activists on "tours" of sweatshops in the Global South. Such tours were important for many of USAS's early leaders, giving them a more personal perspective on the sweatshop problem and fostering ties between U.S. students and Third World workers. According to the USAS member Laura McSpedon (interview):

I think the opportunity to go to other countries and meet workers—the tours that those groups did were really critical in terms of motivating what was probably a relatively small group of students, but still a core group of leadership, who could then communicate that back to other students and motivate folks.

This was important in terms not only of motivating people but also of legitimating the work of USAS members, since their connections with actual sweatshop workers made their claims more credible when challenged by their opponents (cf. Keck and Sikkink 1998). These ties would also play a role in shaping their global strategy (see Chapters 11–12).

A number of USAS members remarked that, despite the influential role of UNITE and its other collective mentors, they respected and encouraged USAS's autonomy, eager to see an independent student movement grow. McSpedon reflected:

> I would say certainly Ginny Coughlin and other folks from UNITE continued to play a really key role in supporting a few of us who were trying to make this work, but they were also really excited that it had taken on a life of its own. [. . .] I never felt like there was hesitation around students having autonomy and kind of taking this where we wanted to take it and being in partnership with UNITE. [. . .] Having done this work now for ten years, it's actually pretty surprising, I think, the level of control that UNITE gave up in the campaign.

Another progressive social movement organization—one that is not part of the anti-sweatshop movement—played an important role: the United States Student Association (USSA), a long-standing student advocacy organization founded in 1947. Through initial contacts at UW Madison, where USSA and USAS coexisted, USSA had a significant impact on USAS's campus strategy. USAS members attended trainings by USSA organizers, in which USSA gave the anti-sweatshop activists a number of analytic tools for analyzing power structures on campus and developing a long-term strategy. In particular, USSA transmitted the campus-level strategy of escalating tactics to USAS that I unpacked in Chapter 5 (Champagne, McSpedon, and Wheatley interviews).

As an organization USAS had to pass on the lessons it learned from its allies and its own experience to new members. Creating such a system of institutional memory is a particularly challenging issue for a student organization such as USAS, with its constant turnover of membership and leadership as activists graduate from college and move on to new things (often other activist organizations). The USAS member Molly McGrath (interview) told me, "USAS does do a lot of training. All the trainings that they do and all the conferences constantly process through all these different students, so I think that is USAS's main mechanism for passing on institutional memory and building skills." USAS holds regular conferences at which attendees were, among other things, socialized into the ideology of the anti-sweatshop movement and trained in USAS's strategic model and the skills needed to run a successful campaign on campus. The first such conference took place in July 1998 in New York City, before USAS was even officially founded.

The USAS national organizer Zack Knorr (interview) went to his first USAS conference in 2005. Before he attended, he said, "I actually didn't even know that USAS was a national organization. I thought it was a group on my campus." He spoke about how inspiring the conference was, seeing the history and very real impact USAS had had:

> I found out that there's this eight-year history of running these campaigns, that we've created this organization—the Worker Rights Consortium—that we've really used our power to support workers in winning really concrete victories. And I think I could see after being there, really see, the strategic vision of what USAS is and where universities fit in. [. . .] And seeing that was really, really powerful for me—just seeing that students could really make a difference.

In 2007, when I conducted my interviews, USAS had two regular conferences: "a bigger one in February, which is more geared toward bringing new people in, and a smaller one [. . .], generally in August, which is more about strategic visioning for the next school year" (Knorr interview). At the larger conference, there were a number of panels and workshops, largely run by students, in which USAS's ideology and strategy were laid out. Training and mentoring happened in both formal and informal venues. On the one hand, there were formal workshops where students were trained in strategic thinking, using a variety of tools (Champagne interview). On the other hand, students formed relationships with more experienced activists from other campuses who could give them advice. The USAS member Thomas Wheatley (interview) said, "It can be pretty empowering to come together and meet other folks who are doing the same kind of thing that you're doing, build that community of people, and then you can go back to them [during the course of a campaign] and say, 'You guys at this school succeeded in your campaign—how'd you get it done?'" I look more at the significance of these relationships below.

These national conferences and networks were all the more important because, as with many campus activist groups, USAS chapters tended to be small. McSpedon (interview) recalled that at Georgetown, "probably, at our most active point, we had fifteen people coming to weekly meetings and hashing all this out and then a larger list of a few hundred who would maybe come to stuff, maybe send e-mails when we asked them to." As a result of both this small size and high turnover as members graduate, campus USAS chapters faced many challenges in sustaining themselves over the long term. For one thing, mentoring new members while simultaneously carrying on the business of the organization could be a challenge. Nick Reville (interview), a USAS member at Brown University, noted:

> It's always hard, with the intake of new people, figuring out how to get them involved, get them to do something that's useful. And it's hard to balance that with the people that are spending a lot of time on things like the [campaign for the] WRC. [It's hard] trying to be really inclusive while getting things done, having the meetings.

The unfortunate fact is that, while some USAS chapters stayed strong for many years, others did not last. Knorr (interview) commented:

> There's some groups that are always there, some groups that are really strong for a while and then fade away for a while; someone new comes in that's really excited and really wants to make things happen, and they start to grow again. [. . .] There's not one kind of common trajectory, but there have definitely been groups that were very, very strong that either dwindled or don't even exist anymore; there's groups that come out of nowhere that never really had that much going on and then all of a sudden they get a few really strong leaders, and they become really big; and then there's groups that have just kind of always been very steady groups, like the University of Wisconsin, Madison, or Georgetown, that have had, like, a very steady presence throughout all ten years that USAS has been around.

Knorr was uncertain whether there were any consistent reasons one could pinpoint for the long-term durability of different USAS chapters but suggested that the individual personalities of the activists involved (which becomes crucial in small groups), the culture of the particular campus, and the density of allied social movement networks (especially labor networks) in the local area around the campus all might play a role.

When a chapter does fade away, this reduces USAS's strength. According to the USAS member Amanda Plumb (interview):

There were many schools where there was a campaign. For example, at UMass they signed on to the WRC, they got a code of conduct, but it hasn't been enforced in years. There's no students enforcing it, so probably if someone went to the student center and looked at where the sweatshirts are from, it may be completely going against the code of conduct or against the agreement, but no one's enforcing that, so who cares?

This problem of chapters fading away has probably grown worse since the 2008 economic recession. As a result of their declining economic standing, student activists have increasingly come to focus on economic justice issues that affect them more directly, such as unsustainable rates of tuition and postgraduation debt. This has meant that there has been less energy for student activism where students are conscience constituents, such as the anti-sweatshop movement.

One way USAS has tried to address this problem of turnover and to sustain membership is to have key members remain involved, at both the national and campus levels, as mentors for a few years following their graduation. McGrath (interview) kept up her ties with the UW Madison chapter even after she graduated: "I know people like myself and David [Alvarado] and people who are not students but part of solidarity groups in Madison who mentor these leaders every year. That helps to develop a really close relationship in day-to-day contact." At the same time, the aim was not for these graduated activists to manage the campus chapters but for the chapters to benefit from the more experienced activists' knowledge and experience while retaining their autonomy. McGrath continued:

> We always made a concerted effort in USAS to transition out. It was like, no, you don't have influence or decision-making powers. We have a new group of leaders, and it's going to be their responsibility to do this. I think I had some influence, and I definitely talked to a lot to people, but I don't think I had any decision-making ability within USAS at that point.

Another way USAS was able to draw on the experience of graduating members was to hire them for the national staff—including as paid national and regional organizers—for a few years before they fully moved on to other things. Knorr (interview), one of these national organizers, said an important part of his job was training younger activists:

A lot of what we do as the [national] staff—and also the other organizers we have that work regionally—is really trying to encourage people to see that the most important thing they're doing is
that they're developing leaders, so to always organize with the idea
in mind that you're trying to organize yourself out of a job, that
you're trying to make yourself unnecessary by helping to train two
or three younger people that can do everything that you're doing.

This, in turn, contributed to the longevity of both individual USAS chapters and the national organization as a whole, ensuring that there were
replacements for people as they graduated and moved on.

An additional challenge to its longevity that USAS has faced are lulls,
or periods when there were no high-profile transnational campaigns in
support of sweatshop workers overseas for the student activists to take
on. USAS dealt with this by diversifying its understanding of what a
sweatshop is and where sweatshops exist, taking the issue closer to home
by campaigning for the rights of workers such as cafeteria staff, custodi-
ans, and even adjunct faculty on campus. The corporatization of higher
education, discussed in Chapter 3, has become one of USAS's major issues,
especially in the forms of the outsourcing of campus service work, low
wages for campus workers, and the rise of faculty in low-paid, low-securi-
ty adjunct positions (United Students Against Sweatshops 2009a, 2016;
Knorr interview).

Decision Making and Communication

Both at the national-level conferences that determined USAS's overall direction and in the organization's individual campus chapters, members
usually made decisions through consensus, a form of participatory democracy that puts a great deal of emphasis on deliberation. This consensus-oriented culture also shaped the relations between the national USAS
and its chapters. McGrath (interview) described the decision-making process on national campaigns (whether to implement a new policy such as
codes of conduct or joining the WRC or targeting a particular company)
this way:

The [elected national] coordinating committee would make the bigger decisions on actions. Campuses, a lot of times, made their own
decisions about what they were going to do locally, but they would
always try to coordinate as much as they could with the national

center. There's always that negotiating back and forth with what national USAS would do and what the campuses would do.

The national USAS would also consult with allied groups in planning these campaigns, "but USAS made its own decisions." At the local level, members of campus chapters would meet and talk among themselves to discuss the best way to reach their goals on their campus, drawing on their local knowledge of the campus, even as they also drew on USAS's standard strategic model of how to conduct a campus-based campaign. When appropriate, they might use a modified form of consensus, delegating certain responsibilities to subcommittees.

As discussed in Chapter 1, a number of scholars (Ganz 2000, 2009; McCammon 2003, 2012; Staggenborg 1989) have argued that such participatory-democratic, deliberative models of decision making foster better strategic decision making than models in which decisions are made from the top down and passed on by fiat to the membership. In addition to the reasons discussed in Chapter 1, Francesca Polletta (2002) suggests that such decision-making methods not only promote the development of participating activists' abilities, as they learn new skills through the process of deliberating with others and taking on new responsibilities, but also encourage solidarity within the organization, as people come to feel they have a stake in the outcome of any action because they helped to shape it.

The experience of USAS activists confirms these claims, although my interviewees also sometimes noted the difficulties with consensus: it can be a time-consuming and sometimes frustrating process, especially when strong differences of opinion exist. In the end, though, they all seemed to feel that the benefits outweighed the drawbacks. McGrath (interview), who described the process of consensus at UW Madison as "tortuous," thanks in part to factionalism, nonetheless contrasted it positively with her experiences at the AFL-CIO Solidarity Center:

> Looking back at it now, I think that it strengthened us, because now I'm part of [. . .] the Solidarity Center, which is extremely hierarchical. If there's just a group of people at the top making decisions, there's no investment of the grassroots. And we need those numbers. It was very educational as far as listening to people talk for hours about their opinions and what they think. I think it did strengthen us.

Even Wheatley (interview), who declared, "I might stick a fork in my eye if I have to go back to that model of organizing now," admitted, "but it really enabled everyone to step up into playing the role and to learn the ropes as you go. I think if it had been more top-down, I probably would not have gotten the experience that I got just being at the table and figuring out strategy."

These campus chapters were not isolated from one another. Members of various USAS chapters not only had contact at annual conferences but also, as noted above, drew on the relationships they formed there and stayed in touch during the school year, sharing information, tactics and strategies, and other ideas. In this, telecommunications technology such as e-mail Listservs and telephone conference calls were important. The period when USAS was first forming was also, it should be noted, when e-mail was coming into its own as a major communications medium. Despite all the hype around the Internet, research on its role in social movements has shown that it is not enough to create long-distance social movement networks on its own; instead, it seems crucial for activists to form face-to-face ties first (as at USAS's national conferences), ties that can then be maintained via the Internet and conference calls (Fox and Brown 1998; Keck and Sikkink 1998; Olesen 2005).

As discussed in Chapter 4, Duke students' decision to carry out the first sit-in demanding public disclosure spurred students at other schools to take similar action. While part of the push came from getting information about the sit-in from the traditional mass-mediated news (whether by television or newspaper), direct communications among students by e-mail and phone were also crucial. The information students shared could be as simple as a flier they had designed or as complex as sharing strategies for a sit-in. Often, the students would discover that their administrations were using similar arguments or delaying tactics (such as referring the matter to a committee, as discussed in Chapter 5) against them, and they could learn from one another's responses to them. Once students at a few campuses learned that committees were a dead end, for instance, intercampus communication allowed the strategy of not agreeing to join them to become part of USAS's common pool of knowledge. It also allowed the student activists to learn this during the school year, in the midst of their campaign, which meant they did not have to wait until the next summer conference. They might also coordinate a common day of action, where students on multiple campuses would all mobilize on the same day around the same issue, simultaneously pressuring their administrators.

Caroline Stoppard* (interview), a USAS member at Indiana University, recalled:

> Nothing we did would have been as effective if it had only been one campus. [. . .] There was a lot of communication as to what's going

on among campuses [. . .] and there continues to be. That's a really important part of the movement. I guess [it's part of] what makes USAS so effective. I sort of take it for granted that everyone's going to know what's going on around campus, but I guess I shouldn't. It is an accomplishment that those networks were established and maintained.

The national staff also played an important role in coordinating actions among campuses and passing on strategic knowledge. Knorr (interview) described his work as a regional organizer, coordinating the campaign among the University of California system campuses in support of the DSP:

> I ended up doing a lot of the groundwork. I would travel to different campuses and hang out with the group leaders, get to a point where we were friends basically, and then I would keep in touch with them about how their campaigns were going, try to offer advice or support, and then we would make our decisions collectively on our conference calls during the week.

It is such organizations and networks, and the knowledge that they hold in their collective memory, that allowed USAS and its allies both to develop such innovations as the WRC and DSP and to wage successful transnational campaigns in support of workers in specific factories, processes that I examine in the chapters that follow.

III

CYCLES OF CONTENTION AND STRATEGIC INNOVATION

8

The Brands Strike Back

*Corporate Social Responsibility and the Creation
of the Fair Labor Association*

The Limits of Corporate Social Responsibility

The major apparel firms were not passive in their response to the student campaigns but actively fought against them. The principal countermeasure the brands eventually settled on were corporate social responsibility (CSR) programs, including both in-house "social compliance" departments and corporate-led NGOs such as the Fair Labor Association (FLA), charged with monitoring their member companies.[1] While factory owners may rely on repression of workers as their favored countermeasure (an issue explored in Chapter 11), in the United States the leading firms are usually not in a position to have thugs beat up their critics, so they have had to rely primarily on countering the students' frame—something at which they have been relatively successful through the use of CSR.

---

1. Note that the FLA is only one of three major monitoring organizations affiliated with the apparel industry. The other two are Social Accountability International (SAI) and Worldwide Responsible Apparel Production (WRAP); of the three, the FLA is generally considered the most credible within movement circles. This is because, while the FLA includes some NGOs and has had to make some concessions to address their concerns, the SAI and WRAP have only corporate members, resulting in standards that are far lower than the FLA's. Ultimately, however, all three suffer from the fundamental flaw of an innate conflict of interest (Esbenshade 2004b; Rodríguez-Garavito 2005). Since the SAI and WRAP are not involved with the chain of events I trace in this book, I do not discuss them here. For a detailed review of their operations, see Esbenshade 2004b and O'Rourke 2003.

Most of the literature on these CSR programs has looked at them primarily in terms of their effectiveness in protecting workers' rights (see, e.g., Barrientos and Smith 2007; Esbenshade 2004b; Locke, Amengual, and Mangla 2009; Locke, Qin, and Brause 2007; O'Rourke 2003; Pearson and Seyfang 2001; Rodríguez-Garavito 2005; Seidman 2007; Tsogas 2009; Wells 2007). While this is an important consideration—and I draw on this research here—in this chapter I suggest that it makes sense to consider these programs as much in terms of their success in allowing apparel companies to frame themselves as socially responsible in the discursive arena of the national mass media, thereby restoring their legitimacy and their brand image following the attacks by the anti-sweatshop movement.

The unfortunate fact, according to the consensus of the scholarly literature, is that CSR programs have not been terribly effective in ending sweatshop working conditions. For instance, Richard Locke, Fei Qin, and Alberto Brause (2007, 20–21) came to the conclusion that Nike's internal compliance program was lacking on the basis of data provided by Nike itself—which, if anything, should be biased in favor of the company. Using a "data set based on factory audits of over 800 of Nike's suppliers located in 51 different countries," they concluded that the results were uneven, at best, with improvements in some factories, but many others showing no improvements or actually deteriorating in their treatment of workers over time. "Interviews with other global brands, NGO representatives, and leaders of the major multi-stakeholder initiatives indicate that Nike's experience with monitoring is by no means unique." John Ruggie, the special representative of the United Nations Secretary-General on human rights and transnational corporations, offered a similarly pessimistic conclusion: "We keep hearing now, from just about everywhere . . . monitoring doesn't work. [. . .] Just about everybody, at least off the record, will tell you that monitoring doesn't work and auditing of supplier factories doesn't work because people cheat" (quoted in Zarocostas 2009).

While CSR programs have been ineffective at improving working conditions, what they have done effectively is acted as a counter-framing tool that has restored the apparel industry's legitimacy. What is worth noting here is that, in a sense, the movement has been successful in that it has forced the industry to respond and change its initial strategic response to the anti-sweatshop movement. The brands' original reply to the movement's critiques was to deny there was a sweatshop problem. When they could no longer credibly do that, they denied that they were responsible, since they were not the actual employers of the workers being exploited and had no way of knowing what was going on in the factories with which they did business (Klein 1999). The progressive journalist Naomi Klein (1999, 197–198) reports the challenge Disney's spokesman Ken Green gave to one journalist: "'We don't employ anyone in Haiti,' he said [. . .]. 'With the newsprint you use, do you have any idea of the labour conditions involved to produce it?' Green demanded of Cathy Majtenyi of the *Catholic Register*." The anti-sweatshop activist Brent Wood (interview) observed:

> When brands tell you today how committed they are in respect to the rights of workers, you always have to remember that it wasn't that far in the past when they had exactly the opposite position. [. . .] That was their position, and it did not work. It didn't protect Nike's reputation. Consumers did not buy it. They were not persuaded by the logic, and it took the brands a while to realize that.

Thus, at least briefly, the anti-sweatshop movement forced the lead apparel firms to the defensive, until they realized they needed to shift gears.

CSR programs create at least the appearance that these companies are sincerely trying to do something about the problem of sweatshops. While I would hesitate to claim that the companies with CSR programs have no interest in fighting sweatshops, it is important to note that they initiated their CSR programs only in response to attacks by the anti-sweatshop movement and that they have consistently refused to address the root causes of the problem, maintaining instead the business practices that force their contractors to cut costs on the backs of their workers.

The Creation of the Fair Labor Association

When students began pushing for labor rights codes of conduct, the major firms actively tried to persuade schools to oppose them, particularly the requirement for disclosure of factory locations, a necessary prerequisite for independent monitoring. The USAS member Laura McSpedon (interview) reflected on why disclosure was considered essential:

> We felt like if there were a public list of factories that produced Georgetown apparel, then a human rights group in El Salvador could look at that list and say, "I'm going to talk to workers in the factory, because I know that this university has said they don't want certain things, right?" People could look at that list and hold these companies accountable in a way that we could never do with supposedly random inspections of a privately held list of factories.

The apparel companies could not, of course, simply defend the existence of sweatshops. Instead, according to McSpedon, they deployed two arguments in their counter-framing:

> They [. . .] tried to make [USAS] out to be a protectionist front for UNITE and used the history of both UNITE and the labor movement as being somewhat protectionist to try to discredit us. [. . . They claimed,] "These students are really nice, but they're just misguided, they're being used by the union."

They also tried to argue that disclosure of factory locations would harm them:

> Their main argument—and administrators totally bought it at first—was "You know we can't tell you where our factories are because it could give away trade secrets." . . . Obviously in an industry like the garment industry it's just an absurd argument. How you make a T-shirt is not like a drug patent.

Indeed, it is quite common for competing brands to use the same contractors and for their products to be made alongside each other in the same factories. The lead firms, however, were able to make a case that many administrators found persuasive, leading them to take the companies' stated concerns seriously.

The industry was not about to regain the moral high ground by simply opposing students' efforts to fight sweatshops, though. It had to offer an alternative solution to bolster its legitimacy and focused on CSR programs as the answer. In this, apparel companies were aided by an outside initiative, which soon came under industry control. In August 1996, responding to the Kathie Lee Gifford scandal and other, similar revelations in the media, the Clinton administration formed the Apparel Industry Partnership (AIP), a task force initiated by Secretary of Labor Robert Reich that brought together a number of representatives of the apparel industry and their critics from the human rights and labor community. The administration's goal was to create a system of independent monitoring that would have the support of both industry and labor rights advocates; its hope was that such a multi-stakeholder initiative could effectively address the problem of sweatshops, particularly those outside the United States, where the government had no formal jurisdiction. The final result of this was the FLA, a multi-stakeholder initiative whose stated goal was to monitor apparel production in an effort to ensure that it was sweat-free (Esbenshade 2004b).

The negotiations were long and arduous, with industry and labor advocates disagreeing on a number of important issues, such as workers' right to freedom of association (i.e., to form a labor union); whether contractors should be required to pay a living wage; and what actually constituted effective, independent monitoring. When it became clear that the AIP as a whole could come to no consensus, a group of corporations and moderate human rights NGOs began to meet separately to hammer out an agreement among themselves, deliberately excluding the unions that had been part of the AIP. The industry groups made two minor concessions to their critics. First, they agreed that they could hire their monitors only from a list accredited by the organization as a whole, thus creating some room for NGO input into who qualified as a monitor. Second, they agreed that the U.S. Department of Labor would conduct a study of whether or not the minimum wage in countries where they had operations was sufficient to meet workers' needs. After reaching a consensus among themselves, they presented their agreement as a fait accompli to the other AIP members. UNITE; the Retail, Wholesale and Department Store Union; and the Interfaith Center on Corporate Responsibility—all AIP members—refused to have anything to do with the agreement. Regardless, the remaining groups went forward and on November 2, 1998, officially formed the Fair Labor Association. The dissenting AIP members publicly denounced the agreement, as did the AFL-CIO. Those NGOs that remained part of the FLA argued that by doing so they could continue to push for higher standards in the future (Esbenshade 2004b; Greenhouse 1998a, 1998b).

As these events were unfolding, so was the first wave of student antisweatshop activism, with the demands for disclosure and independent monitoring. College administrators quickly realized that they simply did not have the expertise or infrastructure to monitor the codes of conduct they created in response to students' demands. They also hoped to find a way to placate the students and bring some quiet to their campuses. Meanwhile, both the Clinton administration and those companies that were part of the FLA began actively recruiting colleges to join the Association in an effort to boost its legitimacy. Nike offered to disclose its factory locations in return for schools' joining the FLA, a powerful incentive, since Nike was one of the principal licensees of many schools at which USAS was active. Since becoming a member of the FLA seemed like the perfect solution to several of the problems college administrators faced, this recruiting effort soon proved fruitful (Esbenshade 2004b).

On March 15, 1999, seventeen colleges and universities became the first members of the FLA representing higher education (Krupa 1999); by late April, fifty-six colleges had joined (Greenhouse 1999b). (As of May

2017, the FLA had 161 university affiliates [Fair Labor Association 2017].) USAS activists were deeply upset by this decision on the part of administrators. They saw the FLA as deeply flawed, for reasons I explore below. They soon began a campaign to push for their schools to leave the FLA, a campaign that would eventually culminate in the creation of the WRC, a truly independent monitoring organization without industry ties.

The Operations of the FLA

To understand why USAS and other members of the anti-sweatshop movement were so critical of the FLA, we must look at how the FLA was organized and operated. As originally constituted, the "FLA's board was to be made up of six NGOs and six companies, plus a neutral chair. [. . . A]ny important change would require a 'super-majority' vote, virtually congealing what was touted as a preliminary arrangement with room for improvement" (Esbenshade 2004b, 182; see also Wells 2007). With the addition of colleges and universities to the organization, the board was changed to give member colleges six representatives, as well (Fair Labor Association 2008a). Companies initially paid membership dues of $5,000–$100,000 on the basis of their annual sales; colleges and universities paid membership dues of 1 percent of their annual licensing revenues, to a maximum of $50,000 (Krupa 1999). The federal government also originally provided some funding, though it was later cut back (Esbenshade 2004b).

The FLA oversaw a monitoring process that certified companies as being in compliance. Participating companies were supposed to monitor all of the factories with which they contracted through their own, internal monitoring system and hire an outside, FLA-approved monitor to regularly inspect a percentage of those factories. These monitors could be either NGOs or accounting firms, despite accounting firms' lack of labor rights expertise; in addition, a number of for-profit monitoring firms sprang up that were accredited by the FLA. For the first three years of a company's membership, outside monitors had to inspect 30 percent of its factories; each year afterward, the monitor would check on 5–10 percent of the company's factories to ensure they were in compliance with the FLA's code. Companies had significant influence over which factories were actually inspected. Such inspections were announced beforehand, which effectively allowed management to clean up its act, eliminating any problems at least for the duration of the inspection. The results of the inspections were considered confidential and not made available to the public (Esbenshade 2004b; Greenhouse 1998a). A typical inspection would last only a day or two, and while the monitors would typically interview workers, they would do so on factory premises, thus denying them the protection of confidentiality (Blasi and Schmaedick interviews).

Many of the NGOs that initially stayed with the FLA in the hope of improving it grew frustrated over time as the industry members vetoed any significant improvements. Eventually, all of the groups with any meaningful connection to the labor movement withdrew. The final group to pull out was the International Labor Rights Fund (ILRF), which resigned from the FLA on October 4, 2001. The resignation of the ILRF, along with the success of the WRC and continued pressure from the anti-sweatshop movement, did finally prompt the FLA to make a number of important reforms to its operations in late 2001 and 2002. Participating companies no longer selected and paid for their monitors; this process was now carried out by the FLA's staff. The system of selecting factories for outside inspections was randomized; inspections were made unannounced; and some degree of public disclosure of the reports was implemented (Esbenshade 2004b). What is noteworthy here is that the FLA felt some need to emulate at least part of the practices of truly independent monitors, such as the WRC, indicating that there are some limits to just how successful CSR is as a legitimating strategy in the face of continued movement opposition unless there is at least some appearance of independence and transparency (Rodríguez-Garavito 2005).[2]

Despite these important improvements, problems remained with the FLA's programs. The monitoring reports, while summarizing the results of inspections, reported only the name of the lead apparel firm, the monitoring organization, the region in which the factory was located, the problems, and the progress being made toward correcting the problems. The public reports did *not* contain the actual name and location of the factory, making it extremely difficult for third parties to verify the accuracy of the reports. In addition, due to a loss of government funding, the number of inspections *decreased*—to only 10 percent of factories during the initial period and 5 percent of factories each year thereafter (Esbenshade 2004b). Monitoring visits were still brief and still did not protect worker confidentiality (Blasi and Schmaedick interviews).

The FLA had a centralized code of conduct by which all member com-

---

2. While it is beyond the scope of this book, it is worth noting that in 2008, the FLA once again revamped its approach, implementing a new methodology at first known as the FLA 3.0 and later as the Sustainable Compliance Initiative (Fair Labor Association 2008b, 2012a). For a defense of this type of approach, see Locke, Amengual, and Mangla 2009, which refers to it as a "commitment-oriented approach." For activists' critiques of the FLA 3.0, see FLA Watch n.d. and Sweat-Free Stanford Campaign 2007.

panies were expected to abide themselves and to ensure that their contractors did so, as well. The code included prohibitions on forced labor, child labor (defined as workers younger than fifteen), harassment or abuse of employees (verbal, physical, or sexual), and discrimination in hiring and management practices. Management was supposed to ensure that adequate health and safety conditions were met and recognize workers' right to form a union and engage in collective bargaining. In paying both standard and overtime pay, employers were supposed to conform with either local law or the prevailing wage in the local industry, whichever was higher. The workweek was supposed to be no more than forty-eight hours, plus twelve hours' overtime, with one day off a week guaranteed; exceptions, however, could be made in the case of "extraordinary business circumstances" (Fair Labor Association 2008c). There were a number of problems with the code, though. It did not deal with the question of freedom of association in countries such as China and Vietnam, where independent unions are illegal, and it contained no provisions for a living wage. In addition, many feared that the exception allowed to the workweek time limit in case of extraordinary business circumstances left a lot of room for abuses (Esbenshade 2004b).

The Movement Critique of the FLA and CSR

The anti-sweatshop movement's critique of the FLA operated on two levels. One was a critique of the association's monitoring and certification practices, which, anti-sweatshop activists argued, were carried out in such a way that their effectiveness was highly questionable. At a more fundamental level, the movement critiqued the FLA for being built on an inherent conflict of interest in that the major apparel companies played a significant role in governing and funding the very organization that was supposed to monitor them. It was, as one newspaper report (May 2000, C4) quoted University of Oregon student Mitra Anoushiravani, like having "a fox monitoring a chicken coop." It was this fundamental conflict of interest that in many ways accounted for the faulty monitoring practices.

In looking at monitoring programs, whether corporate-sponsored or independent, it is important to consider not only their effectiveness in protecting workers' rights but also the rights they are designed to protect. In their analyses of labor monitoring programs, César Rodríguez-Garavito (2005) and Stephanie Barrientos and Sally Smith (2007) distinguish between *protective rights* (or outcome standards) and *enabling rights* (or process rights). Protective rights cover such basic quality-of-life elements as decent health and safety standards, levels of pay, reasonable overtime hours, and so forth. Enabling rights are those such as freedom of association, collective bargaining, and freedom from discrimination that give workers the power to pursue respect for protective rights on their own. In other words, enabling rights are those that facilitate worker empowerment, the main goal of the anti-sweatshop movement.

According to Rodríguez-Garavito and Barrientos and Smith, even if they include both on paper, corporate-sponsored monitoring programs tend in practice to put much more emphasis on protective rights than on enabling rights. Different scholars have suggested different reasons for this disparity. According to Ruth Pearson and Gill Seyfang (2001), protective rights such as child labor receive more media coverage than enabling rights such as freedom of association; since companies are primarily responding to consumer perceptions, they focus on the former. According to Barrientos and Smith, focusing on protective rights is also more consistent with a top-down, technocratic approach with which corporations are comfortable. I would suggest that, while these are doubtless factors, the most important reason is probably that suggested by Jill Esbenshade (2004b): companies' desire to preserve the balance of power in their favor, which supporting enabling rights would undermine. Equal weight is given to both protective and enabling rights only in movement-sponsored monitoring programs such as the WRC (Barrientos and Smith 2007; Rodríguez-Garavito 2005).

Thus, even if CSR efforts were actually effective, they still would have been fundamentally flawed in the eyes of anti-sweatshop activists, for the same reasons that the fair trade movement's efforts are (as discussed in Chapter 6). Corporate social responsibility programs are, at best, paternalistic; because they do not create conditions for worker empowerment, they leave workers vulnerable if interest in such programs ever declines. On the basis of their own empirical research on the effectiveness of monitoring programs, Rodríguez-Garavito and Barrientos and Smith have reached conclusions similar to those of the anti-sweatshop activists, arguing that to be effective, monitoring programs must guarantee workers' enabling rights, countering some of the great asymmetries of power in the global production process and giving workers the power to protect themselves. The FLA failed to do this.

The FLA's Compliance Program

One major point of criticism that the anti-sweatshop movement had of the FLA was the very fact that it certified companies as being compliant with its requirements, a practice activists viewed as highly misleading.

The USAS member Eric Brakken (interview) recalled, "Within the framework of the FLA, people were deathly afraid of that." In strict terms, the
FLA certification simply indicates which participating brands were in
compliance with its monitoring requirements, not that they were sweatfree. As Gay Seidman (2007) points out, though, most consumers do not
have a terribly sophisticated understanding of such certification programs. Even a well-intentioned consumer does not, generally, have the
time to thoroughly investigate what any particular certification may actually entail, so it is all too easy to take a certification such as the FLA's as
an indication that the brand in question is actually sweat-free.

Brakken (interview) explained:

> Obviously the idea of providing labels is a huge incentive. A lot of
> companies, one would think, would want that label with the in-
> creasing scrutiny and consumer concern about sweatshops. But
> there was a debate about whether or not a factory could ever be
> sweatshop-free.

Ultimately, anti-sweatshop activists decided that, even in the case of the
WRC, the monitoring organization they created, they were not in a position to certify anything as sweat-free. The sheer scope of the problem,
both in terms of the pervasiveness of the sweatshop problem and the size
and global distribution of the industry, militated against any surveillance
system that could actually continually monitor factories or firms for violations. And anti-sweatshop activists did not want to mislead consumers
with the idea that the problem could be so easily solved. (As Chapter 12
shows, USAS would eventually back a certification program—the Designated Suppliers Program—but it would have a much more limited scope.)
The FLA apparently did not see these things as major problems.

The monitoring program the FLA used to certify participating companies' compliance was also highly problematic. First, there was the question
of "who the monitors would be again—this question of is it [the accounting firm] Ernst and Young being hired by a company to do a self-assess-
ment or is it NGOs that are explicitly fighting for workers' rights?" (Mc-
Spedon interview). Even some of the monitoring organizations that were
nominally nonprofits, such as Verité, were primarily oriented toward providing a service to the major apparel firms and operate very much like
commercial firms, not workers' rights organizations (Esbenshade 2004b).
In *Monitoring Sweatshops*, Esbenshade (2004b) extensively analyzes the
organization and practices of the commercial and quasicommercial mon-

itoring firms on which the FLA relied so heavily. She found them, for the most part, to be unqualified for the job. While the heads of the monitoring firms may have had some experience with labor issues, most of the monitors they hired did not. Many were recent college graduates, former Peace Corps volunteers, or missionaries, the last of whom were valued for their foreign-language skills. They were insufficiently trained and, at the end of the day, generally had little understanding of workers' rights. Esbenshade found their actual monitoring practices to be inconsistent and sloppy. In addition, private monitoring firms attributed little importance to the violation of such enabling rights as freedom of association and collective bargaining. Both they and the companies that hired them saw what they did as a substitute for unions, ensuring the well-being of workers without the need for intervention of the "third party" of a union.

In addition to the lack of qualifications on the part of many of the monitoring organizations the FLA used, their actual monitoring practices left much to be desired on multiple fronts. The FLA continued not to disclose factory locations, something that has been central to the anti-sweatshops' demands. Instead, the association relied on privately held lists, making independent verification of its reports impossible (McSpedon interview). There was also the fact that the FLA, at least initially, notified factories of inspections in advance, giving managers a chance to cover up violations (Esbenshade 2004b; Brakken interview). While the FLA corrected this in 2001, other problems remained. For one thing, the inspections were usually very brief: according to Agatha Schmaedick (interview), a former WRC investigator, "They take place over just a few days to at most a few weeks," in contrast to the WRC's inspections, which normally take several weeks. Such short inspections did not last long enough to uncover serious abuses, which may require extensive investigation. According to Richard Locke, Matthew Amengual, and Akshay Mangla's (2009) study of one (pseudonymous) apparel corporation, the inspectors for the company's own social compliance department complained that such short visits were ineffective.

Ken Abrams (interview), who has experience with monitoring, also criticized the FLA for the fact that its monitors

> interview workers inside the factory, which hampers their ability to be candid. The managers are there watching those who are being interviewed. That's the standard: 99 percent of all audits done by social control auditors are done based on interviews inside the factory.

The FLA's official guidelines for its inspectors advised them to interview workers in places where they were safe from surveillance by their employers' and not to ask them leading questions. These guidelines, however, were both vague and suggested only; they were not requirements. It appears that, in practice, FLA monitors rarely followed these guidelines closely (Wells 2007). Such lack of confidentiality left workers vulnerable to retaliation—being fired, for instance—if they reported serious problems, a fact that managers in some plants took advantage of. Managers, by contrast, were given a guarantee of confidentiality by FLA inspectors in a double-standard that favored the very party that was least vulnerable to retaliation (Esbenshade 2004b).

The USAS member Caroline Stoppard (interview), who also has experience with monitoring programs, told me:

> That kind of monitoring is just not effective at identifying what the most serious kind of violations are and getting them fixed. They're very good at finding health and safety violations, things like the floor mat should not have been three inches from the door; it should have been four inches from the door. [. . .] But they're almost never going to get to the bottom of problems [having] to do with the freedom of association of workers or harassment of the workers that they wouldn't talk about even if they know or are aware. And then there are all sorts of other problems the factories can cover up—forced overtime, excessive overtime—if they want to.

In other words, the FLA performs best at finding violations of protective rights while failing miserably when it comes to enabling rights.

Stoppard went on to tell me about a report by Bureau Veritas, a for-profit monitoring company, describing conditions in a coffee mug factory in China. Her group had obtained a copy of the report:

> Of course, the only violation they find is that there aren't enough lights by the exits. [. . .] The fact that it's in China—I'm sure there are few more problems than there's not enough light by the door so workers can see their way out. But the best part is in the section on freedom of association. There's this whole two- or three-sentence explanation of their findings on freedom of association, which says something like, "All workers without distinction have the right to form trade unions of their own choosing and bargain collectively." This is in China. You get thrown in jail if you try to form a trade union of your own choosing, bargain collectively, or form any kind

of organization that's not sanctioned by the Communist Party. [. . .] Clearly, they pulled it from some code of conduct and decided it was the right finding and put it in there. It's just a joke. It doesn't mean anything. That's just one report, but that's an example of what this kind of auditing is about, and that's, unfortunately, the majority of the FLA's program.

It should be noted, however, that members of the anti-sweatshop movement were not totally disparaging of the FLA's efforts. Stoppard (interview) said:

They do respond to complaints, which can be helpful at times, especially when the WRC is working on a case, too, and they can reach agreement . . . on what the problem is. They usually reach agreement with the FLA on the problem. The problems are in the documents. It's the action [recommendation] writing that results in a disagreement. But it's still helpful for the WRC to have the FLA acknowledge that the same problem is going on.

While the WRC may be better at detecting problems, the FLA has more weight with the lead apparel companies. If the WRC can persuade the FLA to come on board and bring the lead firms with it, then it is far easier to solve a problem, since these companies have far more influence with their contractors than anyone else does (Esbenshade 2004b; Rodríguez-Garavito 2005).

Corporate Power in the FLA

There is, of course, a good reason that the FLA continually failed to develop an adequate monitoring system: the fact that a number of major apparel firms sat on the Association's board and provided the bulk of its funding. Jim Wilkerson, director of trademark licensing and stores operations at Duke University, who was actively involved with the FLA but withdrew from the organization in 2001 (later to join the WRC), told me:

I personally am quite disappointed in the results achieved by the Fair Labor Association since 2001. They have done some good work, but I don't feel that they have gone after these issues aggressively enough or achieved results that lead to lasting improvements in the conditions in the factories and in the lives of the workers. And I feel that there, over time, has developed too much corporate influence in the

Fair Labor Association, which I think has contributed to a softening of its approaches toward remediating labor rights violations.

The problem is that "private monitoring [. . .] was built on irreconcilable contradictions. These contradictions can be summarized as follows: First, [major companies] are in control of a program meant to discipline them; and second, workers are not participants in a program meant to benefit them" (Esbenshade 2004b, 198). There was an inherent conflict of interest involved in the FLA, which essentially allowed the corporations involved to monitor themselves while creating a façade of independence. It is the corporations on the board that helped set policy—and had veto power over policy changes. While the FLA may have shifted to hiring monitors itself, instead of allowing member companies to do so directly, creating something of a buffer, it was still the member companies that helped define the code of conduct to which they would be held and the standards for choosing which groups would be hired as monitors (Esbenshade 2004b; Wells 2007).

The major apparel companies that sat on the FLA's board have no interest in reforming the system of production that causes sweatshops, since doing so would reduce their flexibility and raise their costs. Nor did they have an interest in a monitoring system that would enforce enabling rights, allowing workers to organize independently and wield some power in the workplace (Esbenshade 2004b). The former WRC investigator Agatha Schmaedick (interview) observed:

> Factories that have taken strides in compliance and have signed path-breaking contracts with workers ensuring meaningful wage increases, health insurance, compliance with local laws—often those contracts are not even fully in force before the factory loses all of its orders and eventually has to shut down or outsource the majority of its production.

Decent working conditions increase contractors' cost of doing business, leading the apparel firms to look elsewhere—even when the contractors' increased costs came about as a result of complying with the lead firms' own codes of conduct.

Esbenshade (2004b, 10) summarizes the problem this way:

> Private monitoring is adapted to the globalized production system, *but it does not challenge that system.* Private monitoring accepts as given the industry's production practices—such as mobility and hidden chains of production—and its multilayered structure, both

of which foster sweatshops. Thus, although monitoring purports to, and may minimally, improve conditions for workers, it cannot systematically address the sweatshop problem.

The only long-term solution is the strengthening of both labor unions and public, democratic regulation of the economy, whether through local governments or some transnational system of enforceable labor regulation. Even the monitoring of movement-linked programs such as the WRC is limited in scope, tied to college production. The crucial difference is that the anti-sweatshop movement is aware of the limits of monitoring. Its members generally advocate strong unions and public regulation. They resorted to civil society–based monitoring programs because they believed that, at this historical juncture, they would have an easier time changing corporate policy than government policy. As discussed in the Conclusion, though, they hope that over the long run their activism will lead to changes in public policy, as well, and to a more worker-friendly regulatory system.

The FLA as a Corporate Counter-framing

While the FLA and similar programs largely failed to improve conditions for workers, they did succeed in another way: they countered the success that the anti-sweatshop movement had early on in framing the issue of sweatshops in the national mass media. Indeed, it seems likely that this purpose, and not the elimination of labor abuses, was the primary aim of apparel companies such as Nike and Reebok in developing CSR programs and supporting the FLA. On the basis of his experience as a board member of both the FLA and the WRC, Wilkerson (interview) has concluded that the leaders of the major apparel companies knew that their programs were largely ineffective. When the lead firms ask their contractors to sign on to codes of conduct,

> the factories as a matter of survival say, "We'll do it. We will adhere to the code of conduct." And the companies know that the factories cannot adhere to the code of conduct standards for the price that the companies have dictated to the factory. It's a bait and switch. It's a [public relations] game.

Unfortunately, the switch to emphasizing their CSR programs proved a successful countermeasure for the apparel industry. It is important to remember that the initial victory that the movement won in the discursive arena of the national mass media was an unusual one. The mass media is not an even playing field. Major corporations have a tremendous advantage over movements, not simply because corporations have more resources with which to try to shape the coverage of the issue, though that is a large factor. There is also the fact that most reporters and editors—the people who ultimately decide which frames will be featured in the news and which will be marginalized or ignored—have been socialized, including through their training as journalists, in such a way as to accord corporations and other powerful social actors more legitimacy than they do more marginal groups, such as social movements (Ferree et al. 2002; Gitlin 1980; Ryan 1991). While the sensational nature of the initial exposés of sweatshops may have allowed activists to persuade journalists that they had something newsworthy to say, ultimately journalists were inclined to believe the major firms once they came up with a credible response to the movement's critique.

Here it is worth recalling Seidman's (2007) arguments about the often deceptive nature of corporate monitoring programs, which can create the illusion of an effective commitment to ending sweatshops when there is no such commitment. Indeed, in the experience of some of my interviewees, they can create such an illusion even when it is clear that CSR programs are not actually working. The major apparel firms depict the problem of sweatshops as an intractable one for which they are not actually responsible. This framing of the problem has proved quite successful for the apparel industry. Eric Dirnbach (interview), a staff member at UNITE HERE, observed:

> Just issuing a report talking about the code of conduct and all the factory monitoring really does a lot to reassure reporters and the public that they're trying. And folks will be, like, "OK, I understand they haven't solved all the problems, but they're trying." You know, it looks like they're trying. The Gap puts out a report every year now or every two years. They do thousands of factory monitorings a year. They have ninety people in their social compliance program, with a [vice president] as head of social compliance. [. . .] Yet if you go to the factories and take a look at what's going on, you see the same problems. I think the industry has done a good job of placating the public and the media—that's what we have to figure out how to get past.

Given the credulous attitude most journalists hold toward corporations, figuring out how to get past this framing is no easy matter.

The major apparel firms did not simply use CSR as a generalized defensive frame against the anti-sweatshop movement. They also deployed the CSR frame strategically in particular conflicts with the anti-sweatshop movement to counter individual allegations of labor abuses. Esbenshade (2004b, 57) notes:

> Liz Claiborne and Kathy [sic] Lee Gifford, for example, both used their monitors' findings to publicly repudiate workers' reports of violations. [. . .] Companies such as Nike, the [sic] Gap, and Guess send information to consumers, investors, those who have signed petitions against them, and the like, proclaiming their progressive labor practices based on their monitoring programs.

To some extent, USAS managed to circumvent the dominance of the industry's framing in the national mass media by waging its battles in the discursive arena of the college campus. But, of course, it is not as if USAS's audiences were isolated from the national mass media. USAS had to deal with the pervasiveness of consumer culture on college campuses and the resulting valorization of the major brand-name apparel companies among students. It was not just students who bought the corporate framing hook, line, and sinker, though. The college administrators whose decisions activists must shape frequently also have bought into it. A former USAS activist (interview) told me, in some frustration, about her experiences meeting with administrators whom the industry had won over:

> Go to these meetings at universities and you can guarantee that one of these administrators is going to stand up and say, "I think we agree that we all—the university, USAS, the brands, and the WRC—have the same goals. We just disagree about the strategy for implementing them." I'm like, "Are you kidding? You think USAS and Nike have the same goals? I can't believe this." [. . .] Administrators will almost always put the brands and the WRC on the same playing field. They claim, "It's a dispute over the facts— we need to get to the bottom of the facts." They're not thinking, "Nike's making money off of abusing workers' rights and has everything to lose if that's revealed, whereas WRC has no financial stake in the outcome. Maybe the WRC's right."

Despite the frustrations of activists, though, the shift in the apparel firms' framing strategy was an important one. In acknowledging their responsibility for working conditions in their contractors' factories and setting up their own codes of conduct, the brands made themselves vulnerable in certain ways they were not before. When a factory used by a company is caught clearly violating the company's own code of conduct, activists can highlight this hypocrisy. This can prove very useful in solidarity campaigns with workers struggling in sweatshops (Esbenshade 2004b).

The Creation of the Worker Rights Consortium (WRC)

Innovation in Action: Crafting the WRC

Having analyzed why exactly the U.S. anti-sweatshop movement found the Fair Labor Association so problematic, we can now look into how the movement responded to its formation, our first major cycle of innovation. This process produced the Worker Rights Consortium, a genuinely independent monitoring organization whose creation added a significant new layer to the strategy of the corporate campaign (discussed in Chapter 4) on which anti-sweatshop activists had been relying to pressure apparel firms. According to Eric Brakken (interview), USAS's first staff person, the WRC was originally simply a paper proposal, meant as a conceptual alternative to the FLA, but it took on a life of its own as it became the focal point of the movement's response to the apparel industry.

As with many strategic innovations by social movements, the development of the WRC was spurred by the obstacles the movement encountered. The USAS member Jess Champagne (interview) spoke about the student group's main motivation for creating the WRC:

> We felt that it was important to have something clear to offer to universities that would counter-balance [the FLA]. [. . .] The universities were telling us that they were going to join the FLA. We thought that the more universities joined, the more effective it would be in covering up what was actually happening on the ground. So we decided that we needed to make a clear alternative

that would bring universities together, that would have an impact on sweatshops.

The student activists saw the FLA as a barrier to the effective use of the corporate campaign strategy. An important part of corporate campaigns is delegitimizing the target, especially in the case of companies such as Nike and Adidas, for which their brand image is their primary asset—and thus one of their most vulnerable points of attack. As discussed in the previous chapter, the FLA, with its façade of social responsibility and involvement of multiple stakeholders, did much to enhance the legitimacy of the member corporations. USAS believed that by designing an alternative to the FLA that was truly an *independent* monitoring organization, it could undermine the FLA's legitimacy. Such an alternative would also strengthen the position of the anti-sweatshop movement, both in the framing contest that was ongoing in the national media and in bargaining with college administrators. If it did not want colleges to join the FLA, USAS had to be able to present journalists and school officials with another option.

It is likely, however, that, even without the formation of the FLA the student anti-sweatshop movement eventually would have been pushed to create something like the WRC. The USAS member Thomas Wheatley (interview) recalls, "At the beginning we were really focused on disclosure. [We thought] we just needed to have the names of the factor[ies]; that if we had the names of those factories, people all over the world would bring up the list, look up those factories," and undertake the monitoring and investigations themselves. Local labor rights groups, however, were not likely to get easy access to the places they wanted to inspect simply because the factory was on a list that said it was producing for certain colleges that had codes of conduct. Factory owners would have little incentive to admit such groups to their facilities, particularly if they did have something to hide. USAS's various organizational mentors saw the problems with leaving monitoring to local groups before the students did. Wheatley (interview) said:

> The more we dug into it, the more we understood. The more students went to visit [and] did research, the more information we got from our allies in the movement. Nikki [Bas of Sweatshop Watch], Medea [Benjamin of Global Exchange], Charlie [Kernaghan of the NLC], and other folks [said], "This is great, but what are you going to do next? How are you going to do this? We need to talk about how we enforce these codes. This is really fabulous. Congratulations, kids! Now comes the hard part."

The WRC thus represented an alternative not only to the FLA but also to monitoring by individual schools, none of which—including the wealthiest universities—had the resources or expertise to properly monitor the implementation of their codes of conduct. By pooling the resources of member schools, the consortium would have the ability to monitor the implementation of its codes in a way no school could have managed on its own, no matter how serious it was about doing so.

Without this pooling of resources, it would have been considerably harder for USAS to use the leverage it had over the schools to exercise leverage, in turn, over the lead apparel firms. It was one thing for students to pressure their schools' administrations into adopting codes of conduct. It was another for that to translate into pressure on the schools' business partners to change their actual conduct. For this to work, a critical mass of schools needed to put pressure on the lead apparel firms to mend their ways. As discussed below, when the campaign for the WRC first began, Nike responded by canceling its contracts with a number of schools that had joined the consortium. But later, when a sufficient number of schools had joined the WRC, Nike found itself compelled to respond to students' demands that it put pressure on its contractors to allow workers to unionize in cases such as the Kukdong factory in Mexico in 2001 (see Chapter 11). College students were too important to Nike's marketing strategy to just cut out that major section of the market because of monitoring programs that the company believed impinged on its ability to operate freely. Instead, Nike at times had to concede to pressure from students via their schools. The WRC itself, it should be noted, did not engage in protest actions, but their shared membership in the consortium facilitated collective action by member schools to pressure their licensees, even if many schools did so only under pressure from their students.

The existence of the WRC not only facilitated USAS's ability to apply leverage to apparel firms. It also was crucial in conflicts over the legitimacy of the movement versus the industry. By refraining from engaging in protest, engaging only in monitoring and remaining independent not only from corporations but also from labor unions, the WRC avoided any appearance of a conflict of interest. The WRC's factory inspections were thorough compared with the FLA's, taking place over several weeks or even months and using local and international experts. This gave its reports a great deal of legitimacy, which meant they could potentially damage a company's brand image a good deal. USAS could then draw on this legitimacy, using the WRC's reports to justify its protests and giving the group more power to pressure school administrations and apparel companies.

The process of designing the WRC involved consultations among a wide range of groups in the anti-sweatshop movement, working more or less through consensus. Brakken (interview) noted, "By this time, the students [. . .] were the group that all the other anti-sweatshop groups were paying attention to. We were the grassroots energy happening around the country." Thus, USAS had many allies who wanted to work closely with it to design the response to the FLA. This pattern of a wide range of groups working together to coordinate campaigns and develop new strategic innovations is seen repeatedly in the history of the movement. As discussed in Chapter 1, having such a wide range of groups involved—and thus, people with a wide range of knowledge and experience—strengthened the movement's ability to innovate creatively (Ganz 2000, 2009; McCammon 2003, 2012) as it designed the consortium.

The people involved in crafting the WRC—both students and veteran anti-sweatshop activists—held a series of conference calls, paid for by UNITE, and met face-to-face immediately before USAS's official founding conference in July 1999 (Brakken and Wheatley interviews). The relationship between the student wing of the movement and the veteran activists was a complex one. As USAS member Nick Reville (interview) recalled, the more experienced activists

> were trying to take sort of a backseat role because they didn't want to be seen as dominating student movements; they wanted the students to have autonomy. But in a lot of cases, they were the people that we were getting our information from. How do we even know what's happening in these countries? We know through other organizations. [. . .] We needed those groups. We needed their professional expertise [and] their understanding of what we are trying to do.

One thing worth noting is that the groups involved at this stage were all based in the United States. The workers with whom USAS sought to act in solidarity were not directly involved in designing the WRC. All of the more established groups, however, had extensive contacts with labor unions and labor rights organizations in the Global South; drawing on these ties, they were able to relay the concerns and priorities of Third World activists to the USAS members involved in designing the WRC. The USAS member Laura McSpedon (interview) told me, "I just remember feeling that the NGO partners—like Global Exchange, the National Labor Committee and Sweatshop Watch—they were the people with the relationships on the ground in other countries, and that was the key to making this happen." At the same time, some individual USAS members did have their own ties to groups representing sweatshop workers. The USAS member Alyssa Caine (interview) said:

> There are some people in USAS that had their own relationships. Marion Traub-Werner took [two years] off and worked for STITCH [a group building bridges among female workers in Central America and the United States], so she had contacts. [. . .] Miriam [Joffe-Block] really helped forge a lot of the relationships in Thailand as a USAS activist who got a Fulbright and spent time there. Agatha [Schmaedick] spoke Bahasa Indonesian and decided to go to Indonesia and had some relationships there.

Despite this, USAS had no institutional ties with groups in the Global South. As Chapters 11 and 12 show, this changed as the movement grew. USAS would develop close, consistent ties with groups abroad, and these groups would come to be more directly involved in planning by USAS and its allies.

As one might expect, given the circumstances, the discussion among anti-sweatshop activists as they designed the WRC was very much shaped by the FLA in the sense that the WRC emerged out of critiques of the FLA. The substance of these critiques, however, was shaped by the movement's ideology. One area where this is clear is in the movement's understanding of the main cause of sweatshops lying in the structure of the apparel industry and the need of companies—both lead firms and contractors—to maximize profits. The most obvious aspect of this was the strong belief of all of the groups involved that corporations should have no role in the governance or funding of the WRC. This reflected not simply a desire for the WRC to appear independent and thereby have more legitimacy. As discussed in the previous chapter, according to USAS's analysis, it was sweatshops' centrality to the apparel industry's profit strategy that prevented the apparel companies from taking the steps needed to eliminate sweatshops. Including corporations in the WRC would have undermined activists' ability to design the organization so that it emphasized enabling rights, such as freedom of association, alongside protective rights.

Activists' understanding of the structural and therefore pervasive nature of sweatshops also shaped the strategy they designed for the WRC's inspections—specifically, what they called the "fire alarm" model of monitoring (see Chapter 10). According to Brakken (interview):

> One of the things the FLA wanted to do [was] put a tag on the clothing saying it was sweatshop-free or FLA-approved. [. . .] The debate

within the anti-sweatshop movement around the FLA was whether a label would actually work. Could a product actually be certified sweatshop-free? [. . .] So I think part of the framework of the WRC came out of the [realization that] there's thousands of factories around the world; we're a limited organization; we're never going to be able to have a permanent presence that would actually be able to certify these factories. [. . .] The WRC was [. . .] primarily set up to respond to workers' complaints and to be reactive, instead of proactive. I think that was a result of those early debates.

The WRC has not historically certified factories as sweat-free or given them a seal of approval, although this began to change with the design of the Designated Suppliers Program. Activists feared that this would create the illusion that a monitoring program alone, rather than a restructuring of the apparel industry and the fostering of independent labor unions, could prevent sweatshops.

This interpretive-analytic process of evaluating the limitations of the FLA through the lens of the movement's ideology of worker empowerment using a deliberative, participatory process resulted not only in a better design for the monitoring organization but also in the deepening of that ideology. Reflecting on the significance of this process for himself, and for many of the others involved, particularly students but also their NGO partners, Brakken (interview) said:

Going through some of those questions, it definitely changed my worldview around. I hadn't really thought about the long-term vision of how people would be empowered. The question isn't whether American consumers are going to be able to dictate the needs of the apparel workers in China or El Salvador. The questions are whether Salvadoran or Chinese workers have their own needs that need to be dealt with and need a good way to deal with that stuff. At that point at time, for some people, it was a little bit of a learning curve. [. . .] It definitely affected a lot of students' worldviews.

What Brakken and the others involved in designing the WRC ultimately concluded was that the end goal was not simply to create a U.S.-based monitoring organization but to create an organization that could help foster "a permanent organization of workers who could monitor [the factory] themselves on a day-to-day basis. That's called a union" (Brakken interview). In other words, guaranteeing enabling rights alongside protective rights became central to the WRC's mission through this process of reflection. It was an issue that not only the students "had to grapple with; [. . .] the other organizations [. . .] had to do it, too" (Brakken interview).

Over the course of these discussions, the participants developed a "white paper" that

> outlined a case for why [the WRC] was necessary, a case for why this was possible, and some principles, like monitors ought to be independent, they ought to be within or connected to the local community, and workers ought to be interviewed off-site, and those kind of things. (Wheatley interview)

On October 19, 1999, USAS made its white paper and the WRC public, calling on all colleges and universities to withdraw from the FLA and join the consortium (Greenhouse 1999c). The WRC's founding conference was planned for April 2000. In January 2000, the network of anti-sweatshop organizations hired Maria Roeper (interview) to bring the organization to life before the April conference.

What the creation of the WRC did was add a new element to corporate campaigns, with its monitoring program working in a way that bolstered the legitimacy of the movement and undermined that of the industry. The movement had made limited use of independent monitors before, but such monitors were the *outcome* of a successful campaign, designed to keep an eye on one or a limited number of factories, when a deal was reached with a company to make sure it lived up to its commitments to activists (Armbruster-Sandoval 2005; Esbenshade 2004b), not a strategic element *within* a campaign. (Strikingly, none of my interviewees referred to these previous monitoring agreements when they discussed the creation of the WRC.) The WRC changed how independent monitors operated as an element of the anti-sweatshop movement. Although they did not engage in protest campaigns, the WRC's staff's independent monitoring and verification of workers' complaints of abuse provided valuable legitimacy to the claims of those who were protesting, since they could point to the work of a relatively neutral third party to back up their claims. This is particularly important in getting school administrators to agree to sanction their licensees, since such officials are usually reluctant to damage their relationships with their business partners.

The Campaign for the WRC

Simply because the WRC was potentially a better monitoring organization than the FLA did not mean schools were going to sign on to it. As discussed in Chapter 3, most school administrators have close relations with major corporations through interlocking boards of directors. They also value their commercial contracts with corporations such as Nike and Reebok and were loath to offend them by taking action such as signing on to an organization designed by some of their most vocal critics. The USAS member Caroline Stoppard (interview) noted:

> It was something that was proposed by student activists, and universities were being asked to commit tens of thousands of dollars to an organization that was basically designed to go around and embarrass their business partners that had sweatshop conditions in their factories. But somehow we got them to do it.

Another obstacle, as we saw in the previous chapter, was that many school administrators seemed genuinely to believe that the major apparel firms were truly interested in ending the sweatshop exploitation of workers and that it was important to work cooperatively with them in doing so.

USAS therefore was going to have to pressure the school leaders to sign on to an alternative approach, using the same confrontational tactics as were necessary to get schools to adopt codes of conduct in the first place. At the same time, USAS would have to fight a framing battle with the major apparel firms, contesting the legitimacy of the FLA versus the WRC's approach to monitoring factories for sweatshop conditions, each side claiming that its approach would be more effective. USAS was thus in the position of fighting simultaneously battles with their own schools' administrations in the social arenas of college campuses across the country and with apparel corporations in the arena of the national mass media.

The 1999–2000 school year was marked by another wave of intensive student activism, again culminating in a wave of sit-ins in the spring semester, with the goal of compelling school officials to join the WRC prior to its official founding conference in April. According to Caine (interview):

> Students took that founding conference as an opportunity for their campaign. They built sit-ins and hunger strikes and all that stuff around the founding conference, saying, "We want our colleges and universities to join the Worker Rights Consortium before the founding conference." It became a kind of deadline.

It was also intended as an incentive to the schools: if they took part in the conference, they could play some role in shaping the WRC (Caine interview).

In pressuring college administrations to join the WRC, USAS used the same range of tactics and the same strategy of escalation it had used in its campaigns for the codes of conduct over the previous two school years. It had the problem, however, of convincing administrators to join an organization that, unlike the FLA, did not actually exist and had no significant financial backing. This created a major legitimacy deficit. According to Reville (interview):

> It was this bootstrapping thing—how do you go from nothing to something? We needed schools to sign on, but they wanted to sign on to something. So we were basically trying to convince them to sign on to this document that nobody had signed on to. It was like agreeing to join an organization that didn't exist. It was kind of a funny situation, but we had to do that in order for [the WRC] to start existing.

The first school to officially join the WRC was, in fact, Reville's (interview): own school, Brown University. This struggle had actually begun in the spring of the previous school year, when students began pressing President E. Gordon Gee to withdraw from the FLA. Reville recounted:

> We went to them and said, "OK, here's the issues we have with the FLA—we want you to withdraw." And then we said, "Okay, how about if they don't make improvements on these issues in the next six months, then we'll withdraw." And I think we said that because we felt like we did not have an alternative to offer, so just saying, "Let's pull out," was not as credible as that might be. So they agreed to [the six-month test period].

Of course, after six months the FLA had not improved at all, but Reville and the other USAS members at Brown now had the proposal for the WRC to present as an alternative. The Brown students used Gee's promise to withdraw from the FLA and the threat of a sit-in as leverage to force him to come to an agreement. They settled on a compromise, in which Brown would remain in the FLA but also join the WRC (Reville interview). Gee made this public on October 19, 1999, the same day the anti-sweatshop network officially released the WRC white paper, inviting schools to join (Marklein 1999).

Within USAS, the compromise the Brown students struck with Gee was controversial. Reville said:

I think there were a lot of people at other schools that thought that was a bad idea and felt that it furthermore set a bad precedent. [. . .] To me it seemed like it was much more important to get schools into the WRC rather than getting them out of the FLA. Even if you got all the schools that had USAS chapters out of the FLA, you still would have had a bunch of random schools in it— and it would still have that legitimacy of having schools in it. [. . .] I think getting that first school on was crucially important. It's not clear what would have happened if we hadn't gotten on there, because I know that a lot of [USAS chapters] used us as an example and relied on us in order to get their school to sign on. I think especially being able to take advantage of this Ivy League cachet, that was always something that helped other schools.

The first few colleges and universities to join the WRC after Brown were also small Ivy League schools. By mid-February 2000, with the WRC's founding conference less than two months away, only Bard College, Loyola University in New Orleans, and Haverford College had also signed on (O'Neill 2000). While their Ivy League status lent the WRC legitimacy, these schools gave the students little leverage over the major apparel firms, because their licensing programs were either small or nonexistent (with only procurement programs instead). What the movement needed as a next step was for some of the major sports schools to sign on, which would put far more pressure on the big apparel companies. On February 15, 2000, USAS chapters on many campuses began to systematically step up the pressure on their administrators. As a result, they netted their first three big sports schools: the University of Indiana, University of Michigan, and UW Madison. This did not happen without significant confrontation, It took sit-ins at Michigan and Wisconsin and the threat of one in Indiana (backed up by news reports of sit-ins elsewhere) to get the schools' administrators to agree (Caine and Stoppard interviews). According to Caine (interview):

> The administrators talked together, and they then affiliated with the WRC at the same time, all together. I think it was fear of going it alone and going up against Nike specifically and the fact those Big Ten schools were able to join together, I think, made it possible for them join. That was a big boost to the credibility of the [WRC].

According to Roeper (interview), the WRC "went from three to forty-four schools" between January and the April founding conference, with the ten-school University of California system affiliating with the WRC the day before the conference.

Neither the FLA nor the apparel industry reacted positively or passively to these developments. Their primary response was to try to frame the issue in a way that allowed them to maintain the moral high ground both in the arena of the national mass media and with college and university officials within the arenas of college campuses. While representing themselves as respectful of the students' efforts, various groups affiliated with the FLA argued that the WRC would have neither the resources nor the reach to properly engage in monitoring. They argued that including the companies in the FLA gave it the necessary means to monitor effectively (Greenhouse 1999c). Roberta Karp of Liz Claiborne said, "You need buy-in from the people who have a stake in this. [. . .] Corporations have a stake in protecting their names and making sure the facilities they contract with are operated fairly, efficiently and effectively" (quoted in Snyder 2000, B1). Some companies, such as Liz Claiborne and Reebok, claimed to be well ahead of USAS in terms of fighting sweatshops, pointing to their own CSR programs as evidence (Krupa 1999; Snyder 2000).

Representatives of the apparel industry also objected to the lack of corporate involvement in the WRC and its policy of unannounced inspections. Vada Manager of Nike said:

> We object to the Workers [sic] Rights Consortium because it does not provide a seat on the table for companies. [. . .] Another issue is it has a "gotcha" monitoring system, which in our minds is not a serious way to achieve the common goal that we all want to achieve, which is to eradicate sweatshop conditions. (Quoted in Greenhouse 2000a, A16)

Here again, as in the previous chapter, we can see the lead apparel corporations using CSR programs as a means to avoid and obfuscate the real issue—the structure of the industry whose commanding heights they control—while presenting the appearance of caring about and trying to solve the problem of sweatshops. They tried to make the case not only that they were willing to be partners in the quest to end sweatshops but also that without their involvement—and on their own terms—the movement could not succeed.

Nike was not only particularly vocal in its criticisms of the WRC as it attempted to reframe the issue but also took countermeasures that went beyond those of other companies. In April 2000, the company began actively retaliating against schools that joined the WRC—specifically Brown

University, the University of Michigan, and the University of Oregon. Nike started by canceling its contracts with Brown and Michigan (Asher and Barr 2000; Greenhouse 2000b), the latter of which was a Big Ten sports school whose "contract extension would have been worth between $22 million and $26 million over six years. [. . .] That would have made it the most lucrative such deal in college sports history" (Asher and Barr 2000, A1). In the case of Oregon, the retaliation was of a more personal sort. Nike's president Phil Knight was an alum of Oregon, and over the years he had donated $50 million to the school. In response to the university's decision to join the WRC, Knight canceled the donation of an additional $30 million he had pledged (Asher and Barr 2000; Greenhouse 2000a, 2000b). Even as the students were exercising leverage over their administrations through sit-ins, Nike was trying to exercise its own leverage by pulling out of licensing agreements that school officials valued.

On one level, Nike's retaliation seems to have been successful. The University of Oregon's administration, which had never been very committed to the WRC, soon withdrew from the organization (Steffan interview). On another level, however, it backfired. According to Caine (interview):

> It brought more attention to the issue and gave the WRC a different legitimacy, too. [. . .] This is the Worker Rights Consortium. It's just a small organization starting up. There was nothing to say that they were going to be able to do anything, but if Nike's going to cancel a $30 million [donation] over it, then it makes it seem like they really could do something. So that was a bad campaign strategy for them to try to prevent the WRC from going forward. It made the WRC look more legitimate, not less.

Nor did Nike's decision cause Michigan or Brown to withdraw from the WRC. Michigan, in fact, made a lucrative deal with Nike's rival, Adidas (Steffan interview).

The Foundation of the WRC

Even as this campaign was unfolding, Roeper was doing the work needed to prepare for the organization's founding conference, including setting up an office and finding a fiscal sponsor for the grant that had already been secured for the WRC. But her job involved more than just paperwork. She had to establish a distinctive identity for the WRC so that it was clear that it was autonomous not only from the apparel industry but also from USAS and the labor movement, particularly UNITE. "I was supposed to be in the role of establishing an organization with the credibility of a research organization, not an activist one," she said. This was necessary to create a group that colleges and universities would feel comfortable joining, one that they felt they had some ownership of and that was not simply the tool of the student activists who had been occupying their offices or a labor union such as UNITE, which many administrators saw as having dubious, protectionist motives (Roeper interview).

At the same time, the activists involved in creating the consortium wanted to ensure that it remained true to its original purpose. Thus, according to Wheatley (interview), the group drafting

> the initial framework for the bylaws, which was probably all of three paragraphs, [. . .] wrote it intentionally to make sure that universities would never have a majority of their own; they would have to share power with external advocates, who were not the most radical of them. It wasn't UNITE or Charlie Kernaghan [of the National Labor Committee] but Kate Pfordresher [of the People of Faith Network], David Schilling [of the Interfaith Center on Corporate Responsibility], and folks like that.

The founding conference took place on April 7, 2000. Attendees were organized into three caucuses—USAS members; an advisory board consisting of advocates and scholars who had long been involved in the anti-sweatshop movement, including representatives of groups from the Global South; and college and university administrators. Members of each caucus were to elect members to the WRC's board of directors and four working groups that would finalize the bylaws and help define the details of the WRC's policies. The conference itself consisted of a day-long meeting, featuring a panel of activists and scholars who had been instrumental in creating the WRC, taking questions from the audience about how, exactly, the consortium would work and what the working groups' tasks would be (United Students Against Sweatshops 2000). The situation was an unusual one, because in this forum the anti-sweatshop activists were clearly in command of the situation. While USAS and its allies were well organized, the college and university administrators were meeting with one another for the first time; they had to request more time to organize themselves and decide how they would elect members from their caucus to the governing board and working groups (Featherstone 2002; United Students Against Sweatshops 2000).

School officials also had concerns about various aspects of the WRC, raising a number of issues with the presiding panel. Some were basic questions about how the advisory board's membership had been selected. Others were about how much the proposed structure of the WRC was open to change. College and university administrators were particularly concerned that the consortium be open to engaging in dialogue with major apparel firms and that USAS's firm anti-FLA position not be that of the WRC. Many schools also belonged to the FLA, with officials from those schools arguing that the goal should be to reform the association, not undermine it. The panel explained that many of the details of the WRC were open to negotiation and that the consortium was certainly open to dialogue with industry; certain core features, however, were not negotiable, such as the absence of industry representation on the WRC's board to avoid compromising its independence. The panelists also indicated that USAS's anti-FLA position was its own and would not be the position of the consortium. At the request of one school official, the number of working groups was expanded from four to five to address some of these concerns (United Students Against Sweatshops 2000). As the chapters that follow show, the WRC did indeed maintain a cordial relationship with apparel companies and the FLA, engaging them in dialogue and working with them, as long as doing so did not compromise its principles.

Through the founding conference and the working groups, college administrators were able to have some role in shaping the WRC—and thus to develop a stake in the organization—but in a way that the consortium remained true to the ends for which the anti-sweatshop movement had created it. The bylaws were finalized by late 2000, and the board hired Scott Nova as the WRC's executive director.

The next chapter looks at the organization of the WRC and its fire alarm approach to monitoring sweatshops. Subsequent chapters look at the international work that the WRC, USAS, and other anti-sweatshop organizations have accomplished in collaboration with groups in the Global South. What we have seen unfolding in the past few chapters is a conflict between the anti-sweatshop movement, on one side, and the apparel industry and the FLA, on the other, made up of a series of strategic moves and countermoves by the social actors involved, each trying to exert leverage and legitimacy against other social actors, including not only one another but also college officials.

In the crafting of the WRC as an innovative, strategic response to the FLA, we have also seen in this chapter the dialectic between ideology and experience that is at the heart of the development of strategy by social movements. The U.S. anti-sweatshop movement had been taking action based on its existing strategy of corporate campaigns and seeking new points of leverage over the apparel industry—in particular, experimenting with codes of conduct for college licensees as a means to this end. As it did so, it ran up against obstacles: the realization of the impracticality of relying solely on local labor rights groups to carry out monitoring and the apparel industry's formation of what USAS saw as a deeply problematic monitoring organization in response to the movement. The movement then took the time to analyze its experiences, reflecting on them in light of its ideology of worker empowerment. It did so collectively, drawing together activists from a range of groups, with different constituencies, experiences, and networks, thus greatly broadening the range of insight it could draw on, far beyond what any one individual or group would have brought to the table alone. In doing so, the anti-sweatshop movement generated a new strategic innovation—not simply the WRC as an organization, but a new model of monitoring that could complement the existing model of corporate campaigns. It also deepened its understanding of worker empowerment and its relevance to the anti-sweatshop struggle, coming to understand that monitoring would never be enough and that workers needed to be able to exercise voice and power through their own organizations.

Embedded Autonomy and the Fire Alarm Model

The Organization and Monitoring
Practices of the WRC

The WRC's Embedded Autonomy

Although it was USAS and other members of the anti-sweatshop movement who pushed for the creation of the Worker Rights Consortium, once the WRC was created, college and university administrators formed a significant part of its constituency. If the WRC was to have credibility in the eyes of this group, it had to take into account their perspectives and concerns, as well as those of the anti-sweatshop movement. This meant that it had to have some autonomy from USAS and the other organizations of the anti-sweatshop movement. It could not be seen as a simple extension of USAS, something that was a real danger early on. As the previous chapter showed, school officials were particularly concerned that the WRC engage in dialogue with the apparel industry and the FLA instead of taking a purely oppositional stance to them, as many USAS activists were inclined to do. The WRC has, in fact, been willing to engage the apparel industry in dialogue and show some sensitivity for its concerns; indeed, the WRC's staff have found this to be a strategically wise choice and central to their success in many ways. At the same time, to accomplish its goals, the WRC had to maintain ties with an extensive network of anti-sweatshop groups, not only in the United States but also throughout the Global South, wherever factories producing licensed goods for schools are found. These groups in the Global South formed the WRC's "eyes and ears" (Schmaedick interview); they alerted the consortium to cases of potential labor rights violations that it should investigate. Thus, the WRC forged a wide, strategic network of ties with both industry and the anti-sweatshop movement while remaining relatively independent from the organizations that make up both sectors.

The WRC's relationship with other groups, particularly in the anti-sweatshop movement, is perhaps best characterized by a phrase Peter Evans (1995) coined in a much different context: *embedded autonomy*. Evans used the phrase to refer to the relationship that successful industrializing states (such as Japan, South Korea, and Taiwan) have with other social groups in their countries, particularly business elites. In much of the Third World, states have been *captured* by local business and landed elites—that is, the state is largely under their control, following their dictates. In most of these cases, such elites are too short-sighted and too focused on their immediate self-interest to strategically promote anything like a coherent industrialization program. To promote successful, broad-based industrialization ("economic development"), states must instead have some independence from these elite economic interests so they can shape the policies of the business sector with a combination of regulations, incentives, and central coordination. However, while being captured by business interests will not let the state do this, neither will being completely isolated from such social actors. Instead, government bureaucrats in charge of promoting industrialization must develop dense social networks with business leaders by both formal means, such as joint state-business councils that determine industrial and economic policy, and informal means, with retired state bureaucrats assuming positions in industry. These ties allow government bureaucrats to negotiate and coordinate with leading capitalists to define their goals vis-à-vis industrialization and the strategic policies to reach those goals. This relationship is what Evans meant by "embedded autonomy": the state was embedded in a set of social networks without being controlled by any of the other social actors in these networks, instead maintaining its autonomy.

Using this frame of reference, it is clear that the FLA was captured by business interests from the moment of its creation. The structure of its board and the nature of its funding have allowed business to play a disproportionate role in shaping the association's policies, resulting in successive monitoring programs that have been largely ineffective at addressing the problem of sweatshops (though they have been quite effective in allowing business to maintain its legitimacy, arguably its main goal). Indeed, "capture" may be the wrong word, since this implies that at one point the FLA was independent, although it never has been.

In contrast, the WRC was designed to be autonomous from industry—no representatives of business sit on its board; nor does the WRC take money from the business community. Instead, its board was made up of five representatives each from three constituencies—college and university administrators, United Students Against Sweatshops, and the independent labor rights experts who make up the WRC's Advisory Council (Worker Rights Consortium 2007b). As shown in the previous chapter, this autonomy from business was fundamental to the way anti-sweatshop activists conceived of the WRC. Thomas Wheatley (interview) of USAS played a role in crafting the WRC. He said of the FLA, "It's the fox guarding the chicken coop. You can't have the people who have it in their interest to drive wages and working conditions to the bottom guarding the door of the monitoring process that is designed to do the opposite. Structurally it just doesn't work." Looking at the WRC versus the FLA and other, similar corporate-sponsored monitoring programs, the USAS member Ken Abrams commented:[1]

> The WRC just represents universities; [it's] multi-university. The fact that [it's] independent of industry allows the WRC to be more aggressive in pressing companies because no one has veto power over what [it does] publicly. [In a]ll these other organizations, either through formal or informal means, there are very powerful voices of the companies in determining what gets said, what gets done.

Despite this emphasis on autonomy from industry, the WRC maintained connections to apparel companies. In particular, when inspections revealed that a contractor had been violating workers' rights, the WRC tried to work with the companies involved—both the lead apparel firms and their contractors—to rectify the problems. This means that the WRC needed to maintain open lines of communication with the FLA and the apparel industry, particularly companies' social responsibility departments. We explore this relationship with companies in more depth below after examining how the WRC carried out its inspections.

Through the university and USAS caucuses, as Abrams said, it is members of the higher education community who had the most weight with the WRC. Affiliated schools paid an annual fee to the WRC, which varied from school to school, depending on the nature of an institution's licensing program. These fees made up 45 percent of the WRC's budget, with the bulk of

---

1. Other corporate-sponsored monitoring programs include Social Accountability International (SAI) and Worldwide Responsible Apparel Production (WRAP). For more information on these organizations, see Esbenshade 2004b and O'Rourke 2003.

the remainder coming from federal and foundation grants (Worker Rights Consortium 2007a). Although the WRC had a model code of conduct (Worker Rights Consortium 2007c), member schools were not required to follow it. Instead, they could implement their own codes of conduct. Such codes had to include disclosure of all factory locations and provisions regarding "basic protection for workers in each of the following areas— wages, hours of work and overtime compensation, freedom of association, workplace safety and health, women's rights, child labor and forced labor, harassment and abuse in the workplace, non-discrimination and compliance with local law" (Worker Rights Consortium 2007a). One point of contention that remained between the university caucus, on the one hand, and the USAS and labor rights experts caucuses, on the other, was that many schools' codes of conduct had provisions that required only the local minimum or prevailing wage (which usually is a paltry sum), not a living wage (though a living wage was part of the WRC's model code of conduct).

Through the involvement of USAS and its advisory council of labor rights experts, the WRC was also embedded within the network of organizations that make up the anti-sweatshop movement. Yet it was careful to maintain some autonomy from the movement, as well, a strategic necessity to maintain its credibility. In particular, said the WRC staff member Jeremy Blasi (interview), "We don't take money from unions on purpose because we want to maintain our position as an entity that can assert itself as a neutral investigative body." In the eyes of both the university caucus and many publics, close ties with the labor movement would be as suspect and delegitimating as close ties with the apparel industry. This is particularly important given that "the Fair Labor Association tried to make [the campaign for the WRC] out to be a protectionist front for UNITE and use the history of both UNITE and the labor movement as being somewhat protectionist to try to discredit us" (McSpedon interview). The WRC also was careful to remain distinct from USAS, with which it could all too easily be identified, given that USAS was instrumental in its creation and in pressing school officials to join the consortium. According to the WRC staff member Nancy Steffan (interview):

> USAS is just a different kind of organization. They're the student anti-sweatshop movement. We're monitors and investigators. So [USAS has] a very different relationship with the universities. [. . .] We don't do protests. We don't condone protests. We don't work directly with unions or on behalf of unions. [. . .] We do different kinds of things. But then we can also talk to universities and brands and get a very different kind of reception than USAS does.

Again, we see that the WRC's autonomy was crucial to its work. But so were its ties with the anti-sweatshop movement. As we explore below, the network within which it was embedded was essential to alerting it to problems it should investigate. And if it could not work with companies to solve a problem, it was this network (*not* the WRC) that mobilized to pressure the companies to change their course.

Both labor unionists and USAS members understood and appreciated the strategically distinct role that the WRC played in the anti-sweatshop movement—and thus the necessity for its embedded autonomy. Eric Dirnbach (interview) of the apparel union UNITE HERE said of the WRC, "I think they have helped probably a dozen unions at a dozen factories organize a union. [. . .] We actually are able to help workers in a number of factories organize, and that's tremendously important in this kind of issue, where that is almost impossible to do." The USAS member Nick Reville (interview) observed that it was extremely exciting for student activists to see something as concrete as the WRC and its monitoring program come about as the result of their efforts. He saw the WRC as "lock[ing] in our wins," creating an institutional presence that, through colleges' and universities' ability to suspend and cancel licensing agreements, had some enforcement power. There was no sense among the people I interviewed that the WRC was potentially vulnerable to capture by universities, but an understanding that the WRC was strategically placed to carry out a role— credible, independent monitoring—that no other organization in the anti-sweatshop movement could perform.

The Fire Alarm Model: The WRC's Monitoring Practices

Just as the WRC's structure and relationship to other groups differed fundamentally from corporate-sponsored monitoring organizations such as the FLA, so did its approach to monitoring. The FLA and its kin relied primarily on some form of certification, whether of factories or of companies (Esbenshade 2004b). As noted in Chapters 8 and 9, anti-sweatshop activists saw serious problems with this practice, fearing it could mislead consumers into believing that goods so labeled were genuinely sweat-free. Maria Roeper (interview), who was hired to bring the WRC to life, noted that when the consortium was being created, there was some confusion around this point among rank-and-file USAS members: "Many people tried to say, 'Join the WRC and be sweat-free.' And many of us in the leadership [of the movement] were saying, 'We won't actually be sweat-free, because you don't overnight have perfect working conditions anywhere. It's a long, involved process. [. . .] They're not going to fix it overnight.'"

Unlike the FLA, the WRC did not regularly inspect factories. Instead, it responded to news of possible violations of workers' rights and relied heavily on its local networks of their allies for such news.

The WRC's staff members referred to their approach toward monitoring as the "fire alarm model." Rather than relying on regular inspections of factories, followed by certification, the fire alarm model as a strategy involved investigating factories in response to complaints by workers or their advocates or other reports of potential code of conduct violations. According to Steffan (interview), "We work with local organizations to check out the factories where we have received complaints of problems and where there's local interest in working with us to improve working conditions."

One of the first things the WRC had to do following its official founding in April 2000 if it wanted to effectively carry out its goal of independently monitoring conditions in apparel factories was develop a network of contacts with such local organizations throughout the Global South. As the USAS member Laura McSpedon (interview) said, when the WRC was being designed, it "seemed important that there was someone who was not at a 202 [Washington, DC,] area code phone number for workers to call." It was not enough for the consortium to have a relationship of embedded autonomy with anti-sweatshop groups in the United States; it had to develop a similar network of relationships with groups that were in contact with the workers it hoped to aid. These groups were the consortium's "local eyes and ears on the ground," in the words of Agatha Schmaedick (interview), a former investigator for the WRC. "They have contact with the workers, and if there's a problem at a factory they get word of that, and they pass it on to us." Groups and people who served as the WRC's local contacts included "unions, community organizations, faith-based organizations, women's rights organizations, doctors who work in occupational health and safety—there's a whole gamut of individuals and organizations that are constantly hearing worker's grievances" (Schmaedick interview). The WRC's inspection program also relied on the expertise, both professional and local, of these groups and individuals to aid in factory inspections. As part of maintaining its autonomy, however, the WRC had to be careful not to use contacts who had reported potential labor rights violations to do the investigative work on the same cases, as that would involve conflicts of interest. In describing these networks, I am relying primarily on reports by WRC staff; I am not in a position to evaluate how successful they were in developing these relationships. I can evaluate only what their intentions were in doing so.

Workers filing a complaint could do so either directly with the WRC or through the intermediary of one of the consortium's local contacts. The complaint process was meant to be worker-friendly (Esbenshade 2004b), not one that involved large volumes of paperwork or working with a labyrinthine bureaucracy. Thus, the means of submitting the complaint was purposefully flexible: it could be verbal or written and could be delivered to the WRC through any medium (phone, fax, postal mail, e-mail or a form on the WRC's website). Further, the complaint did not need to go into the technical details of how the alleged labor rights violations contravened the codes of conduct of the WRC's affiliate schools. It was enough that it was clear that serious problems had occurred. The complaint did, however, have to be specific about what the problems were. Throughout the ensuing inspection process, the consortium and its partners protected the confidentiality of the complainants to guard them against retaliation by management (Worker Rights Consortium 2007d).

According to Jeremy Blasi (interview):

> A substantial percentage of our complaints involve workers who've been fired for trying to organize their union or organize in some other way in their workplace to improve the conditions, eliminate violations. So case after case after case, the actual work of what we're doing involves, in part, documenting the ways in which the firing of these workers, who are seeking to improve things in their factory, was illegal, because you can't fire someone for organizing a union or trying to improve conditions in your factory. And then [we try] to get those workers reinstated into the factory, if that's what they want, so that the efforts, the collective efforts of workers in these factories to improve things, can go forward.

Officially, the WRC had jurisdiction only in cases in which collegiate apparel was being produced. In practice, it ended up dealing with a wide range of companies, many of which did not produce college-licensed goods because any one factory might produce goods for several different corporations and thus would be producing goods for the general market alongside college apparel (Blasi interview). The WRC's influence was therefore wider than the small part of the apparel market over which it had formal surveillance power. Many of the noncollegiate firms with which the consortium dealt had plenty of incentive to cooperate with the WRC's investigations—they cared about their brand images, and there was always the danger that, if they did not deal with the WRC, they would have to deal with USAS or other, more confrontational members of the anti-sweatshop movement.

As discussed in Chapter 8, members of the anti-sweatshop movement were generally critical of the brevity of the inspections done by the FLA, which usually lasted only a few days. Such short inspections prevented not only the investigators from doing a thorough job but also the inspectors from building and drawing on ties with local groups and helping them build their own capacity to carry out monitoring. The WRC carried out its inspections over a period of several weeks. Once the inspections were complete and the reports were issued, the consortium remained in touch with the local actors, trying to ensure that its recommendations were actually implemented—something the FLA historically has not done. Thus, the WRC was usually involved with a particular factory for at least a few months; in some cases, where either the factory's management or the companies that patronized it were resistant to changes, the consortium could have remained involved for years on end, as it did with the BJ&B factory in the Dominican Republic (though this was an extreme case). Regarding her experience as one of the WRC's field representatives and monitors, Schmaedick (interview) told me:

> I used to spend months' worth of time in Asia, and then I'd come back to the [United] States for a month, and then I'd go [to Asia] again for a month or two. There's a lot of back and forth. Obviously, I wouldn't be working on just one factory. I'd work on several. It's a lot of time to build up the trust and the rapport and to make sure we understand what the problems are and then, more importantly, that the recommendations that we put forward make sense in terms of actually addressing the issue at hand.

Steffan (interview) noted, "The first step is never going to a factory and doing inspections. It's always talking with workers. That's the only way to get the real information about what's going on and make sure we do something meaningful, that people want to happen and are going to [. . .] try to [work with us to] obtain the truth." Again, we see a monitoring strategy that was meant to be worker-centered and emphasized building local relationships. The WRC's representatives also took care in putting together their inspection teams. Although the consortium consulted with unions representing the workers on what problems needed to be addressed and the best way to do so, union representatives were never included in inspection teams because of the obvious conflict of interest (Steffan interview). As noted above, any advocacy group that filed a complaint with the WRC in relation to a particular case was barred from the inspection team working on that case, though the inspectors might consult with the group in the same manner they did with unions. Any inspection team had to include both representatives of the WRC and representatives of local groups who had relevant expertise. In a case in which there were charges that labor laws were being violated, the team would include lawyers with expertise in local labor law; in a case where there were charges of health and safety violations, the team would include doctors who specialized in occupational injuries and diseases and so forth. The consortium might also draw on people with expertise from outside the region (Worker Rights Consortium 2007d; Schmaedick interview, 2007)—for instance, Mark Barenberg, a law professor at Columbia University who specializes in labor issues, has been involved in a number of WRC inspection teams.

The WRC's inspection teams relied on a wide range of means to gather data, including actually visiting and inspecting the factory, as well as going through the factory's records—for instance, going through its payroll records to look for evidence of failure to pay workers their wages properly. The inspection teams also relied heavily on interviews with a wide range of concerned parties. Particularly central to the inspections, as already noted, were interviews with workers. Chapter 8 discusses how the anti-sweatshop movement critiqued the FLA and corporate CSR programs for failing to protect workers' confidentiality in such interviews. The basic inspection protocols of the Worker Rights Consortium (2007d), by contrast, mandated such confidentiality. The protocols also required the monitoring teams to approach workers for interviews outside of work, through intermediaries such as local advocacy groups or sympathetic doctors that the workers knew and trusted. Without this, workers have no way of knowing that the WRC's assessment team was not actually affiliated with factory management or the major companies that contracted with the factory—and without such knowledge and trust, workers would have plenty of reasons to be less than candid, if only to protect themselves from retaliation by their employers. The investigation protocols also required the consortium to redact quotes from workers in their final reports in such a way that all information that might identify individuals was removed.

In some cases, it was important to get information out promptly, before the investigation was complete. Regarding the case of Kukdong, a maquiladora in Mexico (see Chapter 11), the WRC's executive director, Scott Nova (interview), told me:

> Union leaders were fired during the [organizing] campaign. It was critical that they were reinstated. The purpose of the firing was not just to deprive workers of their leaders, but to scare the hell out of those who hadn't been fired. So it was critical that the chilling effect be halted [. . . ,] which required responsiveness on our part. So we were able to investigate very quickly and issue a preliminary

report within a matter of a day clearly outlining the obvious violations, the illegalities of the firings.

If the union leaders had not been reinstated promptly, they would have
been forced by economic necessity to find work elsewhere, eliminating the
workers' leadership over the long run. Groups such as USAS were able to
use this preliminary report (Worker Rights Consortium 2001b) to put
pressure on the lead firms, such as Nike and Reebok, that did business with
Kukdong's owners to reinstate the fired workers. Meanwhile, the WRC continued with a more in-depth investigation, eventually putting out a full
report (Esbenshade 2004b; Nova interview).

     As part of its long-term orientation toward monitoring, the WRC—
unlike the FLA and many other corporate-sponsored monitoring programs—tried to remain involved to see that its recommendations for correcting labor rights violations were actually implemented. In Chapter 8, I
noted that part of the movement's critique of the FLA was its failure to see
that problems that its inspectors found were addressed. For Schmaedick,
such follow-up was central to any successful monitoring program:

> Finding violations, unfortunately, is almost too easy—the viola-
> tions are so blatant. But the follow-up ensures that promises that
> are made are kept. Moreover, say, for example, the issue is excessive
> overtime or excessive, forced, and even unpaid overtime. Often it's
> easy to correct the unpaid part. People can be paid. But to correct
> the "excessive" part means the restructuring of the factory produc-
> tion lines and the workday and spreading out production over more
> time, more days. That takes longer, and sometimes you think you
> have addressed it; then it shows up in other problems where people
> aren't making the production deadlines or something, so you need
> to readjust, you need to reassess. That requires going back and forth
> and finding solutions that actually address what you were trying to
> address rather than creating new problems.

Monitors who do not surveil conditions over the long term are unable to
see whether management has made the recommended changes and whether these changes adequately address the problems found and to build the
long-term relationships with factory owners, workers, and local advocacy
groups that ensure such changes are carried out. The WRC, with its long-
term commitment, had a much better chance of accomplishing this.

     The WRC also sought to build the capacity of local groups with which
it worked so they were better able to address labor rights violations on

their own (Worker Rights Consortium 2007d)—again a major difference between it and programs such as the FLA. Schmaedick (interview) told me, "It's all really about capacity building [. . .]—especially in setting up internal grievance systems within the factory that really work, making sure there's new respect [. . .] formed between management and the workforce and that the workforce has a voice, an organized voice, in the workplace, so they can address grievances in real time and rely less and less on external monitors such as myself." The WRC was also interested in building the capacity of local advocacy groups besides unions so that these groups could both work with the consortium on future investigations more effectively and act on their own to fight sweatshops more effectively (Worker Rights Consortium 2007d). The WRC, a small organization, had the capacity to be involved in only so many investigations; thus, building the capacity of local groups meant there were fewer cases in which it needed to intervene directly, and it could use its limited resources more effectively.

The WRC thus developed a large network of contacts—its "eyes and ears"—throughout the Global South with which it tried to maintain mutually beneficial relationships. Being embedded in this network was essential for the WRC if its monitoring strategy was to have any hope of real success. In turn, the WRC offered its partners a means of strengthening their own hand in the battle for labor rights. If it was not embedded in these networks, the WRC would have been a far less effective organization. At the same time, it needed to maintain its autonomy for its factory inspections and reports to have credibility. Its wide range of contacts meant that it was not dependent on any one organization in its network when it carried out an investigation. Not only did the WRC have a wide range of experts with whom it could work, but it could also avoid conflicts of interest that would compromise its integrity.

Issuing Reports and Working with Companies

While the WRC worked with anti-sweatshop groups in the context of its investigation of alleged abuses of workers' rights, it primarily worked with companies—both the major apparel firms and their contractors—in the context of trying to correct the abuses it found. Roeper (interview) told me that, unlike in USAS, there was "a fair amount of talking and working *with* the companies rather than *against* them," especially their CSR departments, in the case of the WRC. Such lines of communication needed to be kept open if the companies were to take the WRC's recommendations seriously and even consider implementing them. Thus, the consortium needed to remain embedded in a set of relationships with the apparel industry. At the same time, it worked to ensure that its autonomy was never compromised. As noted earlier, corporations were barred from sitting on the WRC's board and donating money to the consortium, and the WRC placed a high value on transparency. Unlike the FLA and other corporate-sponsored monitoring groups, which treated reports as the confidential property of the lead apparel firms (Esbenshade 2004b), the WRC made all of its reports public, documenting the violations it found. The consortium tried to maintain this balancing act of both keeping good relations with industry and transparency by giving the companies involved in any particular case the chance to correct labor rights violations *before* the consortium published the report and acknowledging any such corrective action in the report. However, if the companies failed to address the problems the WRC inspectors raised, the WRC published this failure, as well, leaving the companies vulnerable to campaigns by USAS and its allies.

The investigative teams' reports were the nexus through which the WRC both worked with companies to persuade them to comply with its recommendations and maintained its public transparency. These reports not only documented violations of labor rights and codes of conduct but also included recommendations for actions on the part of the companies involved, put together by the monitoring team in consultation with local advocacy groups. The WRC's office in Washington, DC, then went through the reports to prepare them for the final public release, editing them as necessary and clarifying points that might be obscure to those uneducated about workers' rights. Steffan (interview) told me about a report on Cambodia she had just completed in which she had to justify why some problems were actually problems so the report would stand up to critiques by detractors of the anti-sweatshop movement in the college or industry sector:

> For example, maybe there's a factory in Cambodia where one of the problems was verbal abuse by this supervisor in the embroidery department and one of the things she was doing was screaming at workers who would leave work at the end of the shift, even if they hadn't [met] their quotas. You can't legally force workers to work past their shifts, even if they haven't finished. [. . .] Well, the skeptic here might say, "Well, the person didn't finish the work. Of course, the [worker] should have gotten yelled at" [. . . ,] so I had to put in a footnote saying that it is a violation of Cambodian law. [. . .] We have to make sure we're thoroughly explaining why everything's a violation because there's always going to be someone who

says, "Well, that doesn't sound so bad to me." Clearly, these are people that have no idea what it's like to be a low-wage worker in Cambodia. We're taking the problems as workers describe them to us [. . . ,] but we have to make sure we're explaining it in a way that's airtight, and see whether they're a violation of law, a violation of codes of conduct, a violation of [International Labor Organization] principles. It's got to be described in that way and in relation to something that's not controversial.

In some cases, the reports might have served to strain relationships with the companies the WRC needed to work with by publishing things those companies would prefer not to be known. It was, however, the principle that was important. According to Roeper (interview), "It was a big, big issue early on in the creation of the WRC that all of these other monitoring organizations—the FLA, Verité, etc.—did not make their reports public. Part of the concept of the WRC is that public accountability is very important. Disclosure of factory locations is important, as is public disclosure of information." Even if few people read the reports thoroughly, the fact that they were public made them available to those groups—such as USAS or the Solidarity Center—that might launch a campaign against a company that failed to deal with the problems in good faith. If the WRC's efforts to work with companies by making recommendations did not lead to public accountability, such campaigns might have been able to do so—an issue explored in the next few chapters.

According to Schmaedick (interview), after the report was compiled, but before it went public, the strategy would follow this course:

> We give a copy . . . to the brands involved, to the factory management, and to the workers who filed the complaint or the trade unions, depending on what the situation is with labor at the factory. We give the main parties involved a chance to look at everything before it goes public. We say these are the violations and there are some very serious ones, but if you agree to these recommendations, we will definitely put that in our public report. It gives everybody a chance to save face. [. . .] I led a lot of those initial visits with brands, where we would report our findings to them quietly at first, and they still knew we were going to go public with it, but they started to feel, over time, that if there was cooperation from them in the beginning, it would fare far better for them in the long run.

In addition to working with companies, the WRC at times worked with the FLA (see Chapter 9). The FLA's public view was that the two organizations play complementary roles in fighting sweatshops. Auret van Heerden, former executive director of the FLA, said about the relationship, "The WRC has great connections on the ground and an early-warning system that is invaluable at times. There is an obvious synergy emerging. They can uncover problems. We can get the brands to get us both in the door" (quoted in Esbenshade 2004b, 195).

The WRC staff people I spoke with felt that they had successfully established cordial, constructive relationships with the factory owners and the lead apparel firms, achieving some degree of respect from them. Steffan (interview) told me, "The brands were very skeptical at first; then we went through a period where we were developing good relationships with them, at least in terms of specific factory cases. If there was a problem that we had documented at a factory, we could generally count on at least the bigger brands to intervene—they're more sophisticated with corporate social responsibility programs." Obviously, the relationships the WRC had with the brands, and even with the FLA, were never as tight as those it had with the anti-sweatshop movement, since the consortium's purpose was to act as a watchdog over those companies. In any such relationship, there was bound to be some degree of strain. And those relations—with both the companies and the FLA—grew more strained over the years as the WRC pursued implementing the Designated Suppliers Program (DSP), which asked more of the major companies than simply fixing violations at the factory level. It asked them to change the way they do business, an issue I look at more closely in Chapter 12. In addition, in 2015, Nike announced it would no longer cooperate with the WRC in granting it access to the factories with which the company contracts, making it next to impossible for the consortium to monitor these factories to check whether they are in line with its member schools' codes of conduct (Jamieson 2016; Nova 2015). As a result of a campaign by USAS and its allies, in which several schools cut their ties with Nike, the company retreated from this position and, in August 2017, signed an agreement facilitated by Georgetown University's administration pledging to work with the WRC to guarantee access to the contractors' factories (Gearheart and Newell 2017; Segran 2017; Worker Rights Consortium 2017).

Clearly, there are marked differences in how the WRC related to other organizations in the anti-sweatshop movement and to the companies it monitors. In both cases, however, the relationships may be characterized as embedded autonomy, though with more emphasis on embeddedness in the case of the anti-sweatshop movement and on autonomy in the case of the apparel industry. To pursue its monitoring strategy effectively, the WRC needed to maintain relationships not only with a wide range of organizations, including anti-sweatshop and workers' advocacy groups that alerted it to problems and helped it carry out its task of monitoring, but also with the companies that were being monitored, to find ways to address the problems that its monitoring program revealed. At the same time, to maintain its credibility as a watchdog organization, it could clearly not be beholden to any other organization or set of organizations that had a stake in the wider conflict over labor conditions. In many ways, the WRC has proved an effective monitor. Indeed, one of the signs of its success is that it was usually able to say in its public reports that the companies involved had taken steps to fix the problems found. This was not, however, always the case. In cases in which companies were not compliant with the process, the wider anti-sweatshop movement would take advantage of the information the WRC documented to undertake campaigns against them. I look at these campaigns in the next chapter.

Transnational Solidarity
Campaigns

The campaigns I have examined so far—to win codes of conduct for licensees at colleges and universities and to establish the Worker Rights Consortium—were not fought for their own sake. These local, campus-level campaigns were fought to give the anti-sweatshop movement more leverage in its global efforts to support workers in sweatshops fighting for their rights, particularly the right to form labor unions, so they can exercise power and voice on their own. To do this effectively, U.S. groups must work closely with the workers they want to support, letting those workers set the main agenda. In other words, the U.S. groups must find ways to act in solidarity and seek to empower the workers not only in their own workplaces but also in the transnational campaigns against sweatshops. Such solidarity and empowerment include not only engaging in specific campaigns to help workers at specific factories but also finding ways to establish long-term relationships between U.S. groups and groups representing the workers they want to help. While the majority of its campaigns were in support of workers in the Global South, United Students Against Sweatshops engaged in at least one major campaign to support workers at a U.S. facility: the New Era Cap factory in Derby, New York. In this chapter, I explore the global political opportunity structure within which these campaigns took place and the strategic models that guided USAS and its allies in these campaigns.

While every solidarity campaign is different, common threads run through all of them. Each campaign was waged in a similar set of social arenas, trying to use similar points of leverage. In other words, the POS within which the movements fought these battles was more or less the same across campaigns, with differences primarily due to the nature of the companies involved and their relationships to one another. The movement also developed a standard strategic model for such solidarity campaigns, although, as with its strategic model for waging campus-based campaigns, USAS and its allies would adapt it to suit the circumstances of the individual campaign.

When we examined campus campaigns, the POS was relatively simple in that we were looking at one social arena: the college campus. At its most complex level, as in the battle for the WRC, the struggle was fought in parallel on multiple campuses, with students coordinating their actions across campuses while also fighting a secondary battle in the arena of the national mass media. Even in this case, though, we can more or less understand what was happening by looking at how the campaign was waged on individual campuses. Solidarity campaigns in support of workers at factories producing college-licensed goods involved a much more complex POS, one that was fought in multiple social arenas—the actual factory where the workers labored, the major companies that did business with these factories, the schools with licensing agreements with these brands, and the national U.S. mass media. In addition, the governments of the countries where the manufacturing took place might get involved, whether to repress the workers or (more rarely) support their right to form a union. The battles here made use of two main points of leverage: the workers' ability to disrupt production at the factory—for instance, through a strike—and colleges' and universities' licensing agreements with the lead firms. They also made use of one main point of delegitimation: the brands' desire to maintain their good public image, which students could sully on their campuses and the U.S. movement as a whole could sully in the national mass media. The licensing agreements and public image intersected with each other on the college campus, since licensing agreements in many ways are a highly specialized marketing strategy. The battles of this campaign were then fought at various locations, both geographically and socially: the production site in the factory, the marketing site in the mass media, and an important site of consumption on college campuses.

Solidarity Campaigns

The first major solidarity campaign that USAS undertook after the establishment of the WRC was in support of workers at Kukdong, a Korean-owned factory in the town of Atlixco, Puebla, in central Mexico. The plant, owned by a multinational that also had factories in Indonesia, Bangladesh, China, and South Korea, produced goods mainly for Nike and Reebok, both of which had licensing agreements with colleges that had signed on to the WRC (Hermanson 2009; R. Ross 2006). The long-time labor solidarity activist Jeff Hermanson (interview), who at the time was with the AFL-CIO Solidarity Center's Mexico office and participated in the Kukdong campaign, told me, "This was really the campaign in which USAS and the WRC established themselves as effective players in the global sweatshop arena—very effective players."

When Kukdong was opened in November 1999, the managers recruited workers by promising them better working conditions at their factory than were available elsewhere in the region (Hermanson 2009; R. Ross 2006). Particularly attractive was the promise that management would provide free breakfast and lunch—a strong draw when many families did not have enough money to feed themselves adequately (Worker Rights Consortium 2001c). As with most such factories, the employees at Kukdong were predominantly young women—85 percent of the eight hundred-person workforce were women age sixteen to twenty-three (R. Ross 2006). Conditions at the Kukdong factory proved to be less than ideal. Managers, many of whom were inexperienced and had little training, both physically and verbally abused the young women working there. The wages did not even meet the minimum required under Mexican law, let alone reach a level sufficient to support a family. Workers were denied both maternity leave and sick leave. Clean water for drinking was often unavailable, and the bathrooms were filthy. Even the promised meals were problematic. The lunches were made from rancid food, served on dirty plates, causing a number of workers to fall sick. The breakfast consisted of only coffee and bread in a region where the cultural norm was for breakfast to be a substantial, nourishing meal (Hermanson 2009; Worker Rights Consortium 2001c).

In May 2000, the Kukdong workers also discovered that, without their knowledge or consent, management had struck a deal shortly after opening in December 1999 with the Confederación Revolucionaria de Obreros y Campesinos (Revolutionary Confederation of Workers and Peasants [CROC]) to "represent" them as their union. CROC is the smaller of the two unions that are associated with the Partido Revolucionario Institucional (Institutional Revolutionary Party [PRI]), which ruled Mexico when it was a de facto single-party state from 1929 to 2000. Even after the transition to a multiparty system following the PRI's loss of the presidency in December 2000, it remained dominant in many areas—including Puebla. Given its close connection with state power, CROC cannot be considered a genuine, independent union. Indeed, in most cases, as with Kukdong, it made no efforts to actually represent the workers enrolled in it. Instead, it signed contracts with management that guaranteed workers only the wages and so forth that are the minimum requirement under Mexican law while providing that any worker who refused to join the union and pay dues would be fired. The union officials made their living off these dues, while in return they helped management control the workforce and repress dissidents (Hermanson 2009; R. Ross 2006; Worker Rights Consortium 2001c).

On December 15, 2000, five workers organized a one-day boycott of the cafeteria, demanding better food. On the basis of trumped-up charges, Kukdong's management fired the leaders of the boycott on January 3, 2001, sparking a larger revolt, as six hundred workers (out of an eight hundred-person workforce) walked off the job on January 8. They escalated their demands to include not only better food and the reinstatement of the fired leaders but also the right to join an independent union instead of CROC. On January 11, the police and thugs working for CROC attacked the workers as they camped out around the plant in the middle of the night. The young women sat with their hands in the air, singing the Mexican national anthem, as they were beaten up. Seventeen ended up in the hospital, while the assault was broadcast on Mexican national television (Hermanson 2009; R. Ross 2006; Worker Rights Consortium 2001c). Management and CROC refused to allow many of the striking workers to return to work; others were required to sign loyalty oaths to CROC or were forced to resign (Worker Rights Consortium 2001c).

Upon receiving word of the start of the strike, USAS and other U.S. anti-sweatshop groups began to mobilize. The day immediately following the attack on the workers, Evelyn Zepeda, a Salvadoran American USAS member at Pitzer College in California, arrived in Atlixco to help coordinate actions between the workers and USAS via the Internet. She remained there for the duration of the campaign, with the financial support of the Solidarity Center, staying with Marcela Muñoz, one of the fired leaders (Hermanson 2009; R. Ross 2006).

USAS also began mobilizing in the United States, sending out an e-mail that urged its members to take action, targeting both Nike and Reebok as Kukdong's major customers and those colleges that had contracts with the two companies. The USAS member Molly McGrath (interview) noted that by this point, of the anti-sweatshop groups in the United States, USAS "was the one that had the most ability to turn out the grassroots arm. [. . .] Whatever USAS decided to do as far as actions on campuses or sending public messages to companies had a lot of influence."

USAS pressured its schools' administrations to follow up on their commitments as members of the WRC. By this point, most administrators were relatively responsive to USAS. They had been through enough sit-ins and other such actions that they knew there could be trouble if they did not respond to students' demands. Thus, USAS members needed to do little more than hold educational events and public rallies (McGrath and Stoppard interviews). In addition, now that they had joined the WRC, a minority of administrators genuinely felt they had some stake in this issue and in seeing that Nike and Reebok actually abided by their agreements (Nova interview). At this stage, USAS was not asking schools to suspend their contracts with Nike or Reebok—just to get in touch with them and let them know about their concern. The threat of suspended or canceled contracts was certainly in the background of these conversations, though, and both Nike and Reebok knew there could be unpleasant consequences if they did not follow through on their commitments to maintain high labor standards among their contractors (McGrath and Stoppard interviews). On the advice of the Solidarity Center and USAS, the workers at Kukdong filed a formal complaint with the WRC on January 18, 2001. As a result, the consortium began to prepare to investigate the situation on the ground (R. Ross 2006; Worker Rights Consortium 2001c).

As a result of the pressure on them, Nike and Reebok, in their turn, began to pressure Kukdong's management to reinstate the fired leaders. On February 19, 2001, these tactics succeeded in persuading the company to reinstate the workers and recognize an independent union (Brigham 2003; Hermanson 2009). As a result, three of the five leaders of the striking workers were rehired. Following this, they set out to persuade as many workers as possible to return to the job (and their worried parents to let them), with the goal of continuing the struggle from within.

Under pressure from Nike, Kukdong's owners also agreed to a joint delegation by representatives of the WRC and Verité, an FLA-accredited monitoring firm (Brigham 2003). Given the urgency of the situation, the WRC put out a preliminary report on January 24, 2001, stating that the Kukdong employees' right to freedom of association had clearly been violated and that the striking workers, particularly their leaders, should be reinstated immediately (Worker Rights Consortium 2001b). If this was not done, the workers would need to find work elsewhere, thus endangering the efforts to set up an independent union (Nova interview, 2007). Meanwhile, the WRC continued with its investigation in preparation for a more in-depth report, which was published on June 20, 2001. As became the custom with its future reports, it noted in its June report the steps Nike, Reebok, and Kukdong had taken toward dealing with the problems and discussed how they still fell substantially short of their obligations (Worker Rights Consortium 2001c).

Over the summer of 2001, Nike began significantly cutting its orders with Kukdong, publicly attributing this to a seasonal drop-off in demand. As a result, management was forced to lay off large numbers of employees, reducing its workforce to 350 (R. Ross 2006). This pressure convinced the factory owners that they had to find some way to get rid of the government-backed CROC and work with an independent union if they wanted to retain their business. To do so, Kukdong formally closed down and re-opened as another company, Mexmode. It paid CROC off—officially, it compensated the union for damages—while it negotiated with the work-ers, who created a new independent union, the Sindicato Independiente de Trabajadores de la Empresa Mexmode (Independent Union of Workers of Mexmode [SITEMEX]). Mexmode's management and SITEMEX finally agreed on a union contract on September 30, 2001, nine months after the initial strike (Hermanson 2009).

While tensions between management and workers certainly remained, the situation improved considerably. "The first contract at MexMode [sic] had a nominal 10% wage increase, in recognition of the losses the com-pany had suffered during the nine-month struggle and as a show of good faith by the new union" (Hermanson 2009, 12). The contract also con-tained language that clearly protected workers from abuse by supervisors. The contract lasted only six months, so it could be renegotiated in March 2002, when management hoped to have the factory back at full produc-tion again and be able to provide the workers with better compensation (Hermanson 2009). Nike, however, initially refused to return its orders to the factory to the prestrike levels. A group of Mexmode workers went on a tour of the United States, speaking at a number of colleges with which the brand had licensing agreements. As a result of renewed public pres-sure, Nike significantly increased its business with Mexmode (R. Ross 2006). SITEMEX and Mexmode's management signed a new contract on April 1, 2002, which gave the workers a 38 percent bonus—effectively a substantial raise that made them among the best-paid workers in the re-gion (Hermanson 2009). Thus, USAS and the WRC—in alliance with a number of other groups, such as the Solidarity Center—were able to sup-port the workers in their struggle for justice.

The Kukdong campaign was not the only major solidarity campaign that USAS and its allies undertook. Two other important campaigns, which I review here only briefly, were in support of workers at the BJ&B plant in the Dominican Republic and at the New Era Cap plant in New York State.

The BJ&B campaign began before the establishment of the WRC, in 1997, just as USAS was coming together as a national organization. The BJ&B factory was owned by the Yupoong company, based in South Korea. It produced baseball caps for a wide range of customers, including universities, professional sports teams, and some of the major brand-name companies, including Nike. As with most sweatshops, the vast majority—95 percent—of the two thousand workers were young women. And as with most such factories, conditions were highly abusive: workers complained about verbal and physical abuse, sexual harassment, undrinkable water, forced overtime, and poverty-level wages. In 1997, a Dominican union, the Federación Nacional de Trabajadores de Zonas (National Federation of Free Trade Workers [FENATRAZONAS]), contacted UNITE for help. The U.S. union, in its turn, published a report on the situation in 1998, specifically orienting it toward students, to pull the newly developing USAS into the struggle on the side of the workers—a sensible strategy, given that a significant portion of BJ&B's production was for U.S. colleges and universities. UNITE also organized a U.S. tour for two workers from BJ&B—nineteen-year-old Kenia Rodriguez and twenty-year-old Roselio Reyes—which included a number of speaking events at colleges. Unfortunately, the Yupoong company was highly resistant to making any meaningful concessions, and the struggle dragged on for years (Esbenshade 2004a; Garwood 2011; R. Ross 2006).

After the WRC was founded, it investigated the situation in January 2002 as a renewed unionization effort began at BJ&B. Zepeda, the USAS member who had spent the duration of the Kukdong campaign in Puebla, also went to the Dominican Republic to coordinate between the union there and USAS. BJ&B's management engaged in retaliatory firings of the union's leaders and publicly accused them of being terrorists. The WRC persuaded Nike (BJ&B's largest customer) and the FLA to come on board and join it in pressuring the factory's management. Even with this pressure, management resisted negotiating with the union or even treating its workers decently. It was not until March 2003 that BJ&B signed an agreement with the Sindicato de Trabajadores de la Empresa BJ&B S.A. (BJ&B Company Workers' Union [see Esbenshade 2004a; Garwood 2011; R. Ross 2006]).

The New Era Cap campaign was a bit different from most other USAS solidarity campaigns because its focus was on solidarity with workers at a factory in the United States (in Derby, New York), rather than overseas (although New Era has contracted other work abroad). New Era produced baseball caps both for major league sports teams and a number of colleges and universities. The company started off as a small, family-owned business, with generally good relations between management and employees. As the business grew and became more impersonal, these relations soured. By 2001, there were three major points of contention between the roughly 350 workers and management. The first was that working conditions did not meet proper ergonomic standards, leading to pervasive on-the-job injuries and work-related ailments, such as carpal tunnel syndrome. Often, workers did not report these injuries and ailments for fear of being fired. After the workers at the Derby plant voted to affiliate with the Communication Workers of America (CWA) in 1997, management responded with persistent union-busting tactics. It also became clear during the course of the struggle that management simply had no respect for the workers, which in many ways was the straw that broke the camel's back. Although representatives of the CWA tried to persuade the workers to take less confrontational actions (such as working to rule),[1] in July 2001 they voted overwhelmingly to go on strike—a strike that lasted eleven months (Carty 2006; Worker Rights Consortium 2001a, 2002; Howald and Palmer interviews).

Even before the strike began, the CWA had begun contacting other groups in the hope of mobilizing a solidarity campaign behind the New Era workers. Through the local chapter of Jobs with Justice, a national organization that focuses on building ties between the labor movement and progressive community organizations, the Derby workers got in touch with USAS. After interviewing workers and documenting pervasive on-the-job injuries and union busting, the students concluded that the New Era factory qualified as a sweatshop. They began a national campaign against New Era, urging their schools to suspend their contracts with the company until the labor dispute was resolved. New Era workers spoke at college campuses across the country and at USAS's annual national conference. After the workers filed a formal complaint in May 2001, the WRC also undertook an investigation, with which New Era's management initially refused to cooperate. The consortium thus published an initial report in August 2001, documenting the problems and management's refusal to cooperate. As more and more schools began suspending their contracts, New Era's management eventually came to the bargaining table and reached an agree-

---

1. "Working to rule" is a tactic that unions frequently use when they believe that a full-out strike is not appropriate. With this tactic, workers follow management's rules for production precisely, with no deviation. Inevitably, production slows down considerably, since the rules reflect neither the flexibility needed to ensure that the process goes smoothly nor the fact that workers frequently perform tasks outside their formal job descriptions.

ment with the workers in March 2002, recognizing the CWA and correct-ing the ergonomic problems. Afterward, the WRC followed up on its previous investigation and issued a new, final report, which reported that New Era's management had fixed the bulk of the problems and was work-ing in good faith on the others (Carty 2006; Worker Rights Consortium 2001a, 2002; Howald and Palmer interviews). David Palmer (interview), a national organizer with the CWA who was deeply involved with the New Era campaign, told me, "It is my belief—and I've told USAS people that were involved—if it was not for the student movement, I do not believe we would have been successful at New Era Cap. They did one heck of a job. The student movement was a key piece of CWA strategy."

Unfortunately, neither the Kukdong/Mexmode nor BJ&B victory proved lasting. This follows an all-too-common pattern in the anti-sweat-shop movement. The problem, as has been noted, is that once conditions for workers improve, their employers' cost of doing business goes up, and its patrons among the major firms look elsewhere for cheaper factories (Armbruster-Sandoval 2005). In the case of Mexmode, it has lost a good deal of business to China, where prices are generally lower to begin with and independent unions are illegal (Robert J. S. Ross, personal communi-cation, 2010). In the case of BJ&B, shortly after the victory at the factory, Yupoong began shifting production to factories it owned in Vietnam, where independent unions are also illegal, and to Bangladesh, which has export-processing zones, another site where unions are banned. BJ&B's major patrons, Nike and Adidas, began moving their orders to these new factory locations, as well. In February 2007, Yupoong abruptly shut down BJ&B without giving the workers the necessary legal notice time. In addi-tion, the company refused to negotiate with the union on terms of their legally required severance pay. Instead, it required workers to sign an agreement stating they would not press for more severance pay, in return for which Yupoong would provide only what it was legally required to pay them under Dominican law. Nike meanwhile continually misrepresented the situation, insisting that Yupoong had come to a negotiated agreement with the union. It was only after more pressure was applied to Nike and Adidas that Yupoong finally agreed to negotiate with the workers and give them decent compensation (Clean Clothes Campaign 2007; Garwood 2011; Nova 2007b). The temporary nature of these victories was one of the major factors that led USAS, the WRC, and others in the anti-sweatshop movement to reconsider their strategy and design the Designated Suppli-ers Program (see Chapter 12).

Having examined these individual campaigns, we can now look at the common elements that underlie these struggles. I begin by taking a closer look at how the structure of the global apparel industry shapes the political opportunity structure of USAS and the anti-sweatshop movement—what kind of mobilizing opportunities they have, where they have points of leverage, and so on—before moving on to the common strategic model behind these campaigns.

Social Arenas and Mobilizing Opportunities

As discussed in Chapter 2, most of the lead firms in the apparel industry do not manufacture. Instead, they market, an orientation that allows them to control the most profitable points of the production system and thus gives them the lion's share of power. That has led many activists to refer to them as the "brands." Given this power, whatever brand-name corporations were involved in a particular struggle constitute the key social arena in that struggle. These companies, McGrath (interview) told me,

> [have] been able to just shut down a factory where a lot of people are organizing. Brands don't own the factories, but brands have a tremendous influence over the factories in that they can just take their orders out of them. There's nothing a factory really can do. A lot of times the business relationship is so important that factory owners will just do whatever the brands tell them to do.

As discussed in Chapter 2, however, the lead firms rarely actually tell their contractors to keep workers' wages down and implement sweatshop conditions. Instead, they tell them to keep manufacturing costs as low as possible—a condition that almost inevitably leads to sweatshop conditions but allows the major apparel corporations to plead ignorance. Nonetheless, because the major apparel companies hold so much power, their decisions have important consequences for those located in other social arenas. The contractors, by contrast, have relatively little influence on decisions made in other arenas.

The challenge for anti-sweatshop activists was that, regardless of their relationship to the production process, whether as workers or consumers, they have no direct access to the social arenas constituted by corporations. These organizations are highly antidemocratic, closed systems that make little room for outside voices to be heard. Thus, activists had to find ways to indirectly affect the decisions made by the lead firms' boards of directors and major executives. Students, as we have explored, could, with the right strategy, exercise a fair amount of power within colleges and universities, which are a major site of marketing and consumption. U.S.

activists more generally could, with the proper strategy, influence the framing of a particular company in the U.S. mass media, thereby undermining its legitimacy and negatively affecting its all-important brand image. Given the centrality of both the national U.S. mass media and college campuses to the brands' advertising strategies, these companies could not simply shrug off what happens here in the way they can with their contractors. They had to take the mass media and college campuses seriously as social arenas if they wanted their marketing to succeed. While they could abandon one contractor in favor of another, they could not abandon the national U.S. mass media; nor were they willing to give up the college market, and they were usually very reluctant to surrender any school to which they did have access through a licensing agreement.

Hermanson (interview, 2007) told me that press coverage of anti-sweatshop campaigns

> [had] been critical in the development of anti-sweatshop consciousness and, at certain times, critical in the development of certain campaigns. [. . .] The BJ&B campaign in the Dominican Republic is an example where a mention in the press was important, mostly because of its impact on the companies that control the brands that you're trying to influence. They don't want to appear in the press, so when they do appear, they try to fix it.

Getting such press was not easy. The former USAS member Trina Tocco (interview), who was with the International Labor Rights Fund (ILRF) when I interviewed her, said, "In order for us to even call up the *New York Times*, I feel like I have to have a fourteen-year-old chained to a sewing machine." The problem was that the sweatshop issue has become "old news"; therefore, it took an extraordinary hook to get coverage for a particular instance of sweatshop abuses (cf. Ryan 1991). The Kukdong campaign could get such coverage because it was the first investigation undertaken by the WRC, an organization whose very creation had been controversial. The Kukdong campaign was therefore novel and interesting—and Nike and Reebok, as companies very much invested in their brand image, were particularly sensitive to such coverage.

Workers have access to the factory as a social arena, something that is not true for other groups, which can influence what happens there only indirectly. Like the college campus, the factory as an arena is undemocratic; unlike the college campus, there is little tradition in most factories of management listening to and having to take into account the opinions of workers the way college officials must do with students, however reluctantly. Trying to exercise power in such conditions is not easy, to say the least, and often involves risking one's life. Workers trying to organize face a number of challenges. Unlike students on college campuses, their ability to form autonomous organizations through which they can mobilize is highly restricted; if they do mobilize, they are likely to face repression, from both their employers and, more often than not, the state; and even if they can successfully pressure their employers, their employers may have relatively little power to change working conditions, given their dependence on keeping prices low. Hermanson (interview, 2007) summed up the position of the large multinational manufacturing companies (such as the owners of Kukdong/Mexmode) this way:

> The multinational production companies [. . .] have a lot of capital relative to workers' organizations. They have relationships with local governments, often corrupt relationships. The weakness of the production companies is that, although they have a lot of capital, it's limited—it's not unlimited capital, and therefore they need to make a profit just about every season in order to sustain their operations. [. . .] They treat each factory as a separate profit center. If it's not making a profit, they close it down. They'll have big losses. They're very vulnerable to worker action because the conditions are so bad and so uniformly bad, which means that a single spark can start a prairie fire. It just doesn't take much to disrupt production in a Korean factory in Guatemala, Honduras, or Bangladesh.

Social arenas differ not only in their decision-making structures and the rules that guide framing contests but also in the mobilizing opportunities those within them have. Workers in Third World sweatshops typically have very little space to organize. While college administrators recognize the right of students to form their own autonomous groups, including ones that press for changes in policy at the college, most factory owners do not recognize the right of workers to form independent unions. The factory owner may well have signed on to a code of conduct requiring recognition of such unions, but in practice such measures are usually ignored or the company will try to substitute a "yellow" union—one controlled either by the company itself or (as with CROC at Kukdong) by the government.

When the lead firms have engaged in countermeasures against the anti-sweatshop movement in the United States, they have primarily used framing strategies such as corporate social responsibility programs. In most sweatshops, however, the first countermeasure employers will rely on is brute repression, often with the backing of the state. The USAS member Liana Dalton (interview) spoke about her experience working in the Philippines with workers facing government repression:

> The Philippines was really an intense experience for me, because I was sleeping on picket lines with people who were wanted by the military and who couldn't go home just because of their involvement in organizing. It really struck me one time because I met with this guy who was organizing an auto parts factory. He was telling me about his organizing drive, and he was [saying], "Oh, I actually want to tell you about the log I've been keeping." [. . .] He said he wanted me to be an added witness, and I said, "OK." He detailed things like, "October 12th, 7:00–9:00 P.M., two armed gunmen on motorcycles outside my house." He said he was keeping this log, and he had one copy in his house and one at the union, so when he was murdered by the military we [would] have some documentation that proves they were involved and we could actually attack the government more concretely for killing him. How do you respond to that? He's already creating evidence for his eventual murder investigation that hasn't happened. But he says he's still standing and we're still organizing and we're going to get this union won.

The overall effect of these various factors that create limited mobilizing opportunities for workers can be devastating. While in some cases workers are able to organize and persevere, more often than not this is not the case. Dalton (interview) also told me about her experiences in Cambodia, where the labor movement was less well organized not only because of repression but also because the unions had been in existence for much less time:

> In Cambodia, for example, you've got strikes that last for a few days or a week or a month, and then people get bought off because their children are going to starve and the campaign strategy and organizing are not comprehensive enough to maintain very long-term struggles in many cases. They're going to take the money; you can't really blame them for taking the money. Most people would take the money in the absence of a clear plan to win. But this reality, compounded with the repression, makes it an uphill battle for unions.

One of the main goals of the U.S. anti-sweatshop movement was to alter the POS by increasing the mobilizing opportunities open to workers in these factories to increase their chances of creating an autonomous, independent union that could bargain effectively with their employers. I heard this again and again from the activists I spoke with. For instance, McSpedon (interview) said:

> I think for me the ultimate long-term goal was to create the room for workers to organize in this industry. Ultimately, what workers need to guarantee better working conditions and better pay and all of that is a union contract. So for me, [. . .] that was the long-term goal: to create a structure and to create systems that opened up that space, in a way that it was closed when we started. [. . .] Not that any code of conduct or any monitor was going to be able to create good working conditions—that, we know, is not true—but they could create the possibility of workers' organizing and being able to appeal to these structures that support that.

The long-time labor solidarity activist Stephen Coates (interview), executive director of U.S. Labor Education in the Americas Project (USLEAP), not only concurred with this approach but also saw the work of USAS as having contributed significantly to it—though the problems remained great:

> The weakness in the labor movement in these countries makes it very difficult to achieve the progress on the ground that we would like to see with respect to worker organizing. I think an important development of the anti-sweatshop movement over the last fifteen years has been the emergence of [. . .] USAS. I think they've been extremely powerful in putting a lot of pressure on companies and helping create this space for improved conditions—or, at least, to create a space where workers can organize for better conditions.

The U.S. movement could not directly affect the decisions made by the managers of sweatshops. They could, however, influence the decisions made by the lead firms. And these firms, in turn, could significantly influence the decisions made by sweatshop employers. The USAS member Jessica Rutter (interview) noted:

> [The major apparel companies] pretty much have the power to determine everything that happens below them in the supply chain. We have seen the power of brands' being able to say one word and have something happen. There was a worker who had been fired for

months for union organizing, and the brand stepped in and said, "Hey, you guys have to rehire this worker." It would happen the next day. So this is something that we knew from experience and also just from analyzing what the supply chain looks like. It's very obvious that the brands themselves are the ones that have the most power.

It is worth noting that governments also play a significant role in this—in the eyes of the anti-sweatshop movement, mostly not for the better. In addition to aiding in the direct repression of workers, the legal structure governing the formation of unions has a large effect on the mobilizing opportunities open for workers. In the case of the workers at Kukdong, they had the right to form an independent union, at least in theory, even if the local government did its best to obstruct that process. In China or Vietnam, however, workers would not even have that much freedom, since unions not affiliated with the state and the Communist Party are illegal. Jeff Hermanson (interview) observed that, as a result, "government repression was not as powerful [in Kukdong] as it is in China. They put down the strike, but then they didn't station troops there." In many countries, such as Guatemala, Honduras, and El Salvador, the very fact that there has been a long history of military governments using extreme levels of violence against the labor movement has left a repressive legacy, even after the transition to formal democracy. The labor movements in these countries remain weak, workers are often fearful of the consequences of organizing, and, while conditions have improved, violence against progressive activists remains very much part of the political situation of those countries (Armbruster-Sandoval 2005).

Occasionally, the government of a country may intervene in a positive way. For instance, in a 1992–1994 campaign in support of workers at the Bibong factory in the Dominican Republic, the reformist, pro-union Secretary of Labor Rafael Albuquerque played a supportive role; he also backed unionization elsewhere in Dominican export-processing zones (Jessup and Gordon 2000). Such cases are the exception to the rule, though. In the vast majority of cases, governments back business if for no other reason than that they are desperate to attract investment and want to create as business-friendly a climate as possible.

Leverage and Legitimacy

Having identified the arenas in which it was crucial for activist groups to affect decisions, the obvious question becomes how those groups actually shaped those decisions. If anti-sweatshop activists had no direct access to the very closed, antidemocratic arena constituted by a major corporation, how did they manage to get corporate leaders to make decisions that favor workers? Activists need to find ways to exercise leverage—that is, they must find structural points of vulnerability to which they can strategically apply pressure to coerce authorities into changing the sorts of decisions they make—and they must attack the legitimacy of (or "name and shame") their targets. In the anti-sweatshop movement, such leverage came at both ends of the production process. Workers exercised leverage by going on strike, thereby disrupting the production process. Most U.S. activists attempted to attack the legitimacy of lead apparel firms by linking them with sweatshops, thereby damaging their brand image. Given that such brands are often the lead firms' major asset, such attacks on legitimacy can, in fact, become points of economic leverage. USAS, with the help of its allies, found a more powerful point of leverage: they relied on the nexus of brands' concern for their image and their desire to have licensing agreements with colleges and universities to pressure the major apparel companies. Importantly, no one point of leverage alone was enough. If workers simply went on strike on their own, they were unlikely to succeed. Instead, the most common course was for them to be repressed and for the rest of the world to hear little or nothing of it. However, U.S. activists could do little to help workers if those workers were not already organizing and fighting on their own. It was essential for both sets of activists to work together and struggle in the arenas they had access to if they hoped to achieve anything.

The sort of leverage that workers can exercise is fairly straightforward: if they are not working, nothing actually gets produced. When they go on strike, they disrupt the production process. As we have already noted, this is far more threatening to the contractors than to the major companies that actually hold the power. Even the large manufacturing companies with multiple factories make a limited amount of money and need to ensure that each factory turns a profit. Smaller companies may consist of only one factory, meaning that in the case of the strike the owner has no other source of profit. In some cases, companies will simply shut down, lay everyone off, and reopen under another name, but this may mean moving to another location and losing the money they sank into setting up the factory in the first place. The lead firms, by contrast, can simply walk away from the conflict, because they have invested none of their own resources in these factories, and there are many more contractors looking to do business with them. Thus, the workers can, with some degree of effectiveness, put pressure on their immediate employer, the manufacturing company;

they have no leverage, however, over the major companies that actually hold the real power. For this they must rely on allies in the United States and Europe. However, U.S. and European anti-sweatshop activists have no way to pressure the contractors directly. They can do so only indirectly. And there is no way that the workers can be empowered if they are not fighting themselves. The goal, after all, is to get the contractors to bargain in good faith with an independent union representing their workers. If the workers are not organized, there is no such union.

According to Liana Dalton (interview), it was during her time working with USAS's allies in Hong Kong and elsewhere in Asia that the importance of workers' organizing really became clear for her: "A code of conduct is just a piece of paper, and I really learned at the time how important it was for workers to be empowered and workers to be enforcing that code of conduct. No matter how good of an external monitor you had or how good a code you had, it didn't matter if the workers on the ground weren't fighting, especially in the context of China, where there really is no public, independent organizing." By contrast, David Palmer (interview) of the CWA, who worked with the local union during the New Era strike, told me that the union itself did not have the power on its own to settle the strike with New Era Cap: "It was really going to be the pocketbook of New Era that was going to settle this thing. [. . .] As the colleges one at a time started coming on board with suspending their contracts with New Era, the pocketbook thing started to come into play." If a relatively strong, well-funded union such as the CWA, working in the United States in a social environment in which labor activists do not normally need to fear for their lives, could not win the fight against a company like New Era on its own, the difficulties a smaller, more poorly funded union in a place where violence against labor unions is the norm become even clearer.

The main vulnerability of many major apparel corporations, which the U.S. anti-sweatshop movement sought to use as a pressure point, is their brand image. As briefly discussed in Chapter 2, a brand is a form of nonmaterial capital and the major asset of many of the best-known apparel companies. Much of their time and many of their resources are spent in trying to manage consumers through means such as advertising and marketing to ensure that they associate positive symbolism with the brand image (Arvidsson 2006; Klein 1999). When the anti-sweatshop movement succeeds in associating a brand with sweatshops and all the ills that go with them, they are doing damage to the company in question's main asset, its main way of turning a profit. Thus, these companies find such actions extremely threatening. Despite the potential threat posed by anti-sweatshop groups, however, it is important to remember that the brand-name apparel corporations nonetheless maintain the upper hand in most cases. Eric Dirnbach (interview), of UNITE HERE, described the situation this way:

> It's very, very difficult to get regular consumers—not activists, but folks going about their business that are not necessarily consumed by this issue—to be aware of what's happening. And we don't have a billion dollars for advertising like the industry does; otherwise, we could run commercials and have billboards. All we have are people handing out leaflets and maybe, hopefully, getting a news article, putting stuff on the websites, putting out an e-mail. That's what activists have. It's disseminating information, and it's people-to-people contact.

Nonetheless, the brand-name firms feel threatened by such campaigns. Some activists I spoke with believed they had done permanent damage to the brand image of some companies. The anti-sweatshop activist Brent Wood (interview) told me:

> As long as Nike is around, people will have it in the back of their minds that somehow Nike is related to sweatshops—and that has hurt their brand image, to some extent irretrievably. It's still a really powerful brand image, but it is somewhat less powerful because of the sweatshop issue. They can never completely overcome that, although it is extraordinarily difficult to quantify what it's cost them financially. They probably try to keep it private, but there's no question it has cost them something significant, and more importantly, there's no question that they believe that it cost them something significant.

Other activists were more skeptical of having had much impact. Mc-Spedon (interview) said:

> I wouldn't guess we had any financial impact on these companies. I think their fear of us having financial impact was almost disproportionate to what would happen in reality. The amount they spent fighting it was an indication of how sensitive they were. The other companies didn't want to be Nike, right? Nike had been painted with the sweatshop brush—and Kathie Lee [Gifford] and Walmart had been—and they didn't want that to happen to them.

Even if the financial impact was minimal, as McSpedon thought, both she and Wood noted that the brand-name firms are still terrified of the potential damage to their image. So whether the financial damage is real or not, the anti-sweatshop movement has been able to turn harm to these companies' brand image into a major point of leverage.

In some cases, they were able to hit firms at sensitive moments in their marketing strategy. The New Era campaign, for instance, happened just as the New Era Cap company was trying to move from being a largely anonymous producer of baseball caps to one with greater visibility and brand-name recognition. Jane Howald (interview), president of the New Era workers' CWA local in Derby, recalled:

> They didn't want a blemish on their mark. They didn't want people to know New Era is a bad place. The way they designed the New Era flag, in our advertisements, we used it against them. They said, "We designed the New Era flag to represent the hardworking American workers," and we said, "So why are you treating us with disrespect? Don't label yourself a true patriotic company when you're sending all your work overseas, and don't say it represents the workers when you won't even pay us a fair wage." We used their own words against them during a lot of the strike.

It should also be emphasized that there are many apparel companies that do not focus their marketing strategy on branding, such as Hanes, whose marketing strategy is based on offering inexpensive products rather than having a particular image. Such companies represent much more of a challenge to the anti-sweatshop movement. The anti-sweatshop activist Ken Abrams (interview) noted:

> If it's a brand, it has a public reputation that it cares about; if its strategy is selling its stuff on the basis of that image—useful, sexy, etc.—then it's vulnerable. If its main strategy is selling stuff cheap, then the consumer typically doesn't care whether it's Fruit of the Loom or Hanes, because they're just buying a white T-shirt or some underwear, and they're not as vulnerable for obvious reasons. So it's much harder. The main thing I'm focusing on these days is a case in the Dominican Republic. Hanes owns a factory with dismal conditions and treatment of workers, and it's been really hard to get Hanes to respond. They just don't care that much. It's not part of their business strategy to appeal to a real sexy image, so it's harder to threaten that image.

Even in the best of circumstances, a campaign to damage a brand's image is an uphill battle. As Dirnbach noted, activists are handing out leaflets and working to get the occasional news story in an attempt to counter billion-dollar advertising budgets. What was important about USAS for the anti-sweatshop movement was not simply that it mobilized a grassroots base in a way that the movement had not been able to do before, but that they were able to exercise leverage in a way that the movement had not been able to before. In Chapter 3, I discussed the crucial nature of licensing agreements to many companies' marketing strategies. It is this very deep investment in cultivating the college market that gave USAS much of its power. Rutter (interview, 2007) said:

> In terms of actually affecting Nike as a company, there's not really so much that you can do as an individual consumer. But if you bring in the university as a consumer, as an institutional buyer, [it helps]. We could very much more easily influence our universities than the brands themselves, so the campaigns are structured in ways that we're kind of going up against the brands, but we're more going against our universities to make them demand that the brands do certain things, which is just a much more effective strategy.

While this strategy was based in part on an ideology of worker empowerment, it was also rooted in USAS's belief in achieving concrete results and a very hard-nosed assessment of where they could actually exercise power in a way that accomplishes something. A number of USAS activists I interviewed spoke about this need to calculate where you actually had leverage to exert power and making that central to your strategy. For instance, the USAS national organizer Zack Knorr (interview) said:

> For the four or five years that we're students, the place that we have the most power is our universities. So we should use that power as strategically as possible to move universities. That's why the initial focus was on university licensing—because that's the most direct power that universities have over these companies. [. . .] Our analysis has always been that you use the power you have in the place where you're at.

In the right circumstances, such campaigns could have a profound impact. Palmer (interview) could very much see the results of USAS's solidarity campaign unfolding as the CWA tried to bargain with New Era:

As the campaign went on, I believe the final total was ten or thirteen major universities that do business with New Era [. . .] actually suspended contracts with New Era because they would not negotiate in good faith with their employees. I remember the night that we settled the contract. Their biggest collegiate customer was Ohio State. Through the work of the student movement, I got a phone call from the students at Ohio State at ten o'clock one night—and they let me know that I had the ability to go back to the employer that night at the bargaining table and tell them that if we didn't get the deal done tonight, Ohio State was the next college to go off-line. We got the deal done that night. It was really a nice moment for me. You don't get many of those types of moments when you do this work.

USAS members and their allies were also very much aware of the limits of this form of leverage, though. It had a real impact only on corporations that placed importance on having licensing agreements with colleges and universities. Like many of my interviewees, however, McSpedon expressed the hope that USAS's campaigns might have a wider impact, despite the limited scope of their leverage:

Our thought was it's not a majority of the garment industry; it's not even a terribly huge percentage. But if we could at least create the space for workers to organize and improve conditions in the factories that made collegiate apparel, that would spill over into other factories—because these companies have factories beyond the ones that just make collegiate apparel, but also because they're often clustered together in free trade zones. So if there's a way that our creating the space in this section of the industry can impact a larger piece of the industry, [that's good]. It was just biting off that piece where we had a more significant amount of leverage over [collegiate apparel producers] than we did as individual consumers against these other brand names.

The Strategic Model for International Solidarity Campaigns

Having examined the power structures within which the anti-sweatshop movement had to operate, we turn to how they actually maneuvered—their strategic model for solidarity campaigns and how they made decisions about ways to implement and modify this model in specific cases.

While the political opportunity structure may present possible points of leverage and delegitimation, they exist only potentially until activists find ways to activate them—that is, until activists take actions that the targeted companies find actively threatening in some way. The anti-sweatshop movement's strategic model for solidarity campaigns helped it to identify such points of leverage and delegitimation and the means by which it could activate them to put pressure on the firms, both lead firms and contractors, involved in any particular case of worker rights violations. The strategic model that underlay anti-sweatshop campaigns drew on several older strategic models: labor struggles against a particular employer, corporate campaigns, and international solidarity campaigns.

Over time, the ability of activists to apply this strategic model has grown more sophisticated as they have discovered new tools they can use in their campaigns. Hermanson (interview, 2007), for instance, told me, "I think that there's been a constant learning curve. I think the Phillips–Van Heusen campaign [discussed in Chapter 2], for example, was the first time we involved Human Rights Watch. [. . .] That was when I began to see the importance of the NGO community as opposed to the labor movement itself." USAS was responsible for one of the key elements in such campaigns: the ability to use college codes of conduct to pressure companies, both major firms and contractors, to respect workers' rights. Unfortunately, there were many campaigns in which USAS's ability to exert leverage via universities did not come into play, because the factories involved produce little or no apparel for WRC member schools. In those instances in which college codes did come into play, however, they often made a crucial difference, giving the movement power over its foes that it would not otherwise have had, changing the terrain of struggle just enough that the movement could often gain the advantage—though not without a great deal of organizing and campaigning.

An integral part of the strategic model for such campaigns was how the international networks are organized. The initiative for any real solidarity campaign must come from the workers on whose behalf it is being waged; otherwise, it is not truly a solidarity campaign. And the workers' efforts at their own workplace must play a central role in the struggle because they are the ones with the most direct leverage over their employers. While the workers' allies both in their own countries and abroad play an essential role in the struggle, there is in many ways no campaign without the workers themselves. On the basis of this insight, the U.S.-based activists who were involved in a struggle attempted to put the workers on whose behalf they were campaigning at the center of the network, letting their strategic decisions be shaped by the workers' priorities rather than those of some other group, such as the Solidarity Center or USAS. This, in turn, was rooted in the anti-sweatshop movement's ideology, with the emphasis it placed on solidarity and worker empowerment (see Chapter 6). I argue in this chapter not only that this approach makes sense in terms of the ethics of the movement but that it was also a strategically important decision, contributing to the movement's successes in its international campaigns. As Francesca Polletta (2005) reminds us (see Chapter 1), it is a mistake to draw distinctions between the instrumental and ideological.

The Boomerang Effect

In addition to the principle of solidarity, a central element of the strategic model for transnational solidarity campaigns was what Margaret Keck and Kathryn Sikkink (1998) call the *boomerang effect*. This dynamic is central to a number of movements that are transnational in scope, including the human rights, environmental, and women's movements. The boomerang effect comes into play when local activist groups, generally in the Third World, find that the POS is closed to them but potentially open to international allies, particularly those in the First World. These international allies have the power to bring pressure to bear where domestic activists cannot, potentially tipping the balance of power in favor of the movement. In the case of the anti-sweatshop movement, workers find that they cannot effectively pressure their employers, because these contractors actually have very little power. It is their patrons—major apparel firms such as Nike and The Gap—that hold the real power in these relationships and whose policies force contractors to cut costs in any way possible, including by violating workers' rights. To exercise power over their employers, workers need the help of First World activists who may be able to exercise leverage over companies such as Nike. The boomerang metaphor refers to the fact that the transnational networks' strategy involves going out of the country where opportunities are closed, striking another target that is vulnerable, and then relying on that target to turn around and put pressure on the original one. The means of pressure is elliptical instead of straightforward. Since workers cannot effectively pressure their employers (the contractors) alone in the case of the anti-sweatshop movement, they rely on U.S. and European activists to put pressure on the employers' main patrons (the major apparel firms). The goal is for these firms to turn around and put pressure on the original target, the contractor, to deal fairly with the workers. Rather than simply being directly targeted, the contractors are targeted in a roundabout way.

Other scholars have built on and critiqued this basic model, arguing that Keck and Sikkink (1998) rely too heavily on the example of the human rights movement and fail to take into account how different issues may shape the nature of transnational campaigns. Julie Stewart (2004) has pointed out that in many campaigns, it is not simply that local activists choose to go transnational because of a closed domestic system, but that transnational actors were involved from the start. This is certainly the case for the anti-sweatshop movement, where transnational apparel firms are, in fact, the most powerful players. John Dale (2008) and Shae Garwood (2011) note that, while Keck and Sikkink focus on how activists bring pressure to bear on nation-states, many movements (including the anti-sweatshop movement) increasingly focus on corporate instead of state targets. Armbruster-Sandoval (2005) has cautioned that, while the aid of transnational actors is certainly important, Keck and Sikkink tended to downplay the importance of the agency of local actors. Keck and Sikkink tend to depict local actors as being able to do little more than contact international allies for support. Armbruster-Sandoval, by contrast, emphasizes that the activism of local groups is as important as that of their international allies, and neither alone can succeed. If workers do not go on strike, they cannot hope to win against their employers, even if that alone is not enough.

What all of these theorists have in common, however, is that they emphasize the importance of transnational activist networks, including members from both the Global South and the Global North in challenging inequalities in power on the ground in the Global South. The activists I spoke with were well aware of the role of the boomerang effect (even if they do not use that term) in solidarity campaigns. For instance, Dirnbach (interview) said:

Why do workers in developing countries need us? They can organize unions on their own. Do they need us? Well, I think they do need us. We need to work together. We can't do this alone. They need to be organizing. They can't do it alone. They need us to put pressure on the companies in the United States that have the power in this industry. That is the benefit that we bring to the table here. We're in the United States, the largest media market, the largest apparel market in the world, and the headquarters of almost all the major apparel companies. There's some power to doing activism here in the United States, right? [. . .] So that's what we bring to the table here.

In some sense, the boomerang effect was at work even in a domestic campaign such as New Era. The New Era workers could not succeed against the company alone and therefore had to enlist outside supporters both in their local community and nationally. Activists from groups such as USAS took a model from transnational campaigns with which they were familiar and applied it to this domestic one, with successful results. This basic division of labor between sweatshop workers and their U.S. allies was rooted in how their social locations gave them access to different points of leverage in the political opportunity structure. Only workers can apply leverage directly to their employers by disrupting production, but only their allies from the Global North can hope to exert leverage over the dominant companies that hold the real power—and can compel the contractors to change their labor practices in the face of the high economic disincentives they have for doing so.

Framing Battles

Given that many apparel companies' principal weakness is their brand image, fighting framing battles that damage the brand's legitimacy was absolutely central to the strategic model underlying solidarity campaigns in the apparel industry. One important tool that activists had in such framing battles was issuing reports based on research. In many ways, this was one of the most important things the WRC did: documenting the specific violations of workers' rights in any one case. More than that, the WRC used the implicit threat of a report containing negative information to get companies to make concessions in return for positive coverage when the report was published. The WRC staff member Jeremy Blasi (interview) explained:

> We try to not just publish things for the sake of publishing them. Transparency is a goal, and we're the only [monitoring] organization that has a public disclosure database, with all of the factories listed. [. . .] But at the same time, you want to use it as a tool; the threat of publishing your report is a way to get a company to do something good. And you make every report a positive report because you used the threat of public disclosure to get them to take some action. By the time you're ready to publish, you can report that they've done all these positive things. So if you look at most of our reports, a substantial number are actually positively toned. They're the final product along the process. In other cases, the case

might be totally intractable. The company's not responding, so there would be value to get [the report] out as soon as possible.

Such was the case with the preliminary reports the WRC published on both Kukdong and New Era—reports that then played a valuable role in the larger struggle over the framing of the issue.

The WRC, however, was not the only anti-sweatshop organization that did research and published reports. It was also an important part of what groups such UNITE HERE and the ILRF did. Like the WRC, they would send representatives overseas to investigate conditions in factories and publish reports on the results. They were, however, less concerned about using their reports as a direct means to pressure companies to change their behavior in the way the WRC did and more concerned about using them to mobilize their grassroots base to pressure the companies in question. Regarding the then ongoing campaign against Walmart, Dirnbach (interview) said:

> You take that research, that basic information, and you convert that into public-friendly material. You put together fliers; you might put together a press release. You'll send versions of that to the media. You want to get the word out there to consumers and the media to raise consciousness about the sweatshop problem. You'll go to the store, and you'll leaflet. You'll do it again and again. And companies are annoyed by that.

Another central tool in framing battles was bringing the workers involved in a particular struggle on tour in the United States to speak about the conditions they face. Keck and Sikkink (1998) argue that direct personal testimony plays a powerful role in framing struggles, humanizing the debate and providing legitimacy to the work of groups in the Global North that reports simply cannot. With reports, it is always possible for the movement's opponents to claim that the movement, however well intentioned, is out of touch with the workers on the ground. When the workers themselves are speaking, this charge is much more difficult to make. Speaking not only of the BJ&B campaign but also USAS's initial efforts to get its schools to implement codes of conduct, McSpedon (interview) said:

> A big turning point for us on campus was a delegation of workers from the Dominican Republic who came in about April 1998: Roselio Reyes and Kenia Rodriguez, two workers from a factory [that] made baseball caps for schools, including Georgetown, came and

spoke on a couple different campuses on a tour sponsored by UNITE. That really for us totally changed the dynamic of the campaign. You know, we'd been saying for four or five months that these sweatshops existed, that they made Georgetown apparel, but to have two workers say, "Yeah, I've seen your logo before. I've sewed it onto a bunch of caps," made a huge difference. We had a huge event in the middle of campus with three or four hundred people who came and heard them speak. It was the first time the administration actually agreed to sit down and meet with us—and with the workers.

When I asked the activist Caroline Stoppard (interview) about the difference between the WRC's reports and tours by workers, she said:

I think people have a different reaction to workers speaking about their personal experiences than to reading it in a report. If someone talks about the experience of getting screamed at by their supervisor because they wanted to leave work at the end of the day, that's very compelling. But when the WRC puts it in a report, [. . .] it's dry, it's coming from a U.S. organization. [Some people will think,] "Who are these people? Why are they making these claims about certain things?" [. . .] I think the same person who would criticize something in a report, once they're face-to-face with the worker, would probably not say the same thing because it wouldn't be appropriate. And then also because they are more compelled in that kind of situation to understand why the conditions are bad.

When I asked her about whether the audience—an administrator reading a report versus a student at a public talk by a worker—made any difference, Stoppard replied, "It might. Most of the people who hear workers who come on tour are not university administrators. They're activists. But even when we bring workers to speak with administrators, they generally have a pretty strong reaction."

When such framing tactics were successful, they often represented a quite direct threat of delegitimation for the major apparel companies, which could be especially damaging to those, like Nike and Reebok, that have invested a great deal in cultivating a certain brand image. The success of such framing battles had a significant impact on anti-sweatshop activists' ability to exercise leverage in a way that would make the lead apparel firms perceive them as a potential disruptive threat to their flow of profits. In the case of USAS, at schools that had joined the WRC, success in these framing battles put college officials in a position in which they felt compelled to do something to deal with licensees who were violating the school's code of conduct. Often they needed to do little more than speak with the companies, with the implicit threat of a suspension or cancellation of the licensing agreement hanging in the background—that is, the threat of the disruption of the consumption process through the loss of prized institutional consumers. In cases in which the U.S. anti-sweatshop movement could mobilize such pressure, this often proved to be one of its most effective weapons.

While at this stage in the game USAS was able to get its school administrators to take such action mainly through skillful framing and moderate levels of mobilization—petitions, public rallies, and so on—this ability was founded on past on-campus struggles that involved substantial levels of disruption through means such as sit-ins (see Chapter 5). Thus, a legacy of disruptive activism gave USAS an implicit form of leverage over college administrations that it might not need to exercise, since the threat hung in the background. Thus, we see in solidarity campaigns something similar to what we saw in campus-based campaigns: they rely on both disruption and changing the prevailing discourse—that is, both leverage and delegitimation—for their success, not one or the other.

The Organization of Solidarity

In ensuring that a campaign is genuinely a solidarity campaign, it is important to seek not only to empower the workers involved at their workplaces but also to include them in the campaign's decision-making processes from the beginning. Indeed, such involvement in the decision-making process is as important an aspect of empowerment as exercising power and voice in the workplace. How well this process of decision making works depends on the network of relationships that connect the groups involved in any campaign.

In transnational solidarity campaigns, a global network is involved in planning the strategy. Speaking about the Solidarity Center's international allies, Hermanson (interview) told me:

> In Taiwan we linked up with a group called Focus on Globalization, which was just a marvelous group. They were academics; they did research; they held demonstrations; they went to the stock market and a meeting of Nien Hsing [a manufacturing company targeted by the anti-sweatshop movement]; they went to the meeting of Tainan [another such company] when we had that campaign. It was a very

great organization, added a tremendous amount. And I must say this: these organizations don't just provide us with an understanding of what's going on in their country. They also participate in the development of a global strategy. They're students of the global production system just as much as we are in the United States. I think it's a real misconception to think that the strategy is developed in the United States, and then you link up with organizations in other countries to carry it out. Quite often, the reverse is the case.

Transnational solidarity campaigns are not, then, U.S.-centric affairs but genuinely transnational in their organization, conception, and execution.

A particularly important element of these international networks is the workers themselves. In the eyes of anti-sweatshop activists, they ideally would be in a leadership position in determining the direction of the campaign. In practice, the picture was more complicated. While the workers could make clear what their priorities and goals were, and other groups could seek to organize around them, the workers in any particular sweatshop had only limited expertise about the global terrain in which the movement had to maneuver, and they knew even less about conditions on the ground in the United States, where the major apparel companies were located and could be most effectively pressured. Thus, there was an inherent tension in the organization of such campaigns. How successfully these two elements were balanced probably varied somewhat from campaign to campaign, though all of the solidarity activists I spoke with seemed sincerely committed to trying to make sure that they were ultimately accountable in some fashion to the workers on whose behalf they were campaigning. At least in the New Era campaign, they seem to have been relatively successful. In speaking of her experiences with USAS and other allies, Howald (interview), the president of the New Era local, said, "They were very open to our suggestions on our activities; they worked hand in hand with our members. If our members didn't feel comfortable doing something, there was never any pressure on our members. [. . .] If USAS said we were going to protest this, and somebody said they didn't like that, they would back off." While Howald and the other leaders of the local union, who had little past experience with organizing and protesting, needed to rely on outside expertise even to help them to understand how to run their strike locally, Howald never felt as though these more experienced allies were imposing anything on the local union. (For accounts of transnational anti-sweatshop campaigns centered on sweatshop workers and their perceptions of and experiences with transnational alliances, see Anner 2011; Armbruster-Sandoval 2005.)

However, according to Tocco (interview), "You're often working with unions that don't have experience or even understand the potential that could exist in using students as a tactic or just as part of a broader campaign. They don't read the articles; they don't know when sit-ins happen. There's just a lack of cultural understanding of what that means." The workers, because of their circumstances, had no way to know what it was possible to achieve on the ground in the United States. This brings us back to an issue discussed in the chapter on the WRC's network of allies: the importance of local expertise, both in the countries of the sweatshop workers and in the United States, where many of their allies were. The workers had a good sense of the local terrain—the plant they worked in and the surrounding community. While they may have had some sense of the local political terrain, it was likely that they would have to work with allies in their own country to help them maneuver in that terrain. Many of these allies were the same organizations—or at least the same sort of organizations—that the WRC worked with. They were all part of one international network: the anti-sweatshop movement. In terms of planning strategy in the United States, groups based in the Global South—whether the workers themselves or their domestic allies—simply could not have the detailed understanding of the political opportunity structure in the United States. As Tocco notes, they were not going to fully understand the role of brands in youth culture and college campuses and why this gave a group like USAS leverage over the brand-name companies. Therefore, of necessity U.S. groups had to plan much of the U.S.-based strategy themselves, working with the workers in any particular campaign to help them understand how, precisely, a particular strategy might affect them and discussing how it might be beneficial or harmful.

If communication was good, however, the workers should at least have had a sense of what sort of impact any actions in the United States were likely to have. From there they could make informed decisions about whether or not a particular line of action made sense, given where they were. Coates (interview) told me, for example, "We had a couple of conflicts with partner organizations that wanted to call for a boycott. We said, 'Well, that's not what the workers want. You may think that that's effective, but it's sort of a knee-jerk response that's not going to work here.' I think most people come around to that view."

Workers are generally concerned that boycotts could end up putting them out of work permanently. This is not what they want. Rather, they are looking for ways to pressure the major apparel companies that will not result in a loss of orders for the factory they work in, if that can be helped. USAS, for instance, preferred to rely on the threat of suspension of apparel firms' college licenses; an actual suspension was a last resort, and USAS never sought a permanent severing of ties with a particular company. The goal was to ensure that workers could continue producing college-licensed goods, only under better conditions, not to end their relationship with colleges. This involved walking a fine line in terms of pressuring companies, but, according to Howald (interview), USAS was sensitive to this problem:

> The students were pushing for contracts to be eliminated with New Era, but they also understood that if it happened, it could impact us and our return to work. So they put more pressure on universities to reach out to New Era and say, "Look, solve the differences with the union that represent the members, recognize that it's there, work on the health and safety issues that the union has brought to light, and see what we can do about getting this into a working relationship." USAS was highly, highly effective in doing that.

All that said, there have been some instances in which USAS called for what were essentially boycotts, urging schools to suspend or cancel contracts with Russell Athletics in 2009 (Garwood 2011; Greenhouse 2009), Nike in 2010 (Greenhouse 2010), and Adidas in 2012 (Blaskey and Gasper 2012; MacLaren 2013). The difference in these cases was that the workers had nothing left to lose, as they had already been laid off by the contractors who employed them. In the case of Russell, USAS successfully pushed for the workers to be rehired; in the cases of Nike and Adidas, USAS successfully pushed for them to receive severance pay they were owed.

In planning strategy, the international network involved in any particular campaign relied on a process of consensus decision making that, perforce, relied very heavily on telecommunications—e-mail and more recently the Internet phone service Skype. "There would be long e-mail chains with a lot of CCs in which strategies would be discussed and debated and developed and assignments suggested and accepted or rejected. And out of that give and take, the strategy would emerge and actions would be taken" (Hermanson interview). While telecommunications has been an invaluable tool in helping activists coordinate globally (see Chapter 7), it works only if key people within the network have met face-to-face and established relationships of trust (Fox and Brown 1998; Keck and Sikkink 1998; Olesen 2005). This is why people such as Evelyn Zepeda and Jeff Hermanson were so essential: they were among the key people in helping forge these relationships of trust, keeping in direct touch with the workers in any particular campaign (even living with them in Zepeda's case), while having close ties to U.S.-based activist groups, such as UNITE HERE and USAS.

One program that was central to building and maintaining these ties of trust was USAS's summer internship program (officially known as the College Apparel Research Initiative [CARI]), which sent students overseas to work with labor unions and labor rights groups throughout the Global South. USAS's internship program started because a number of people among its early leadership realized that it was essential for them to have some personal connections with those workers on whose behalf they were campaigning if they were to be a genuine solidarity organization. As with the WRC's relationship to its partners, I am not in a position to evaluate how well its internship program succeeded in creating relationships of genuine solidarity. It was, however, clear to me that the people I interviewed were all serious about wanting to create such relationships and saw them as of central importance to USAS's work. The relations that were formed through internships had an additional role beyond fostering solidarity and facilitating transnational strategic decision making. They also boosted USAS's credibility, allowing USAS members to counter the claims of some of their critics that the student activists could not really know what workers wanted or what would benefit them.

According to Dalton (interview), CARI was crucial to maintaining USAS's relationships with its partners abroad, although the staff members also played a central role:

> As far as maintaining those relationships, a lot of it does fall on staff because of the student turnover. It's just capacity and access to phones and stuff. I think the other main venue is through our summer international intern program. [. . .] The interns are the ones that actually build the trust and relationships with their host organizations over the course of the two months that they're with them, and then they serve as the liaison throughout the year. We conceptualize our international intern program as not a two-month program but a year-long internship.

While they were in the field the interns served their host organizations in a number of ways, such as lending organizations their English-language skills and computer and other technical abilities, helping the host organizations around the office, and facilitating their ability to communicate abroad. Upon their return to the United States, in addition to maintaining their roles as liaisons, they tried to convey what they had learned in the internship to other members of USAS, both in the leadership and in the grassroots base.

In designing the internship, the first generation of USAS activists were clear on what they wanted to avoid. Eric Brakken (interview, 2007) noted, "A lot of times groups in other parts of the world feel kind of used by U.S. groups. [. . .] They have to take a week out to come and tote a bunch of Americans around, show them all the horrors. The Americans go back, and they do speaking tours and videos on the Internet, and stuff doesn't really change in the country they went to." Instead, the people I spoke with consistently emphasized the importance of building long-term relationships, making themselves practically useful to the groups they worked with, and allowing those groups to set the goals. Indeed, they saw the internships as one of the main means of building the relationships necessary for "seeking guidance in the concrete demands from our partners as much as possible" (Dalton interview). In accordance with USAS's ideology, then, the internship program was first and foremost about building relationships of solidarity and finding ways to empower workers not only in their workplaces but also in the transnational movement against sweatshops.

Simply because there are ties of trust does not mean that reaching consensus is easy. Indeed, it was the difficulty of forging consensus (particularly through a medium such as e-mail, as opposed to the face-to-face meetings where the decision-making method originally developed) that makes such trust so important. Hermanson (interview, 2007) told me the story of one campaign in which anti-sweatshop activists faced a particularly thorny decision. It involved a strike by workers at a factory in El Salvador owned by Tainan Enterprises, a Taiwanese manufacturer that also had plants in Cambodia, China, and Indonesia and that did work for lead apparel firms such as Ann Taylor and The Gap. The question that came up was this:

> Is it ethical to put pressure on The Gap to stop dealing with Tainan everywhere? Or only tell them not to deal with them in El Salvador until the problem is resolved? And there are always different views on that question. [. . .] If you're successful, your pressure results not in their actually leaving Tainan, but it results in their forcing Tainan to fix the problem—which is what happened in the El Salvador case. But if you don't have enough pressure to make a credible threat, you might end up hurting factories that have very little

to do with the basic dispute. So those kinds of things just were argued out, argued out, and argued out. I think in the Tainan case, we went for months before the view that we had to be more extreme or radical and demand a total boycott of Tainan by the brands. It took months before that view prevailed.

When I asked what led movement members to come to this consensus, Hermanson said, "Well, I think the situation of the workers got more and more dire and people became more and more convinced that half-measures weren't going to get the job done. [. . .] And we came to that conclusion reluctantly, but in the end it did turn the trick and brought Tainan to the table, and we negotiated an agreement."

There were also cases in which the network simply could not come to a consensus. Because the network of groups were working together voluntarily, groups that opposed the direction the majority wanted to take could simply opt out of a particular campaign. However, they remained part of the anti-sweatshop movement and could participate in other campaigns with the same groups. In the case of the Designated Suppliers Program (which I look at more closely in the next chapter), the Clean Clothes Campaign, one of the most important European anti-sweatshop groups, came out in opposition to it. The Clean Clothes Campaign thought the DSP was too ambitious and too harsh on the apparel industry (probably because unions and their allies tend to have a less adversarial relationship with corporations in Europe than in the United States). According to Rutter (interview):

> There were a lot of phone calls with them and meetings, to talk through what the program was. [. . .] Unfortunately, we weren't able to ever convince them, even though a lot of their allies were also supporting the program, that this was something that could happen, that it was doable. [. . .] And so, of course, we kept a relationship going, and we would work together on very specific factory cases, but in terms of the larger campaign, they didn't want to endorse something like that.

On the basis of his experiences, Hermanson (interview, 2007) saw this flexibility and the ability of groups to opt out of certain campaigns or programs largely as a strength,

> in the sense that it creates an atmosphere of creativity, where people aren't afraid to disagree or to put out different ideas. I think at

this point in the development of the movement, that's absolutely essential, because nobody's got the answers. If we all had the answers, that would be simple. But I think it could be a weakness if we're not able to bring to bear a critical mass because people don't agree. But that hasn't been the case.

Conclusion

The strategic model for transnational solidarity campaigns was in many ways organized around the boomerang effect. It was what brought sweatshop workers and their local allies into a relationship with activists in the United States and other foreign countries: their local political opportunity structure was largely closed, which created a need to work with groups abroad who had access to openings in the POS that the workers and their local allies did not have. Specifically, U.S. groups could exert pressure on crucial points of leverage that the workers and other Third World groups could not. This did not mean that the workers and their allies did nothing locally. Instead, the strategic model rested on both the workers' pressuring the contractors through strikes and other elements in labor's repertoire of tactics while their U.S. allies attempted to pressure the lead firms employing the contractors more directly by attacking their brand image. Different groups took on different roles, depending on their own skills, connections, and resources and the particular companies involved in the struggle. This allowed for a good deal of flexibility in how the strategic model was deployed from campaign to campaign.

The end goal of all of these activities was to open more mobilizing opportunities for the workers involved and give them more leverage over their employers—that is, to change the POS within which workers must operate. In particular, the goal was to create room for worker empowerment through the organization of an independent union. This was part of what makes the campaigns *solidarity* campaigns: the focus ultimately was on the workers, their goals, and their empowerment.

This focus on solidarity was integral to the success of anti-sweatshop campaigns. With these relationships in place, different groups could negotiate their roles in the various campaigns, what specific actions they would take, while keeping in touch with the workers to ensure that they were actually meeting the workers' needs. This meant that U.S. activists had to make sure that workers were incorporated into the strategic decision-making process in a way that let them define the goals of the campaign.

The next chapter examines the creation of the DSP, which emerged specifically from feedback from groups in the Global South—including unions that had been at the center of some of the successful solidarity campaigns—about the limits of what they were actually achieving and the need to try a new strategy.

The Designated
Suppliers Program

The international solidarity campaigns examined in the previous chapter scored a fair number of successes in that many of them resulted in workers' being able to form independent unions in their factories. The Designated Suppliers Program (DSP) was born out of anti-sweatshop activists' frustration with the limits of such victories. All too often, as happened at the Kukdong/Mexmode and BJ&B factories, a year or two after they had helped workers successfully unionize, members of the wider movement would receive reports that the factory was closing down and the workers would soon be out of work—and the union, consequently, would be no more. As the factory owners reached agreements with their newly unionized employees and improved working conditions, their cost of doing business went up—that is, to do the same work they had done before there was a union, they would need to charge the lead apparel firms more. The reaction of the lead apparel firms—often the same ones that, under pressure from the movement, had pressed the contractor to recognize the union and make a deal with it—would then decide that this cost increase was unacceptable and take their business to another contractor. Soon the factory owner would not have enough customers to stay in business and would have little choice but to shut down. The major apparel companies might be willing to press their contractors to improve working conditions so their factories were no longer sweatshops, but they were not willing to pay what it took to run a factory in a sweat-free manner. Here, we come back to the structural roots of the problem of sweatshops in the basic organization of the international apparel industry. It was this nut that the DSP was meant to crack, at least for college-licensed apparel.

Thus, like the WRC, the DSP was developed as a strategic innovation in the face of new challenges the movement encountered. Unlike the WRC, however, the DSP was not a response to specific actions that the apparel industry had taken. Instead, anti-sweatshop activists were frustrated with the limits of what they were achieving under what was, all things considered, a relatively successful strategic model based on combining corporate campaigns, the WRC's monitoring programs, and the boomerang effect. Spurred on by their growing understanding of the limits of their existing strategic model, they went through an extensive process of innovating, involving widespread consultations, in which they designed the DSP to push past these limits. When it was complete, they publicly unveiled it in 2005 and then began to organize a campaign in support of it. In retrospect, the DSP may have been overly ambitious, for it was met with a sufficient degree of resistance from the apparel industry and its allies in college administrations that it has never been fully implemented. It did, however, lead to a partial success, in that an apparel factory named Alta Gracia that was intended to be compliant with the DSP was opened in the Dominican Republic and continues to operate, with the WRC pointing to it as a model for the rest of the apparel industry. In addition, many of the principles that were central to the DSP were incorporated into the 2013 Accord on Fire and Building Safety in Bangladesh, a legally binding agreement among many major apparel firms and labor rights activists to improve workplace safety conditions in Bangladesh that I touch on briefly at the end of this chapter.

What the DSP was meant to do was "to compel the brands to reward the factories that respect the rights of workers" (Nova interview), instead of effectively punishing them by taking their business elsewhere. Beyond that, it was meant to alter the relations of power among the major companies, their contractors, and workers in such a way that the workers would have more bargaining power than they currently do. The means to this end was to require companies with college licensing agreements to do business with factories that the WRC has thoroughly investigated and approved as generally respecting workers' rights, including the rights to a living wage and to form an independent union. This did not necessarily mean that they would have had to choose from a WRC-approved list. The licensees could have nominated their own choice of contractors, with which the WRC would then work (within reason) to bring up to speed so that they met the requirements of the DSP. As always, the workers could file complaints with the WRC, and if the WRC found that the contractor was not respecting workers' rights, the contractor risked losing its contract and the licensee its license. In other words, the workers would have some ability to decertify the factory at which they work, which would give them some potential leverage over the companies involved that they do not have now. Thus, if the DSP had been successful in meeting its goals, there would have been a shift so that power relations in transnational production chains would not be quite so unbalanced, at least within the limited realm of college apparel. In ideological terms, the development of the DSP involved a reaffirmation on the part of USAS and its allies of the importance of worker empowerment, as well as a renewed emphasis on the structural nature of the problem of sweatshops—and, therefore, the need for a structural solution.

Origins of the DSP

The DSP was, in a number of ways, the product of the transnational network that constituted the anti-sweatshop movement and conducted the solidarity campaigns. As already noted, activists in the network were frustrated with the limits of the successes of the campaigns they conducted. In addition, although the DSP was primarily crafted by U.S. activists, it was specifically responding to complaints by those activists' Third World partners about the limits of what they were achieving, and the U.S. activists consulted extensively with their Third World allies in crafting the DSP, trying to ensure that the new program—while viable in the United States—would meet the needs of activists in the Global South. The transnational solidarity campaigns discussed in the previous chapter thus formed the foundation for the DSP in that the program would not have taken form had it not been for the networks built in such campaigns.

USAS member Jessica Rutter (interview, 2007) explained how the activists began to see the shortcomings of what they were achieving with their international solidarity campaigns:

> So basically what was happening with a lot of the great successes that we had was that the factories were starting to close because as workers organized [, . . .] prices were going up, so the brands were actually starting to divert their orders to other factories. [. . .] With a lot of the really important relationships that had been built with workers at certain factories, those workers were saying, "We really need to keep our factory. That's the most important thing right now."

According to Rutter, this request required a rethinking of USAS's strategy, since it "was really different than anything USAS had ever done before, because USAS generally didn't work to keep business in certain places. That's just not what we did. We supported workers' organizing."

This was not simply a matter of helping workers keep their jobs. It also involved keeping unions alive. When a factory closes down—even if the owners open another factory under a new name—the union no longer legally exists; all of its work comes to naught, and it must start over again. While workers, especially union leaders, may still have organizing skills and ties to allied organizations that can help them, both domestically and internationally, they are likely to scatter to a number of new factories in the search for work. This means that they then have to begin rebuilding the social networks within the factory that are necessary for a successful, democratic union from scratch, which is no easy task. Rutter (interview) said that this pattern of closures "also sends a message to other workers that if you have a union at your factory and you improve conditions at your factory, then your factory will close, which is a really dangerous message to send to workers. It's another kind of intimidation tactic."

There were subtler problems, as well. Winning campaigns in the first place is a time-consuming task. Eric Dirnbach (interview) of UNITE HERE told me, "The scope of the problem is so tremendous that I'm losing patience. You just can't have a two-year campaign to help workers at one factory organize a union." A two-year campaign entails a tremendous investment of resources on the part of anti-sweatshop groups and, in the meantime, limits the resources available to help workers elsewhere. The monitoring *following* a successful campaign has also proved to be time-consuming. Nancy Steffan (interview) of the WRC noted that the consortium found it had to remain continuously involved in many factories, long after an apparent victory: "We would go and write up a report—and then to get the situation fixed takes months. And we're still involved in most of the factory investigations we've done just to make sure things are kept up. If they're not kept up, then we should probably get involved again." This, in turn, limited the number of new cases the WRC could practically take on—and thus its wider impact. As a result, the WRC's executive director, Scott Nova, said in 2006, of the two thousand to three thousand factories around the world producing college apparel, only eight met the WRC's standards fully (Jaschik 2006).

Another problem Steffan (interview) raised is that no progress had been made toward securing workers a living wage:

You probably assumed that at this point the people are getting high wages, but the unions in the industry, the few that exist that are actually bargaining, are generally not bargaining over wages because the factories don't have the money to pay higher wages because they're under so much price pressure from their buyers.

The problem, again, is the structure of the industry, where the lead firms seek contractors that can keep costs as low as possible while maintaining a certain level of quality. As a result, "The actual improvements have a ceiling on them, and then the improvements are actually being eroded over time because there's no reward for improving conditions in the factories" (Steffan interview).

Groups such as USAS and the WRC in the United States thus were getting feedback from their allies, particularly the workers whose lives they had worked so hard to help improve, that made them question the long-term viability of their strategic model. In particular, some anti-sweatshop activists came to believe that the use of codes of conduct and independent monitoring as a strategic model, while valuable, was more limited in its impact than they had initially hoped it would be. This was true in part because the major apparel companies managed to partially co-opt the model via internal corporate social responsibility departments and the Fair Labor Association. Brent Wood (interview) expressed this concern:

> There's been some change, at least on the part of a lot of groups—a move in a direction where that tool of public embarrassment has been made secondary to an effort to use the existing codes of conduct and monitoring systems the brands have developed as a separate tool to promote change. In other words, [there is] a belief that through the codes of conduct and monitoring the brands have opened up so that activists can walk through, that [the brands] can be held accountable to their own self-proclaimed standards, that their own monitoring systems can be used to promote change. And that is true to a degree. The problem is the degree to which it's true is a lot more limited than people recognize.

Again, the reasons for these limits are the structure of the apparel industry. In particular, there is the inevitable conflict of interest involved when corporations monitor themselves and their clients (see Chapter 9). Wood believed that the model based on codes and monitoring "was worth pursuing, because at an earlier time there was more reason to be hopeful. There was less of [an] understanding . . . [that] the way that the supply chain is structured would thwart efforts to use codes towards positive ends. But it's now clear that the level of progress that can be achieved is very limited."

Their experience and their analysis of the apparel industry gave activists a good sense of what they needed to look at to move forward. The DSP aimed to attack this problem head-on by restructuring the supply chain. Steffan (interview) told me that, after the activists realized that "the system just wasn't getting us as much as we thought we could, that it wasn't sustainable over time," they "decided we had to look not only at the labor conditions but also the purchasing practices of the brands—the way they do business, the way their suppliers act, the prices they pay, the relationship they have with them, the way they organize their production to ensure that they're actually in a position to determine working conditions in a factory." It was the focus on these factors that eventually led to the formulation of the DSP.

Strategic Innovation and the Crafting of the DSP

Knowing that you need to strategically innovate and actually innovating are two different things. The process by which anti-sweatshop activists innovated was a time-consuming one, involving widespread discussions and consultations, not only within the movement, but also with outside experts. People came up with a number of proposals, which were discussed and debated in light of the movement's ideology, until they settled on something broadly like the DSP. They then had to hone that model so that it could stand up to scrutiny in the conflict with both the apparel industry and reluctant school administrators that activists knew was sure to ensue.

In many respects, the process of creating the DSP was similar to creating the WRC: there was a participatory, deliberative process of widespread consultation among a number of groups, with those involved drawing on their experiences and working out their differences by means of consensus. Initially, these discussions took place through conference calls and e-mail lists, with people sending draft proposals back and forth and editing them (Dalton, Rutter, Stoppard, and Wood interviews). Rutter (interview) summed up the decision-making process this way:

> We really tried to talk to everyone that we could think of. [. . .] It was a lot of consultation, it was a period of just trying to figure out what could be done, policies that could be helpful, that could address some of these new problems. And so we actually had a retreat

in January 2005 where we tried to bring together a bunch of folks. We brought together students from USAS; we brought together the U.S. unions; we brought together some of the international allies and had this larger summit. It wasn't large—it was like a smaller retreat actually, but maybe fifty people.

In addition, the Solidarity Center and a number of allied academics were involved in the decision-making process (Stoppard interview). After the conference, the activists continued to work on the proposal developed there—the Designated Suppliers Program—and unveiled it in September 2005, the start of the next school year (Dalton interview).

If anything, the network of groups involved was broader than the one that created the WRC, since—thanks to the networks USAS and the WRC had built up over the course of their international solidarity campaigns—groups from the Global South were better integrated. However, this was clearly an initiative led by USAS and the WRC. Although they consulted their allies in unions and at NGOs, those groups were not as centrally involved as they had been in the creation of the WRC (Dalton, Rutter, Stoppard, and Wood interviews). USAS and the WRC had matured as organizations and were in a better position to take a leadership role in this cycle of innovation.

According to Rutter (interview), this process "a lot of times meant having arguments," but she believed that it produced a stronger program at the end of the process:

We had to deal with a lot of different ideas, and a lot of them got incorporated in some ways. And in other ways they were definitely used to create stronger arguments for what we had, so I think in every way that it was good that there was a lot of debate.

In other words, having a diverse range of activist groups and individuals involved created an atmosphere of dialogue and debate that sharpened the interpretive-analytic process by which the groups analyzed their environment, as well as their past successes and failures, and attempted to devise a new strategy that would help them realize their goals and values.

Beyond the use of consensus, there were deliberate efforts to ensure that the decision-making process included allies of USAS and the WRC from the Global South, drawing on both the partnerships USAS had formed and the relationships that the WRC's field staff had developed. As noted in Chapter 11, in such situations there is always the challenge that groups in the Global South do not, and really cannot, fully understand the situation on the ground in the United States—that is, what is strategically feasible and what is not. They can make clear what their goals and priorities are; then U.S. activists must try to find a way to create a viable program that honors those goals and priorities—which necessarily entails some trust between the groups in the United States and the groups in the Global South. The USAS member Liana Dalton (interview) explained how this worked in relation to the DSP:

> I think the core demands come from the unions and the partners in the South. [. . .] The necessity of student organizing has forced us to create this entity, and rather than being this concept of unionized factories and higher prices, it's become the DSP as an entity, as a program. [. . .] A lot of unions don't have a good enough conception of the organizing reality of students' and administrators' relations. They don't understand why some of these decisions are being made. Therefore, it's really difficult to continue that consultation process of keeping them having ownership and decision-making power on exactly what the DSP looks like in terms of the policy document. What's going to be important is for us to keep the policy flexible enough so they can still shape it once it exists, once we've won it.

This shows the careful balancing act that was necessary to maintain transnational relationships that genuinely embodied the principles of solidarity. There were clearly limits to what consultations with unions representing sweatshop workers could accomplish in terms of designing a strategy. The U.S. groups had to be able to act autonomously, using their knowledge of the political opportunity structure in the United States— what rules governed the different social arenas and what points of leverage U.S. groups might have. What this meant was that, in many ways, the DSP was more a project of USAS and the WRC than the groups it was meant to help. Their hope, however, was that it would give their allies in the Global South more room to maneuver—more mobilizing opportunities and new points of leverage.

As noted, in the period leading up to the January 2005 conference, the activists developed a number of proposals. Some that my interviewees described to me bore only a distant resemblance to the final product—the DSP. This contrasts with the creation of the WRC, where the people involved knew pretty clearly from the beginning what they were trying to create: an independent monitoring organization that would serve as a contrast to the industry-controlled FLA. In the case of the DSP, they knew what they wanted to accomplish but were uncertain about what sort of program would help them achieve the goals. Nova (interview) identified their starting point: "We knew we had to do something to create a situation where a factory that treated workers more respectfully could actually survive—and, indeed, thrive—in the industry, and something that would require the brands to change the way their supply chains operated. The initial concept was simply to compel the brands to reward the factories that respect the rights of workers." Here the movement's ideology—specifically, its social analysis—played an important role, helping the activists pinpoint the problem as a structural one, due to the organization of transnational production chains.

According to Dalton (interview), even before the wider anti-sweatshop movement began the conversation that would produce the DSP, USAS was already trying to figure out what its next steps should be. It had taken up a wage disclosure campaign, which, retrospectively, she thought was a poor idea: "But we really didn't know what we were doing at the time in terms of demands. We thought it would be useful, but I think people were kind of floundering around not knowing what to do with the concrete things like demands." Like other anti-sweatshop groups, USAS had identified the lack of a living wage in the apparel industry as a major problem and hoped that, by requiring companies to disclose the wages that workers were paid (just as companies were required to disclose factory locations), it could push the industry to increase wages. Dalton said, however, that eventually "we started realizing that any sort of living wage campaign that we were going to do [. . .] was going to be more top-down than we wanted. Really, what we needed to focus on was unions directly." Here we can see the movement's ideology at play: by looking at the issue through the lens of worker empowerment, USAS rejected a strategy that it feared would be top-down in its approach in favor of one that directly supported labor unions, because the latter approach was truer to its values and goals.

One simple proposal put forward during the deliberations that led to the DSP was to require the brands to make ten-year commitments to the factories that they contracted with, since this would at least stabilize the relationships between the two and keep the brands from switching factories if workers succeeded in improving conditions. It was quickly recognized, on the basis of the movement's past experience, that the lead apparel firms would never agree to such a long-term commitment and that they would need to develop an alternative proposal involving a shorter commitment period (Rutter, Stoppard, and Wood interviews). Dalton (interview) came up with a proposal of her own, on the basis of her involvement with Just Garments, a Salvadoran apparel manufacturing co-op founded by workers who had been fired when they tried to organize a factory producing for Land's End: "I was pretty emotionally attached to the case. [. . .] I wrote a proposal about Just Garments, which was kind of a stupid proposal, fair-tradey almost." As discussed in Chapter 6, many anti-sweatshop activists are critical of the fair trade movement for ideological reasons: they perceive it (rightly or wrongly) as empowering consumers instead of workers. Despite this, Dalton felt there was a core idea in this proposal that was important: "I felt that we should have a third model, and it should be how to support good factories. [. . .] The idea behind it was that we needed some sort of mechanism, once we have good union factories, to support them." This basic notion of developing mechanisms to support good factories would, in the conversations that ensued from these proposals, become a central goal of the DSP. As with USAS's wage disclosure campaign, while many of the initial proposals may have been problematic, they served to clarify the anti-sweatshop activists' thinking, both about what precisely they wanted to accomplish and what might actually be possible, given the political opportunity structure within which they were embedded. Their ideology of worker empowerment helped guide them away from proposals that they felt would not ultimately empower workers through facilitating unionization.

Eventually, they settled on a basic concept of what they wanted. Steffan (interview, 2007) described it this way:

> We knew what the basic idea was: there was going to be a set of factories that were going to operate differently, that the current way the industry operated was just not conducive to respecting worker rights in countries. We needed—hence the term—designated suppliers. We needed to create a new world out there of factories, not geographically in a different place, but a new set of factories that would operate under different conditions, would have a very different kind of relationship with their buyer, and would therefore be in a position to meet high labor standards.

More exactly, they wanted to require that those companies producing college-licensed goods commit to doing business with factories that met particular standards. One of the most crucial of these standards was independent organization of workers—that is, the workers at the factories would have to clearly be at liberty to unionize (or, as an alternative, the factories could be worker co-ops). Moving from this basic concept to a viable program that they could ask colleges and universities to sign on to required a good deal of additional work.

The Proposed DSP

Workings of the Program

We now turn to the proposed Designated Suppliers Program. Since USAS and the WRC have not been in a position where they can actually begin implementing the program, much of this discussion is hypothetical—what the plan of action would have been once they were in a position to initiate the program.

The basic requirements of the DSP were designed to force the major apparel companies to meet the standards of the codes of conduct, not just in the short term, when a campaign found them at fault, but over the long term, whether or not the movement had directly mobilized a campaign around a particular factory. This does not mean that anti-sweatshop activists saw the DSP as a substitute for mobilizing in campaigns. Rather, it was meant to sustain the gains made in campaigns over the long run, without activists' needing to fear that the factory where they helped workers build an independent union the previous year was going to shut down this year. This can perhaps be most clearly seen in the fact that five factories—including Kukdong/Mexmode and BJ&B—were initially grandfathered into the DSP. Licensees that wanted to use these factories for production would not have needed to go through the usual approval process. They were already considered approved as a result of the WRC's extensive past work and positive relationship with them (Designated Suppliers Program Working Group 2006a). After an exchange with the Department of Justice over whether the DSP violated antitrust laws (discussed below), the WRC was forced to drop this element from the DSP (Nova 2011), but it still signals its original intent.

On the basis of their structural analysis of the industry, those involved in designing the DSP identified two major changes the lead apparel firms needed to make in their policies for their suppliers to be able to meet the requirements of the codes of conduct and remain profitable. The first was that the lead firms would have to pay their contractors a price commensurate with the amount they needed to pay their employees a living wage, maintain the factory at suitable health and safety standards, and so on. This meant that the major firms would have to pay their contractors more than they traditionally had, instead of pressing for the lowest possible prices. Second, the major companies would have to make long-term commitments to their contractors—specifically, at least three years—so that the contractors could have confidence that they would continue to get orders if they went to all the trouble of meeting the code of conduct requirements. This requirement represented a promise of job security for both the factory owners and the workers. (There was, however, an escape clause if a company found that the contractor was either failing to meet the standards of the DSP or not producing high-quality products [Designated Suppliers Program Working Group 2006a].)

The distinctiveness of the DSP can be seen by comparing these requirements with those of the Fair Labor Association. The FLA required changes in their practices by contractors, but not by the lead firms (except that they should do business with contractors who met the FLA's standards). While under the newest iteration of its programs the FLA does offer help to contractors so they can meet the required standards (Fair Labor Association 2012b), it does not require its member companies to pay their contractors so they can afford to make these changes. The DSP placed the burden of reform, financially and in policy terms, on those social actors who held the most power and controlled the most resources: the lead apparel companies.

The DSP also built on the traditional code of conduct in two ways. First, it considerably strengthened workers' right to freedom of association—that is, their ability to form a union. Under the DSP, factory owners not only would have had to refrain from union busting, but they also would have had to make it clear to workers that they were welcome to form a union if they wanted one (Designated Suppliers Program Working Group 2006a). "Workers in the apparel industry know that there will be consequences for joining a union," Steffan (interview) said. "So [factory owners] have to take a lot of proactive steps to develop a climate in the factory under which workers could, if they wanted to, join a union." If managers had undertaken union-busting campaigns in the past, they would need to take steps to make it clear to workers that they had turned over a new leaf (Designated Suppliers Program Working Group 2006a). Second, the DSP required participating factories to pay their workers a living wage (Designated Suppliers Program Working Group 2006a). As discussed in earlier chapters, this was a major omission in previous codes of conduct, one that anti-sweatshop activists saw as a major flaw in the older system even before it became clear that their other gains were not sustainable over time. They took the opportunity to create the DSP to remedy this problem. (As discussed in Chapter 8, the FLA did not require a living wage and had a poor record when it came to the right to unionize.)

All monitoring, inspection, and verification of DSP compliance would remain the exclusive province of the WRC, with its autonomy from the apparel industry (as opposed to organizations such as the FLA that had been created or captured by the industry). In addition to conducting the initial inspection when a factory sought approval to join the DS, the WRC would retain the right to carry out inspections at any time, in response to workers' complaints, as it had in the past for all factories producing apparel for member colleges. The WRC also remained committed to transparency: those college licensees that failed to meet the DSP's standards and who did nothing to remedy the situation would find that the consortium would continue issuing reports calling attention to this fact (Designated Suppliers Program Working Group 2006a). They would thus remain vulnerable to being targeted for solidarity campaigns by USAS and its allies.

The DSP and Structural Change in the Apparel Industry

While the immediate goals of the DSP were to benefit the workers in approved factories, USAS and its allies had broader hopes for the program. On the basis of their ideology, they knew that structural changes to the apparel industry were necessary and hoped to use the DSP to accomplish this. Specifically, they hoped that it would be the starting pointing for bringing about an alteration in how outsourcing was done so that it did not involve a race to the bottom in which workers were inevitably mercilessly exploited as the burden of cutting costs was shifted onto their backs. They also hoped that these changes would alter the political opportunity structure for workers, creating more mobilizing opportunities throughout the apparel industry. Ultimately, what they hoped to accomplish was a shift in power within the apparel industry so that workers were on a more even footing with the companies. The USAS member Marion Traub-Werner (interview) said:

> The thing about the DSP that I like is that it's a very structural approach, right? We actually need to change the structure of the industry. [. . .] To force the brands to pay a better price to the factories and so that price can actually get passed on to workers—the reason that doesn't happen is because workers don't have bargaining power. That's also the structure of capital here. This is an unorganized workforce. So can you actually raise their standard of living through this other method? I don't know if you can, but it's definitely worth the try.

It may seem that the potential structural changes would be actually fairly limited, given that the immediate impact of the DSP would be confined to collegiate apparel—which, as discussed in Chapter 3, is only 1–2 percent of the total U.S. apparel market. Originally, USAS and its allies hoped

their codes of conduct would have an impact on the larger apparel industry because college apparel production is widely dispersed. The DSP, if
implemented, would instead concentrate this production. Anti-sweatshop
activists still hoped to have a broader impact on the industry, just in a
different way. The activists I spoke with repeatedly spoke of the DSP as
creating an example that could influence the rest of the industry. Wood
(interview), for instance, said:

> The fact that there are out there a certain number of factories that
> respect workers' rights—it proves that it's possible to do that and
> still make a profit. That will then become the basis for putting new
> pressure on the brands and over time persuading paid observers
> that the brands are full of shit and they can do better than they're
> doing, because here is this shining example that shows that you can.

Dalton (interview) even hoped that the DSP might lead some major firms
involved to put pressure on other major companies: "The brands that are
paying the higher price [under the DSP . . .], they have to pay subsidies to
other brands if they're not willing to pay for the higher standards. So it's
not like the workers get 200 percent wages for producing the university
orders and then 100 percent wages for producing the other orders. All the
workers in the factory get the same wage, a livable wage." To avoid subsi-
dizing other brands, Dalton hoped that the college licensees would start
pressing other members of the industry to raise their prices, as well.

How much of an impact the DSP could have had beyond the college
market remains an open question. Right now, the WRC points to the Alta
Gracia factory in the Dominican Republic, which meets the DSP's standards, as the sort of example, discussed above, of what might be possible
if things were done differently. It is clear, however, that, when they designed the program, USAS and its allies had their eyes on creating structural changes in the industry. In turn, they hoped this would significantly change the political opportunity structure for workers trying to
unionize. As has long been its goal, the anti-sweatshop movement hoped
to create more mobilizing opportunities for workers. Under the terms of
the DSP, not only would contractors have been forbidden to engage in
union-busting activities, but both the lead firms and the suppliers in the
apparel industry would have had to take actual steps to encourage unionization—not something that, in the course of normal business, capitalists
generally do. The DSP was also meant to give workers leverage not just
over their immediate employers, but also over the major firms that dominate the production chains within which the workers are embedded. Any

major company that wanted to sell goods in the valued college market would have to come to an agreement with both its contractors and the union at the contracted factory, paying the contractor sufficiently that the union felt that its members' basic needs were being met. With colleges' codes of conduct and the WRC's independent monitoring of the current system, activists had long sought to expand workers' mobilizing opportunities, but this attempt to give them leverage over major firms was new. Under the codes of conduct, U.S. and Western European groups allied with the workers exercised leverage over the lead companies. This attempt under the DSP to give workers themselves some degree of leverage was consistent with the movement's ideology of hoping, over the long term, to create conditions in which workers and their unions could be largely self-sufficient and did not need to rely on more privileged allies. This is not to say that anyone thought this would happen in the short term solely as a result of the DSP. USAS and its allies planned to remain involved in workers' struggles worldwide for the foreseeable future. But it did potentially represent a step toward that goal.

Shifts in Ideology

The process of designing the DSP produced not only a significant strategic innovation but also a subtle but important shift in the movement's ideology. As was the case with the creation of the WRC, the process of deliberately crafting a new program to counter actions by the apparel industry deepened the movement's ideology—in this case, its social analysis. This involved putting greater emphasis on something that the movement knew was important but had not really accounted for in its strategy. Specifically, it began to examine more deeply the role that the lead apparel firms' practice of outsourcing had on the industry's global structure. According to the USAS member Caroline Stoppard (interview):

> It wasn't like it just suddenly hit us that purchasing practices were something to look at. [. . .] But it wasn't that central to our thinking. We thought we could do this without seriously addressing purchasing practices. We thought that the brands would be forced to address their purchasing practices, even if we didn't impose that on them, because they would recognize that the only way to have their codes of conduct enforced was if they [increased their payments to contractors]— But that was the last thing they actually wanted to change. So that didn't happen. We were running into a brick wall.

The anti-sweatshop movement thus did not make profound changes in its social analysis. Instead, there was a subtle shift in emphasis, with renewed stress being placed on something it had long known but on which it had not focused. This subtle shift in analysis, however, resulted in a major shift in strategy—a move away from simply asking the apparel firms (both the lead marketing and retail firms and the dependent manufacturing firms) to uphold certain standards in their dealings with workers to trying to change the nature of the relationship between the two sets of companies. On one level, the codes of conduct and the DSP were similar in that they asked the companies that constitute the apparel industry to change some of their business practices. On another level, though, the DSP struck deeper than the codes of conduct, targeting practices that are central to the reproduction of unequal power relations in the production process in a way that codes of conduct do not. In other words, through the DSP, anti-sweatshop activists hoped to begin addressing the structural roots of sweatshops, the system of social relations that encourages the gross exploitation of workers. They sought to foster a shift in the balance of power away from the major apparel corporations, not toward their contractors but toward the workers themselves, creating conditions in which the lead companies would have had to contend with strong, independent unions representing workers.

The Campaign for the DSP

The campaign to institute the DSP was much harder than the campaigns on behalf of codes of conduct and the WRC. Indeed, although one factory—Alta Gracia in the Dominican Republic—has been certified by the WRC (Worker Rights Consortium 2014), it remains an isolated "social policy enclave" (Pearson and Seyfang 2001, 67). Beyond that, the campaign largely stalled out, owing to delaying tactics by administrators at some schools (Robbins 2013). There was more opposition to the DSP from industry and schools—because it asked for much more fundamental changes—and the schools had become better at reacting to and containing student protests than they were in the past. This highlights the fact that in developing strategic innovations, coming up with a new plan of action is only half the challenge. Actually implementing it successfully is another challenge in and of itself. In some cases, this may come from the difficulties in mobilizing support in the movement for such a change in direction. In the case of the DSP, the challenge was overcoming the considerable obstacles within the political opportunity structure to its implementation.

USAS launched its campaign in September 2005 by sending a letter to colleges and universities inviting them to join. The vast majority of schools expressed reservations. But over the course of that fall, eight schools— Duke University; Georgetown University; Indiana University; Santa Clara University; the University of Connecticut; the University of Maine, Farmington; UW Madison; and Smith College—signed on to the DSP. Together with representatives from USAS, they formed the Designed Suppliers Program Working Group in March 2006. Jim Wilkerson, an administrator at Duke who had long been supportive of the anti-sweatshop movement, chaired the working group, which included observers from WRC member schools that had not committed to the DSP, as well as the FLA and its member schools and the National Association of College Stores. The initial goal of the working group was to revise the DSP to meet concerns raised by WRC member schools. The resulting document was released in September 2006; it is this version of the DSP that I described above (Designated Suppliers Program Working Group 2006b; June 2006; Wilkerson interview). Some of the changes were made in response to issues raised by schools, by college licensees, and by USAS itself (Designated Suppliers Program Working Group 2006c).

The deep-seated opposition of the apparel industry to the program and the reluctance of many college administrators to do anything that would unsettle their business partners constituted a major obstacle in implementing the DSP. Caroline Stoppard (interview) noted:

> I think that some universities aren't happy with the DSP campaign because they would prefer that the WRC took a more accommodating approach with the industry. Instead, the WRC delivered the unpleasant news that the brands have failed to clean up their act and urged universities to intervene much more aggressively in the industry's supply chain practices, something to which the industry is, of course, extremely hostile. This strained the relationship between the WRC and some schools, not because administrators at those schools lack confidence in the WRC's monitoring work, but because they see the WRC as rocking the boat in an unwelcome manner.

The apparel industry, of course, did not argue against the DSP on the grounds that it would cut into its profits. The FLA questioned the DSP's potential effectiveness. "You can't audit a factory into compliance," argued Auret van Heerden, then the head of the FLA, saying that the DSP would not work because it ran counter to the market organization of the economy (Jaschik 2006). Gregg Nebel, the director of social and environmental affairs for Adidas and a member of the FLA board, objected to the living wage requirement, as well, repeating the long-standing argument that it is impossible to properly measure what would constitute a living wage. He instead touted the FLA's new Sustainable Compliance system, which involved working cooperatively with management to bring factories up to standards (Gaus 2006). This was consistent with the apparel industry's long-standing framing strategy—to claim that it has both a real commitment to ending the problem of sweatshops and, unlike student activists or the WRC, the expertise to do so as a result of its insider position.

When USAS launched the DSP campaign in September 2005, it organized protests on at least forty campuses (Appelbaum and Dreier 2005). To their frustration, however, the members of USAS found it harder to win using the tactics that had been successful in the past The USAS national organizer Zack Knorr (interview) speculated that part of the problem was that the DSP asked for a substantially greater commitment than has been involved with the codes of conduct and the WRC and thus generated greater resistance. He was also concerned, however, that college and university administrators had learned how to adapt to USAS's repertoire of tactics: "Administrations have changed their tactics on sit-ins. The last two years [2005–2007], pretty much all the sit-ins we've done, people have been arrested that day. Administrations are no longer allowing students to stay."

Perhaps the biggest challenge to implementing the DSP was the ambiguous legal status it held until 2011. A number of companies opposed to the program and schools closely aligned with them initially argued that the DSP could violate antitrust statutes. Supporters of the DSP were confident that it could be implemented in such a way that it did not violate antitrust laws—it was simply a matter of finding the correct language. The DSP Working Group initially submitted a business letter of review request to the U.S. Office of the Attorney General, asking for a ruling on its probable legal status (a standard practice). Under the Bush administration, however, the Department of Justice simply would not reply, which antisweatshop activists took as a sign of the administration's general hostility to the whole concept. Fearing that any eventual ruling would result in a rejection, they withdrew the request, waiting for a Democratic (and therefore presumably somewhat friendlier) White House to resubmit it (Nova 2007a). Many school administrations used this as a justification for not signing on to the DSP. In some cases, this was merely an excuse, a sign of general opposition to the whole plan; in others, it reflected the natural caution of college administrators concerned with anything that might put their schools at risk. Even those schools that did make a commitment to the DSP did so in principle: they would not commit to the specific proposal released by the Working Group until its legal status was clarified. After Barack Obama was elected in 2008, the WRC resubmitted the request to the Department of Justice. In December 2011, after the WRC had made some modifications to the DSP at the department's request, the Department of Justice issued a statement that the DSP did not violate U.S. antitrust laws (Nova 2011). By this point, however, much of the momentum of the campaign for the DSP had fizzled out, and USAS had moved back to other, more traditional campaigns to help workers at specific factories (Robbins 2013). Effectively, the opponents of the DSP were able to use the legal limbo it stood in for six years as a stalling tactic, similar to but with much more power than the committees set up by administrators as a bureaucratic delaying tactic during the initial campaigns for the code of conduct and the WRC (see Chapter 5). The fact that the DSP's legal status was genuinely ambiguous meant there was little USAS could do to push schools to implement it immediately, allowing the schools to drag their feet on signing on to the DSP so that by 2011, much of the force behind the campaign was gone.

Conclusion

What we see with the DSP is the need for constant innovation on the part of the anti-sweatshop movement—and how even such innovation is no guarantee of success. We also see quite distinctly how the dialectic between ideology and experience played out. Similar to the process that led to the formation of the WRC, not only did reflecting on their experience in light of their ideology lead the activists to alter their plan of action; their experience also led them to modify their ideology, albeit in subtle ways. While their values—a commitment to workers' empowerment—remained the same, they modified their social analysis somewhat. As my interviewees said, they always knew that the structure of the apparel industry was the root of the problem, but their experiences—the frustration of seeing their hard-won victories melt away—led them to put renewed emphasis on this aspect of their analysis.

This, in turn, led to changes in their norms of action. Supporting workers in their attempts to unionize and acting in solidarity remained central to anti-sweatshop activists, but the DSP in some ways represented a new departure. Traditionally, USAS and its allies emphasized the importance of winning concrete victories. This remains important to anti-sweatshop activists, but they found all too often that the victories were temporary. Thus, they searched for new norms of action by which they could preserve these victories. As a result, they came up with the DSP, which included a form of certification, a practice they had previously looked on warily (see Chapter 9). The certification was not an end in itself, as it is with the forms of certification USAS has criticized in the past. That is, the certification process in and of itself was not meant as a guarantee of good working conditions. Rather, it was part of a larger plan to force the apparel industry to restructure itself, at least within the realm of college-licensed apparel. It was a tool that the movement hoped to use to bring about long-term structural changes so that such programs would not be needed in the future. Thus, the movement's new norms were as much about seeking ways to directly bring about structural change as they were about certification.

Getting the DSP implemented proved to be a challenge. The apparel industry and its allies among college administrators resisted it more than any of USAS's previous proposals, likely because it demanded more deep-reaching changes on their part. This highlights the fact that, no matter how creative a movement is, it must deal with the realities of the political opportunity structure in which it operates. In many ways, the DSP was intended to do just that: it targeted those aspects of the system that present the greatest obstacles to workers in seeking to unionize and empower themselves. The problem was that this same POS prevented them from implementing the program, because the apparel industry seemingly had enough power to obstruct it. Other movements have certainly run up against insurmountable obstacles in their social environment, often after a series of successes. The Civil Rights Movement, for instance, won significant victories in abolishing the Jim Crow system but was unable to bring about the reforms needed to address the problem of widespread poverty in the black community. Part of the problem may also have been simply conjunctural: if a friendlier administration had held the U.S. presidency, the DSP might have received the Department of Justice's approval earlier, and the campaign might not have fizzled out in the same way. This speaks to the complex ways different social institutions interlock to create the POS. Despite the DSP's descent into limbo, many of the ideas underlying the program live on in the form of the Accord on Fire and Building Safety in Bangladesh (Scott Nova, personal communication, 2019). So even if the DSP itself was not a success, the lessons learned from it have proved valuable and have been applied in other campaigns.

Epilogue: The Accord on Fire and Building Safety in Bangladesh

The Accord on Fire and Building Safety in Bangladesh was initially to be implemented over five years, from 2013 to 2018. It was renewed in 2018, until May 2020, in a compromise with the Bangladeshi government. The impetus for the accord came from a series of high-profile workplace safety disasters in Bangladesh's garment factories, in which large numbers of workers died in cases that should have been preventable if the factory owners had followed basic safety protocols. The most notorious were the Tazreen Fashion factory fire, in which 112 workers burned to death after being locked in the building, and Rana Plaza, in which 1,134 workers died in a building collapse after being forced to work there, despite clear signs that the factory was unsafe (G. Brown 2015; Nova 2014). The accord is an agreement by more than two hundred major transnational apparel firms, local and global unions, and a number of labor rights groups (Accord on Fire and Building Safety in Bangladesh 2015; G. Brown 2015; Nova 2014), including the WRC, which has been very actively involved in crafting and implementing it (Rahman 2014). In addition, USAS actively campaigned in support of the accord, pushing college administrators to sever ties with VF Corporation, the parent company of Jansport, when it refused to sign on to the accord (Kitroeff 2014).

The accord creates a system of independent workplace safety inspections and provides for factories that fail to meet the safety standards to be upgraded. The influence of the DSP can be seen in some of the major elements of how this program is being implemented. Although some Bangladeshi factory owners are wealthy and can afford to improve conditions in their factories on their own, others are not. In such cases, the lead apparel firms that contract with them must pay for the improvements. Here we can see the principle from the DSP that the lead apparel firms that control the lion's share of the industry's wealth should shoulder much of the responsibility for improving working conditions, providing their contractors with the funds they need to treat workers in accord with basic labor rights. In addition, the lead firms must continue to do business with these contractors for two years after the improvements are made so that the factories are rewarded for improving conditions, as in the DSP. Representatives of workers, through their labor unions, are actively involved in the entire inspection process. All safety reports are provided to the unions, and workers receive training on workplace safety and their related rights. This means that the accord, similar to the DSP, allows workers to participate in the process of certifying their own workplaces, shifting the balance of power, even if only a little. Finally, the accord is legally binding on the signatory companies (G. Brown 2015; Nova 2014; Rahman 2014). This contrasts with the Alliance for Bangladesh Worker Safety, created by twenty-eight major apparel firms, including Walmart and The Gap, which is not legally binding and does not require the lead firms to commit financially to improving workplace safety conditions (Alliance for Bangladesh Worker Safety 2015; Miller 2014). Scott Nova criticized this aspect of the alliance, saying, "We don't believe that unenforceable commitments are credible" (quoted in "Accord, Alliance or Disunity?" 2013).

Since the process of implementing the accord is ongoing, how successfully it will play out remains to be seen. One challenge is simply the scale of the undertaking, since almost all of the more than 1,800 factories covered have massive workplace safety problems that must be found through inspections, fixed or addressed, and then continually monitored to make sure the improvements remain in effect (Nova 2014). In addition, the accord is limited to workplace safety; it does not cover other labor rights, such as a living wage and freedom of association, although it has pushed the Bangladeshi government to improve legal protections for labor unions. The government is highly corrupt; the country's labor movement is fragmented; and unions are often co-opted by the widespread corruption. Finally, a number of the companies that signed on to the accord immediately after the disasters now regret having done so and have been seeking to water down its provisions. Still, even if the implementation proves uneven, the provisions of the accord and its legally binding nature set new precedents (G. Brown 2015; Rahman 2014) and mean that the DSP lives on in spirit, if not in form.

SweatFree Communities

E ven as USAS and its allies were seeking to innovate in designing the Designated Supplier Program, another group, SweatFree Communities, was engaging in another type of strategic innovation as it sought to take the strategic model USAS had developed and adapt it to a type of social arena other than colleges and universities—namely, city and state governments. Specifically, SweatFree Communities sought to get city and state governments to pass ordinances requiring the companies that provided them with their uniforms to follow labor rights codes of conduct and to set up a consortium—the SweatFree Purchasing Consortium—similar to the Worker Rights Consortium, that could monitor conditions in the factories on behalf of the governments in question. As with the creation of the WRC and DSP, this cycle of innovation took place in the face of a new challenge, but it was a challenge that the movement deliberately sought out—a migration to a new type of political opportunity structure (city and state governments)—rather than a challenge thrust on it by the intransigence of its opponents, as was the case with the creation of the WRC and DSP. The challenge for SweatFree Communities was how the strategic models developed by USAS and the WRC could be adapted to this new social environment while remaining true to the anti-sweatshop movement's ideology of worker empowerment.

An Overview of SweatFree Communities

Just as USAS had its roots in independent efforts by student activists on multiple college campuses to get their schools to do something about the issue of sweatshops, SweatFree Communities grew out of local movements in a number of cities and states. Unlike USAS, which developed its strategy of seeking to use codes of conduct for college licensees on behalf of workers after it began to come together as a national network, the local groups that came together to found SweatFree Communities as a national organization had already been pursuing sweat-free purchasing policies locally. For instance, Bjorn Claessen (interview), the director of Sweat-Free Communities when I conducted the interview in 2007, got his start in the movement in 1996 on the staff of the Central American solidarity group Peace through Inter-American Community Action (PICA), based in Bangor, Maine, which had started a sweat-free purchasing campaign in its town. He worked with PICA on this campaign for nine years, during which time similar struggles cropped up around the country, some targeting city governments; some pressuring school boards over school uniforms; and some trying to get religious congregations to make sweat-free purchases. A variety of groups were involved with these efforts, ranging from Central American solidarity groups such as PICA to labor unions and progressive religious groups. As more of these groups emerged, they began to network and hold conference calls. Their first face-to-face conference was in 2002; in 2003, they received the funding to start Sweat-Free Communities as a national organization and hire Claessen as its first staff member.

SweatFree Communities shared the ideology of worker empowerment and solidarity found in other anti-sweatshop groups, such as USAS. Like USAS, the members of SweatFree Communities came to see the importance of worker empowerment through deliberation among themselves. The trigger for the discussions among the national board of SweatFree Communities was requests from companies such as American Apparel for endorsement as sweat-free. According to Claessen (interview), American Apparel was problematic because it

> pay[s] much, much more than any other garment factory in Los Angeles does, and it has some decent benefits. It turns out, however, that they are vehemently anti-union and, frankly, the owner is a little bit crazy and a megalomaniac. [. . .] He sees himself as a savior for the poor immigrants. [. . .] He adamantly opposes his workers having a union and put down UNITE's attempt to [orga-

nize them] a few years ago. [. . .] They were pretty forceful in terms of telling workers that if you vote for the union, we're going to shut down. We're going to go to Mexico or China.[1]

In response, Claessen said, SweatFree Communities had to make some decisions:

What are the standards? Is it enough that you're not abusive and that you pay a decent wage? How important is it that there is a general respect for workers and their rights? Certainly, I think on the board of SweatFree Communities as an organization we are unanimously in favor [. . .] of workplaces that have genuine rights for the workers to organize and to bargain collectively.

As with USAS, part of this support for worker empowerment means "taking part of our direction and taking our cue from the workers in the communities themselves" (Bartlett interview).

More specifically, SweatFree Communities' goal was to get cities to pass sweat-free purchasing laws, requiring the companies that supply the city government with uniforms to meet certain labor standards, closely paralleling the codes of conduct USAS instituted on college campuses, and to create a consortium similar to the WRC, something the organization succeeded in when it founded the SweatFree Purchasing Consortium in May 2010.

SweatFree Communities' leadership came from a very active national board, whose members consulted with one another monthly via conference calls and once a year at a face-to-face meeting before the organization's larger annual conference. The board members represented a range of activist groups who had been working on the issue of sweat-free purchasing ordinances for some time. Some represented local groups, such as the Milwaukee Clean Clothes Campaign; others represented national organizations such as UNITE HERE (SweatFree Communities 2011). One of the board members, Andrew Kang Bartlett (interview), a representative of the Presbyterian Church Hunger Program, described the setup this way: "Usually the bigger strategy questions are done face-to-face at the board meetings prior to the conferences, where we look at the strategic plans for the year. [. . .] It's really at those face-to-face meetings where we'll make longer-term directional decisions in the process, which [are] then [. . .]

---

1. American Apparel's board eventually fired the owner, citing numerous examples of problematic behavior (Edwards 2015).

honed and further developed throughout the year during the monthly calls." Like USAS, the SweatFree Communities board made decisions through a consensus-oriented, deliberative process that fostered creative thinking.

SweatFree Communities also paralleled USAS in that one of the national office's main jobs was to support local organizing. Liana Foxvog (interview) described her work as SweatFree Communities' national organizer as "supporting [local groups] through developing resources, through maintaining a website, to compiling all their work on the website, to bringing them together in workshops and conferences and conference calls [. . . ,] to [. . .] provide training, to strategize, to bring groups together for networking, to develop shared visions and strategies." Foxvog might provide advice on anything from "how do you start a group when you're only one person?" to the technical details of how to word a sweat-free purchasing law. SweatFree Communities also hosted monthly conference calls in which anyone involved in a local organizing campaign could participate, facilitating the crucial exchange of information and experience. And there was the annual conference. Like USAS, SweatFree Communities' national organization played a central role in spreading the knowledge necessary for local activists to successfully strategize as they sought to pressure city and state governments.

The Political Opportunity Structure in City Governments

Electoral Coalitions

Just as we needed to examine the political economy of higher education to understand the political opportunity structure within which USAS operated, we need to examine the political economy of local governments to understand SweatFree Communities and its strategy. Although SweatFree Communities operated at both the city and state level, here I focus on city politics, because the majority of the group's campaigns took place at the city, not the state, level. Thus, that was the social arena that shaped their basic strategic model. In addition, both the POS and strategic models seem to have been very similar at the city and state level, particularly in small states. On scaling up from the early sweat-free purchasing campaign in Bangor to the state as a whole, Claessen (interview) said, "It involved a little bit more traveling. It involved broadening the coordinating group. But the basic grassroots strategy was intact."

A number of scholars of the workings of city governments (Ferman 1996; Levin-Waldman 2005; Stone 1989; Stone, Orr, and Imbroscio 1991) have concluded that city governments are quite variable in their structure, falling on a spectrum between those that are dominated almost totally by business to others that are more pluralistic, with a broad range of interests represented. In some of the latter, progressive groups may be able to form governing coalitions, although even in such cities business interests still have disproportionate influence due to their control of key resources. When analyzing the governing coalition of a city, it is important to look not only at those in public office but also at businesses and business groups such as the chamber of commerce, foundations, labor unions, community-organizing groups, churches, and other nonprofits— all of which can mobilize resources or votes in support of the election of allied officials or carry out specific projects to reshape the city, whether by promoting affordable housing or through gentrification.

Such governing coalitions form a key element of the political opportunity structure within which SweatFree Communities campaigns had to operate at the local level. Those cities with largely progressive governing coalitions were the ones in which SweatFree Communities was most likely to meet with success, although such success was by no means guaranteed. Activists still had to mobilize leaders and members of groups who formed key parts of electoral coalitions to pressure elected city officials to support sweat-free purchasing laws. Still, the chances for success were much greater in such cases than in cities led by business-oriented governing coalitions, where either most of the population was unorganized and thus not easily mobilized or a strategy had not yet been found that would allow the movement to get a foot in the door of city politics.

Uniform Companies and Purchasing Departments

As one might expect, SweatFree Communities faced resistance to the passage of sweat-free purchasing ordinances from the companies that supplied city governments with their uniforms. The corporations SweatFree Communities clashed with were different from the high-profile brands, such as Nike and Reebok, with which USAS frequently had to deal. While uniform companies such as Cintas certainly care about their reputation, because they do not deal directly with the consumer public, brand image is nowhere nearly as important to them as it is to companies such as Nike and Reebok. Consequently, SweatFree Communities was much less concerned with publicly delegitimating these firms and focused instead on the leverage it could exert when a critical mass of cities and states signed on to the SweatFree Purchasing Consortium. Another wrinkle was that purchasing officials typically use local vendors that, in turn, purchase the uniforms from major apparel companies. Local sourcing is often a result of city laws that promote supporting local businesses. The local vendors, however, are generally small businesses and relatively powerless in the bigger picture. In some cases, SweatFree Communities found it possible to win these vendors over (Claessen interview, personal communication [2011]).

Winning the big, transnational uniform companies over, as one might expect, was quite a different matter. While representatives of uniform companies sometimes testified before elected city officials in opposition to sweat-free purchasing laws, they generally did not oppose the laws directly. Instead, they acted primarily through a key ally within the city government bureaucracy: the head of the Purchasing Department or Procurement Department. Thus, this official was another center of power with which SweatFree Communities had to deal. Purchasing/Procurement Department officials had their own reasons for resisting sweat-free purchasing ordinances: such ordinances would make their jobs more complicated. They also had close ties with the companies that supplied the uniforms and thus were willing to look out for their interests (Church, Claessen, and Schwartz interviews). If the officials decided to actively oppose sweat-free purchasing ordinances, they could undermine the success of a campaign. As Claessen (interview) told me, "If the purchasing people are adamantly opposed, it's all in vain."

One simple way that SweatFree Communities tried to address these issues was by addressing Purchasing/Procurement Department officials' concerns about the complexity sweat-free ordinances would add to their job by meeting with them and keeping them in the loop about what they were trying to accomplish. After activists engaged in some discussion with Purchasing/Procurement Department heads to educate them about the nature of sweatshops and how deeply rooted they are in the apparel industry, some became sympathetic to SweatFree Communities' goals (Church and Schwartz interviews). As Claessen (interview) noted:

> We're trying [as of 2007] to develop a network of supportive government purchasing people, bureaucrats who are responsible for this stuff. [. . .] Right now there are maybe three or so, but we want to grow this group of purchasing officials so we can really network with purchasing officials in cities where there are some concerns. We will link them to colleagues in other cities who can tell them, "Look, this can work. This is doable. This is how we did it."

To further simplify matters for Purchasing/Procurement Departments, the activists worked with the city government of Madison, Wisconsin, in

2014 to develop a model sweat-free purchasing contract. This is a "cooperative" or "piggyback" contract, meaning that any other government agency in the United States can use it as is, removing the need for other city governments or interested agencies (such as school districts) to jump through hoops to create their own contracts. The hope of activists was that having the Madison cooperative contract as a common standard would ease acceptance of sweat-free purchasing laws among apparel firms, since the criteria they would have to meet would not vary city by city but be universal (Chen 2014; SweatFree Purchasing Consortium 2016b).

Sweat-Free Purchasing Campaigns

Like USAS, SweatFree Communities had a basic strategic model that it disseminated to local activists, although this basic model would need to be tailored to the peculiarities of each city or state where a campaign to pass sweat-free purchasing legislation took place. In some ways, the SweatFree Communities model resembled USAS's model in that there was an emphasis on an initial phase involving educational activities to raise awareness and coalition building. However, this coalition building included not only other activist groups but also officials, both elected and appointed, in the very governments being targeted by the campaign. On the one hand, this was a practical necessity, since SweatFree Communities needed allies in the city government who could formally propose the sweat-free purchasing ordinance as a law and then vote for it. On the other hand, city governments—at least in most of the cities where SweatFree Communities has been active—were different from the majority of college administrations in that there were often progressive city officials who, perhaps with some persuasion, were quite willing to actively support the sweat-free campaign.

Although the SweatFree Communities activists might escalate their actions after this phase, the second phase did not involve the sit-ins or hunger strikes in which USAS campaigns often culminated. Instead, they relied on mobilizing their coalition to pressure city officials through such means as constituents' contacting officials to express their support for sweat-free purchasing legislation. While SweatFree Communities' organizers did sometimes stage rallies in support of legislation, they were not the disruptive affairs of a late-stage USAS campaign. Instead, they were designed to attract media attention, both to educate city residents and to pressure elected officials by showing them that there was broad-based, popular support for a sweat-free purchasing ordinance.

These differences in strategy are a result of the differences in the local political opportunity structure, particularly the need to build alliances with city officials. On the one hand, a sit-in in the Mayor's Office would have had a different dynamic from sitting in at a college administration building, one that might actually make it more difficult for SweatFree Communities to achieve its goals. Claessen (personal communication [2011]) noted, "The people we would be targeting in a sit-in are the people we need to gain the trust of and work together with" to develop a long-term relationship to create the SweatFree Purchasing Consortium. On the other hand, elected officials are vulnerable in ways college presidents are not, precisely because they are elected. This gave SweatFree Communities activists leverage over city officials that students simply do not have over college administrators: the threat that they could actually help remove them from office if they were not supportive of the movement's goals. The relatively democratic governance structure of a city (at least as compared with a college or university) creates a different political opportunity structure, which, in turn, created both the possibility and the necessity for a different strategy. One thing this meant was that building broad-based coalitions was even more crucial to the success of SweatFree Communities at the local level than it was for USAS because these coalitions—rather than sit-ins and hunger strikes—became the city-based activists' main means of exerting leverage.

In many ways, educational work and coalition building went hand in hand. Foxvog (interview) summarized the process by saying:

> You're meeting with a number of organizations, seeing how they see their work linked into the sweat-free campaign. You're talking to them about the goals and so forth and doing educational events in the community—having a display at a bookstore about the sweat-free campaign, holding movie nights and film screenings, and [. . .] meeting with the city councilors.

In Portland, Oregon, for instance, such events included the city premiere of the film *Maquilapolis* (about activist sweatshop workers in Tijuana, Mexico) and a house party featuring Carmencita "Chie" Abad, a former sweatshop worker in Saipan who was working with the human rights group Global Exchange (Schwartz interview).

Another important role of educational events such as film screenings was to attract media attention. While SweatFree Communities (unlike USAS) has not yet succeeded in attracting a good deal of national media attention, it did succeed in getting attention from local media in its cities. As with USAS, such press coverage was integral to building support for and legitimating its campaigns. In addition, events such as the premiere of *Maquilapolis* provided journalists with the all-important event they needed as a hook on which to hang a story about some larger issue.

The goal of organizers was to draw in as broad a range of supporters as possible, with the recognition that some groups would be more actively involved than others but that all could provide some form of support. Valerie Orth (interview) of the progressive human rights group Global Exchange, who was the lead organizer for the sweat-free campaign in San Francisco, told me:

> By the end of the campaign, we had fifty-six organizations that were community-based, faith-based, student-based organizations, labor unions and organizations obviously—they were across the board. The idea was to have as broad a coalition as possible, which, of course, impressed the city that they had all kinds of new people coming into City Hall. It wasn't just, like, the usual political-type people. We even had the sex workers in our coalition.

Another important group with whom SweatFree Communities activists did educational work was city officials. Even progressive city officials were very busy and not necessarily well informed about the issue of sweatshops—thus, the need to meet with them and educate them about the importance of the topic, to move them from being potential to active allies. Deborah Schwartz (interview) of the Portland SweatFree Campaign noted:

> Companies say, "Look we have this code of conduct, and it calls for the right to organize, antidiscrimination, etc." One thing that we've done throughout the campaign is that we've used that notorious example of Cintas. We were able to pull out Cintas's code of conduct and articles on workers' deaths they've had on the job, huge [Occupational Safety and Health Administration] violations, large lawsuits. "Let's look at this code of conduct and what they're professing to stand for, and let's look at the reality of the code of conduct implementation. By many different levels this is not effective, and it's not the true word." So going beyond the paper code of conduct to what does it take to enforce those standards, that means looking at implementation, and monitoring is really big. That's a huge myth that we had to address with the director of purchasing in Portland.

Because the purchasing director was affiliated with a green purchasing consortium, he had trouble believing that Portland could be involved in unethical purchasing practices in the form of sweatshops.

In the next phase, the coalitions that activists put together become crucial. The escalation phase could certainly include protests. For instance, Schwartz (interview) described one protest in Portland:

> We had this rally which was covered by ten different media outlets. We were really able to connect the local and international leaders. We had a Salvadoran immigrant who works for UNITE HERE in Portland, we had the vice president of the Portland firefighters' union, two international workers, and the state commissioner of labor speak.

Such protests were geared toward showing elected officials the breadth of support for the coalition. Brian O'Shaughnessy (interview), a SweatFree Communities member active in New York State, said:

> It's one of those things that we would have had to do demonstrations with the former [conservative] governor because you have to get their attention, you have to get them to sit down and negotiate. My experience with organizing and demonstrating is the whole purpose is to get to the negotiating table. We are already at the negotiating table with this new [more progressive] governor's staff, so we don't plan on demonstrations, though it might be needed at some point.

There were additional ways to show popular support. One was bringing representatives of various constituencies to meet with city officials. Sarah Church (interview) of the Progressive Jewish Alliance, who was active in the San Francisco SweatFree Coalition, described the significance of involving leaders of such constituencies as the Jewish community:

> Elected officials may not know the percentage of supporters of sweat-free procurement ordinances in their city. You have to break it down for them. They do know the demographics—the percentage of Jews in our community. And they do know that you can quantify how many people belong to a particular synagogue, so if you get a rabbi signed on for a support letter, for example, that rabbi represents symbolically—and in many cases, actually—the potential support of that whole constituency, which could be thousands of families. So with elected officials you need to break down who their constituency is and let them know what their constituents think about this.

A similar dynamic was at work with the leaders of other constituencies, whether they were religious, labor, or other groups. When elected officials saw groups that were key members of the coalitions that help get them elected to office, they were far more likely to be responsive to the campaign. They knew that if they did not support policies that those groups backed, they risked losing their support in future elections—and, thus, losing their office. This is not to say that elected officials were driven entirely by a mercenary calculus of how they could get reelected. Many genuinely cared about progressive causes. But seeing that their supporters were actively pushing for a progressive cause could prompt them to give it a higher priority than they might otherwise have in their very busy agendas.

In the case of those city officials who proved reluctant to support sweat-free purchasing legislation, the movement could then mobilize its coalition to bring pressure to bear. When City Commissioner Sam Adams of Portland stopped returning Schwartz's calls and was trying to avoid her, the campaign pressed him to support the sweat-free ordinance more proactively:

> We organized a sign-on letter of various grass-top leaders through-out Portland and the State of Oregon—faith [leaders]; labor leaders, including some labor leaders that had donated heavily to his campaign in the past. [. . .] We sent that letter to the press, which ran an article entitled something like, "Anti-Sweatshop Activists Losing Patience." [In t]he next day or so, we got a call from Adams's office saying, "He wants you to come in." We came in, and one of the first things he said was "I'm really concerned about that article that was in the paper." I think that's really been steadfast in our campaign, our use of media. [. . .] He's scheduled to announce this month [September 2007] that he's running for mayor. So really using him as a vulnerable candidate and a vulnerable target has been extremely, extremely useful. (Schwartz interview)

Many times campaigners were able to combine such outside pressure on elected officials with inside pressure from officials who were firmly committed to the campaign. Claessen cited an example from San Francisco, where the mayor and other officials who had been supportive in passing the bill became less so in implementing it:

> At the same time this is going on, the city of San Francisco is a very active participant in this joint consortium steering committee. We

have a good working relationship with the city of San Francisco staff [. . .], the Mayor's Office, Labor Enforcement Office. Then the activists in San Francisco put out an alert, saying, "Call the mayor. Tell him to tell stop gutting the anti-sweatshop law." And, of course, we are, in the first place, an organization that links and connects the activists, so we put out that same alert. It was a tenuous balance. [. . .] It actually worked out to this point. It turns out that, well, some of the city officials felt a little bit taken aback by the alert, at this point having actually pledged funding toward our efforts to organize the consortium. Other city officials [. . .] actually welcomed that alert because it helped them with the other city officials. It's a very interesting relationship. (Claessen interview)

Strategic Innovation

In developing their strategy, the members of SweatFree Communities looked to USAS, the WRC, and the DSP as models of what they wanted to accomplish. They recognized that they did not need to reinvent the wheel, just adapt it to somewhat different terrain. Commenting on the process of deciding to pursue the consortium model, Eric Dirnbach (interview) of UNITE HERE, one of SweatFree Communities' board members, said:

I think there was a bit of discussion about whether that was the right thing to do, but I think everyone recognized that it was. It was easy to recognize that because we had the WRC as a model. [. . .] Everybody in this field recognizes the great strides that they've made, and there's really no alternative to doing that kind of bringing together of cities and states. Otherwise everyone's left on their own and is not able to enforce their ordinance, and we can't have that.

The trick would be adapting this model to the peculiarities of working with city and state governments while preserving the basic purpose of setting up a monitoring system that would empower workers by fostering the growth of independent unions.

As with the creation of the WRC, the practicalities of enforcing pro-labor codes of conduct on uniform companies played an important role in creating a consortium through which city governments could work together and, later, the Madison model cooperative contract. According to Claessen (interview):

Right now [as of 2007], the city of Los Angeles is the only one that actually has a contract for monitoring with the Worker Rights Consortium. It cost them $50,000 to have that contract, so there are a couple of issues here. One is the number of smaller entities that could not pay that kind of money for independent monitoring. But even with that said, the more important issue is that even though the city of Los Angeles has decided to pioneer this effort, on their own together with the WRC, they won't have the kind of impact that we need to have on the industry.

Just as USAS needed to enlist a critical mass of schools to make its codes of conduct and the WRC's monitoring efforts effective, SweatFree Communities needed to get a critical mass of city and state governments involved to make the SweatFree Purchasing Consortium a reality.

Underlying this attempt to adapt the model developed by USAS and the WRC was a shared commitment to the ideology of worker empowerment. Schwartz (interview) explained SweatFree Communities' goal as

challenging the idea, which is so prevalent in free-market doctrines, of going with the lowest bidding and instead asserting the idea that the lowest bidder does not represent what's beneficial to us as a society [. . .] and that we can envision what other values [. . .] that go into the making of a product should be. [. . .] Ultimately, consolidating and shifting power to workers, providing incentives to cities and states to consolidate purchasing where they are independent, democratic unions—we can even get to the place where we have worker-controlled cooperatives. Instead of looking at the lowest bidder, we have to move to a new set of standards.

Following from this, Foxvog (interview) said:

So our strategy and plan really comes from a place that recognizes that consumers need to know where their clothes and other products are coming from [. . .] and workers also need to have a way to be connected to those consumers, share what's really happening on the ground in order for there to be a way to really leverage resources to support worker struggles at those critical moments when the people who struggle need that support.

This explanation closely parallels the explanations many USAS members gave for what they sought to accomplish.

Significantly, SweatFree Communities did not simply adapt what USAS and its allies had already accomplished. Rather, even as the DSP was under development, the members of SweatFree Communities incorporated it into their model for their own consortium. Orth (interview) recounted what happened in San Francisco after the activists knew their sweat-free purchasing law would pass in August 2005:

> The next day, I meet with all these key actors in the sweat-free movement across the country, who all flew to my office in San Francisco. We sat downstairs, and I heard, "Well, actually, this isn't really the best solution. [. . .] That factory closed, and things were not panning out for the sweat-free strategy." I kind of already knew that, but just hearing it flat out, I was, like, "Well, great. I just spent the past year, day in and day out, working on passing this strong policy in San Francisco, and now we know it's not going to work." So then it was, like, "Well, what's the consortium like? Let's talk about a consortium. Let's talk about a Designated Suppliers Program for uniforms, for cities and states, counties and school districts."

The city of Madison's 2014 model purchasing contract also incorporated a number of hard-learned lessons from the WRC, DSP, and Accord on Fire and Building Safety in Bangladesh. It requires full disclosure of all details at all stages of the production process, "allowing city authorities to oversee factories' compliance with national rules on wages and benefits, child labor, employment discrimination and maternity leave, fire and building safety codes, and overtime and maternity leave rules" (Chen 2014). As with the DSP, companies covered by the Madison contract had to take proactive steps to make it clear to their workers what their rights were and that these rights would be respected by their employers. As with the WRC and the accord, the Madison contract rejected the idea of allowing firms to rely only on internal corporate social responsibility programs, owing to the inherent conflict of interest. Instead, participating companies had to channel their funds into the participating government agencies to allow them to oversee the monitoring properly under the auspices of the Sweat-Free Purchasing Consortium (Chen 2014).

It should be clear from Orth's discussion of incorporating elements from the DSP that, in adapting USAS's overall strategy, the sweat-free purchasing movement was not doing so from a distance. Rather, it was embedded in the network that composed the U.S. anti-sweatshop movement, engaging in dialogue with other groups as they sought to expand the movement's reach into new social arenas. This was crucial in helping the activists understand how they needed to go about adapting USAS's strategic model to city and state governments: that it was not enough simply to have codes of conduct; that it was necessary to have a consortium of local governments that could monitor the implementation of the codes; and that because simple monitoring had limits to what it could achieve, something like the DSP was needed. From the outside, the accomplishments of USAS and the WRC look quite impressive in that they helped sweatshop workers in difficult conditions unionize in a number of cases. A more detailed knowledge of these campaigns—particularly of the ephemeral nature of the victories—led to a more nuanced understanding of the strengths and weaknesses of the existing strategy and the need for innovations such as the DSP. SweatFree Communities' close contacts with other groups allowed it to learn about the DSP even as the program was being developed and incorporate it into SweatFree Communities' consortium model rather than finding out about the limitations of traditional monitoring the hard way and having to look for solutions to these limitations on its own.

One interesting aspect of the adaptation process that shows SweatFree Communities was consciously building on the work of USAS and the WRC was its choice to focus initially on uniforms even though the bulk of what city and state governments purchase is electronics and food, not apparel. SweatFree Communities chose to start by targeting the uniform companies because the movement as a whole was more familiar with the workings of the apparel industry; after it successfully created a model for local governments to demand accountability for working conditions in the apparel industry, SweatFree Communities hoped to extend it to other industries doing business with the local governments (Claessen and Foxvog interviews).

Adapting the codes and monitoring strategic model of USAS to city and state governments necessitated some tinkering to fit the new political opportunity structure: the social arenas of city and state governments. In particular, SweatFree Communities had to adapt to the necessity of building coalitions not only with other social movement organizations but also with government officials. Specifically, SweatFree Communities needed to alter the governing structure of its monitoring consortium to meet the expectations of city and state officials, even those who were the movement's allies. In particular, as a matter of public policy, government officials—even those who were highly supportive of the SweatFree Communities campaign—could not agree to a governance structure similar to that of the WRC, in which college and university officials held only one-third of the seats on the board of directors. Government officials had to control a majority of the seats. Nor could they simply form a consortium. Again, as a matter of public policy a city or state government must, at least formally, allow different entities to bid for the right to monitor factories where uniforms are produced.

As a result, a significant part of Claessen's job was working with allied government officials to develop a structure for the consortium that was acceptable to them but still was consistent with the goals of the anti-sweat-shop movement. Claessen and Foxvog (interviews) formed an interim steering committee made up of anti-sweatshop activists and supportive public officials to develop a mutually acceptable structure for the consortium. That way, they could be sure that the consortium's design met basic principles of the anti-sweatshop movement, as well as the concerns of government officials. Once they had such a design, they were in a better position to persuade city and state government members who were reluctant to support strong sweat-free policies to sign on.

Despite SweatFree Communities' willingness to compromise with government officials on the design of the consortium, Claessen (interview) noted there were some places where it would not do so: "The last phone call, we had [. . .] some people entertaining the possibility that businesses be on the board. That's a complete non-starter for us because of the conflict of interest." Here we can see the importance of the movement's ideology, especially its social analysis of the structural problems of the apparel industry, shaping the discussions it had with government officials.

What these examples show is a process of dialogue at work in the formation of the SweatFree Purchasing Consortium. It took place between anti-sweatshop activists and sympathetic government officials who were pooling two different bodies of knowledge. The anti-sweatshop activists were drawing on the extensive social analysis developed by the movement network of which they were a part, an analysis explored throughout this book that looks at how the structure of the apparel industry fosters sweatshops and pinpoints worker empowerment through unions as the solution. What the government officials brought to the conversation was insider knowledge of how city governments work and the standards any sweat-free purchasing legislation and monitoring consortium would have to meet to have a realistic chance of becoming law. The result was something like and yet unlike the WRC and DSP, taking advantage of the groundbreaking work that had been done to design them but adapting the design to a new social arena.

Implementing Sweat-Free Purchasing

Since I interviewed SweatFree Communities members in 2007, they have made significant steps forward, the most important of which was the formal foundation of the SweatFree Purchasing Consortium in May 2010, despite the ongoing economic crisis, which put a severe crimp in city and state governments' ability to fund such an entity. At the same time, Sweat-Free Communities faces a number of challenges in seeing its vision implemented, at both the local level and the national level.

Local Challenges to Implementation

The biggest problem at the local level is that it is one thing to get a sweat-free purchasing ordinance passed and another to get it actually implemented. Many other campaigns, such as those for living-wage laws, face similar difficulties in seeing new legislation they have supported actually put into practice instead of being neglected. Dirnbach (interview) told me:

> I think it's a lack of money and a lack of attention. This kind of stuff will never be the priority for a city or for a state. We have to make it a priority. So once you pass an ordinance or a law or an executive order, it will often languish unless activists make the city and state pay attention to it. Oftentimes it's such an effort to get these things passed that the coalition will say, "OK, we're done," and fall apart. But as we know now, that's really just the beginning of the effort. [. . .] You really need to keep the cities and states honest and make sure they're enforcing it.

One particularly striking example of this occurred in San Francisco. When the city's Purchasing Department solicited bids for uniforms after the ordinance passed, it discovered that none of the vendors for 70 percent of the potential contracts was fully compliant. The Purchasing Department decided that, given this, it should just follow the traditional criterion of going with the vendor that could produce a high-quality product for the lowest cost. Activists protested this decision, arguing that although none of the vendors was fully compliant, some came much closer than others, so the Purchasing Department should use them. While the activists' position might have been more consistent with the spirit of the sweat-free ordinance, their position had no legal basis in the ordinance. What was particularly worrisome to the anti-sweatshop campaigners was that such contracts would last three to five years, so even if the ordinance was amended to require the city to use the most compliant bidder when none was fully compliant, there would be a large chunk of the city's business on which they would not be able to have any impact for several years (Claessen and Orth interviews). This was the situation that led members of the sweat-free campaign in San Francisco to mobilize pressure on the mayor (as discussed above), even as the city was contracting with the WRC to monitor the 30 percent of the contracts for which compliant bidders could be found. The campaign eventually paid off: in November 2007, a couple months after I completed my interviews, the city's Board of Supervisors amended the ordinance to require the Purchasing Department to use the most compliant vendor if none was fully compliant (SweatFree Communities 2007).

The success of this campaign—and the successful implementation of sweat-free purchasing laws in most cities—however, relied on having an organized coalition whose members could be mobilized around these issues. As Dirnbach noted, this was hard to maintain once the ordinance passed. Church (interview) said:

> There have been situations where there's been a paid organizer to help facilitate the coalition passing the ordinance. Then their position ends, and they go on to do another job and can't continue to do that work. In some cases, people have continued to do the work because they've been invested in the issue, but they are no longer paid to do that work.

One reason that the coalition was able to remobilize to put pressure on San Francisco's city government when it became clear that the ordinance would not be enforced for 70 percent of the contracts was that the ordinance also established an eleven-person advisory board to oversee its implementation. The board's membership included activists who had campaigned for the ordinance, thus providing a way for the activist community to remain involved in the process. "But a lot of other cities, they didn't get an advisory group," Liana Foxvog (interview) said. "So once the policy was adopted, there wasn't a way for the activists to actually be involved in a formal way of making sure the city was doing the right thing after it was adopted—so then they kind of stopped." Even when an advisory board was present, it consisted of a small core of activists now working from the inside, leaving most of the activist community demobilized around the issue; that, in turn, led to a situation in which it was still challenging to remobilize them when necessary. Another way activists stayed mobilized and engaged with the issue was to expand outward—for instance, many of the activists involved in the San Francisco campaign got involved in the campaign in neighboring Berkeley. Once the sweat-free movement was successful in the city of Austin, it was scaled up to the next high political entity, Travis County (Foxvog interview). This was not necessarily an option in every location, though. Seeing sweat-free ordinances implemented at the local level thus remains a challenge for the movement.

National Challenges to Implementation

The major challenge at the national level was to get the SweatFree Purchasing Consortium up and running. The first meeting at which Claessen and Foxvog met with sympathetic government officials was held in March 2007 in Harrisburg, Pennsylvania. As noted above, the leaders of Sweat-Free Communities were selective about which government officials they worked with at this stage. Just over three years later, the SweatFree Purchasing Consortium was founded, in May 2010, with Claessen temporarily hired as its first staff member even as he continued with SweatFree Communities.

The economic recession that began in 2008 put a major crimp in the plans to start the SweatFree Purchasing Consortium. The consortium could not be funded in the same manner as the WRC—that is, through contributions by its institutional members (colleges in the WRC's case and cities and states in the case of the SweatFree Purchasing Consortium). Instead, the consortium required only a token $500 contribution from its government members and looked for a means to be self-financing. This was done via setting up a supply chain database that detailed the links between the factories that do the actual production; the transnational firms, such as Cintas, that contract out to them; and the vendors who act as middlemen between the big uniform companies and the cities and states. The database also detailed the working conditions at each factory. This allowed vendors who wanted to sell to governments that had joined the SweatFree Purchasing Consortium to determine which companies they could go through and still be in compliance with those cities' and states' legal requirements. To use the database, vendors and governments would need to pay a fee, which, Claessen hoped, would be enough to properly fund the consortium. To do this successfully, SweatFree Communities needed a certain amount of willingness from the industry to disclose this information. The incentive to participate was access: without the information the database contained, vendors would not know whether companies were compliant, and nonparticipating companies would be shut out of participating cities' and states' uniform markets (Claessen, personal communication [2011]).

Another challenge is membership in the consortium, which remains small—only fourteen cities and three states as of June 2017 (SweatFree Purchasing Consortium 2017). The most recent new member is the city of

Santa Fe, New Mexico, which joined in 2012 (SweatFree Purchasing Consortium 2012). Although the consortium controlled $50 million in purchasing power as of 2011, roughly three-fifths of that came from New York State (Claessen, personal communication [2011]). The challenge in expanding the consortium's membership was rooted in the different political opportunity structure in which SweatFree Communities operated compared with that of USAS. While only one-third of the WRC board consists of college representatives (with the other two-thirds consisting of USAS members and labor rights experts), seven of the SweatFree Purchasing Consortium's twelve board members represent government entities, while the remaining five are labor rights experts (SweatFree Purchasing Consortium 2016a). As noted above, this was a condition the movement's government allies needed in return for supporting the consortium. This meant, however, that SweatFree Communities needed to be more selective about which government entities it brought into the consortium. USAS could simply coerce reluctant college administrators into joining the WRC and remain confident that, even if the majority of schools in the WRC had little interest in the issue of sweatshops, the board's structure would guarantee that the organization remained committed to properly monitoring for workers' rights. The SweatFree Purchasing Consortium presented no such guarantees. For related reasons, it also faced the possibility of a loss of members that was less present in the WRC. Wisconsin, for instance, was once a member of the consortium, but when the time came to renew its membership, the state's newly elected Republican governor chose not to (Claessen, personal communication [2011]).

Despite these obstacles, Claessen seemed optimistic in a 2011 follow-up interview about achieving a critical mass of members in the consortium to make it effective. Doing so would probably require building a critical mass of progressive elected officials willing to support them and able to get their governments to join the consortium. Given the current economic climate, though, many such progressive politicians are probably focused on matters of more local concern, a difficulty Claessen acknowledged.

Conclusion

The Future of the Movement

The anti-sweatshop movement set itself the ambitious goal of achieving a restructuring of the global apparel industry in a way that changes the balance of power, taking some away from the lead apparel firms and moving it to independent unions. Along the way, it both achieved successes and hit roadblocks. In assessing any long-term impact of the anti-sweatshop movement, however, it would be a mistake to treat it in isolation. The outsourcing of production—the main structural cause of sweatshops—is embedded in a host of other practices, carried out not only by for-profit corporations but also by multilateral organizations such as the International Monetary Fund (IMF) and World Trade Organization (WTO), numerous government agencies, and even many nonprofit organizations, which together constitute the system of neoliberal globalization. It seems unlikely that the injustices around sweatshops will be righted in the long term without significant changes in the global economy as a whole, not just in outsourcing practices. Anti-sweatshop activists are certainly aware of this: the anti-sweatshop movement is one of the constituent movements of the larger global justice movement, with members of United Students Against Sweatshops attending protests at meetings of the IMF and WTO and other such summits of world leaders intended to manage the global economy along neoliberal lines. Thus, activism around issues of sweatshops is occurring in the context of widespread global— and, in some cases, highly contentious—activism around a broad range of issues, the common denominator of which is opposition to the larger set of policies and practices known as free markets or neoliberalism.

In seeking to transform the global economy, one thing the anti-sweatshop movement will need to come to grips with is that even its most successful efforts involve private regulatory regimes by nonprofit organizations such as the Worker Rights Consortium and the Accord on Fire and Building Safety in Bangladesh. At their best, these nonprofits create a patchwork of "social policy enclaves" (Pearson and Seyfang 2001, 67) in which only some workers in specific sectors of the industry are protected while the majority remain vulnerable to exploitation. Even the Accord on Fire and Building Safety in Bangladesh, though legally binding, covers only those companies that have signed on to it, and a number of prominent companies have refused to do so, preferring the more voluntary (and therefore, in anti-sweatshop activists' eyes, suspect) Alliance for Bangladesh Worker Safety ("Accord, Alliance or Disunity?" 2013; Miller 2014). USAS and the anti-sweatshop movement more broadly have not found a way to overcome this limitation, instead doing what they can to expand the scope of the policy enclaves and strengthen their ability to protect the rights of workers within them, particularly that of freedom of association. This is so not because anti-sweatshop activists prefer private to public, democratic regulation. The opposite is true of most activists. Rather, it is a result of a pragmatic assessment of where they have the ability to exert power. As discussed in Chapter 2, most anti-sweatshop activists would like to see public, democratic regulation of the economy as a complement to their efforts, and those of unions, in protecting workers' rights. However, at this stage of the game, too many governments remain too deeply committed to neoliberalism to make this an immediately feasible goal. Campaigns such as those of SweatFree Communities at least seek to bring the conversation back into the public sphere, even if they deal with governments as consumers rather than as democratic regulators per se.

In the long run, it will most likely be all of the various elements of transnational global justice activism *together* that will force policy makers to enact dramatic reforms not only to production practices but also to a whole host of other issues and, in doing so, bring them back into the domain of public, democratic governance. One also hopes that the wider social context of deepening economic and environmental crises will persuade all but the most dogmatic elites that serious change is necessary. While anti-sweatshop activists may win important victories that concretely improve the lives of specific workers at specific factories in the short run, in the long run, it may simply be the agitation created by the movement and the pressure this puts on the powerful, rather than any specific victory, that produces change.

I am not belittling the work of the anti-sweatshop movement here. Quite the opposite. The more successful the movement is in gaining specific concessions from elites—the executives of companies such as Nike, Adidas, and Cintas—the more it raises the costs of the current economic model. While the Designated Suppliers Program may remain unimplemented, examples such as the Alta Gracia factory in the Dominican Republic and the Accord on Fire and Building Safety in Bangladesh (see Chapter 12) point the way toward alternative ways of doing business, undermining the frequently made claim that there are no alternatives to the neoliberal model. The anti-sweatshop movement's strategic creativity and its ability to win concrete victories will thus be crucial to any major change in the global economy, even if the ultimate form of that transformation is not quite what anti-sweatshop and other global justice activists had in mind.

Social Movement Theory

Over the course of this book, I have sought to unravel the process by which the U.S. anti-sweatshop movement—particularly USAS and the WRC, with some attention to SweatFree Communities—developed its strategy while positioning this process vis-à-vis the wider political opportunity structure in which the movement must maneuver. In doing so, I have drawn on multiple schools of thought in social movement studies, such as those that favor the concept of political opportunity structure and those that favor what they see as a more interactive, less structural model. While these different schools all provide valuable insights, none is able to stand on its own. Nor do any of these theories adequately explain the process by which movements strategize. As an alternative, I have presented a model of strategic development and a revised model of political opportunity structure that draw on the strengths of the different schools I reviewed in Chapter 1, synthesizing them and adding new elements to fill in the gaps.

Social Movement Strategy

Not all movements necessarily think strategically. A number of interviewees I spoke with said that before they connected with the larger anti-sweatshop movement, they had very little idea of what they were doing in terms of strategy. While they might have been adept at organizing a colorful piece of guerrilla theater on campus, they did not know how to link that up with other actions into a larger, overall strategy to effectively pressure their school's administration to adopt certain policies. According to their own testimony, they were taking an approach that focused on individual tactics (specific, modular actions) without looking at how those tactics fit together in a strategic whole. As a result, they were not terribly successful. A strategic approach differs from a tactical approach in that the tactical approach merely considers individual tactics or frames in isolation, without linking them in any coherent way, while a strategic approach finds ways to interlink the individual movement practices into a larger, coherent whole, with the purpose of exercising power against those responsible for social injustice. Doing guerrilla theater alone is merely tactical; doing guerrilla theater in combination with other actions, as part of a larger, thought-out campaign, is strategic.

But the process of strategizing, by which movements fit tactics, frames, and other elements into a larger plan, remains a black box in much of the literature—one I have tried to open in this book. Looking at the process of strategizing—and not just at the final outcome, strategy—can deepen our understanding of why movement actors make the choices they do and why they succeed or fail. The anti-sweatshop movement seems to be particularly adept when it comes to crafting strategy and, so far, to be relatively successful in winning incremental victories. It is entirely possible that other movements cling more dogmatically to strategies that have become outmoded and are less able to adapt as their social environment changes or they encounter unexpected obstacles. Movements that cannot learn from their experiences are likely to be less successful (cf. Koopmans 2005).

My study of the anti-sweatshop movement appears to show a cyclic nature to movement strategizing, in which activists alternate between reliance on established strategic models and, when the movement runs against the limits of what can be accomplished with the current model, a process of strategic innovation. A successful movement is likely to go through several such cycles over the course of its campaigns, not only as it encounters new threats—something previous theorists have stressed— but also as it deliberately seeks out new challenges, as SweatFree Communities did by entering a new social arena.

As noted in Chapter 1, Francesca Polletta (2005) has argued that it is a mistake to draw a distinction between instrumental and value-rational or ideological approaches to strategy, even if one's take is that movements seek to balance the two. Instead, she argues, determining what is instrumentally effective is a culture-laden process that involves a socially constructed interpretation of the world. My findings confirm this: ideology is central to the process of strategizing, not only in defining what a group's values are and therefore the ends it wants to achieve, but also in helping it interpret and analyze the social systems in which it is embedded and the forms of action that might alter those systems for the better. I find it doubtful that a movement without an ideology to help it make sense of the surrounding world could formulate a coherent strategy.

Here we return to the dialectic of experience and ideology that underlies the process of strategic development and innovation in the anti-sweatshop movement. For a movement's strategy to evolve, the movement must both practically experiment by taking action on the basis of existing strategic models and take the time to reflect on those experiences and their outcome through the lens of its ideology. We can see this process at work in the creation of the WRC, the DSP, and the SweatFree Purchasing Consortium. In each case, members of the anti-sweatshop movement took the time to deliberate collectively about their experiences, particularly the obstacles they were running up against, such as the Fair Labor Association, the short-term nature of their victories, or their attempts to move into a new social arena. In doing so, they used their value of worker empowerment and their analysis of the structural nature of the sweatshop problem—their ideology, in short—to understand what was wrong with the current situation and which new directions might make the most strategic sense. At the same time, a subtler process occurred in the creation of the WRC and DSP, where the activists' experiences and reflection on them helped deepen their ideology and made them see more clearly the imperative to empower workers and (in the case of the DSP) of putting the problem of the apparel industry's structure front and center in their thoughts about strategy. Thus, ideology shapes a movement's actions, but reflection on experiences can also shape a movement's ideology.

The emphasis scholars have put on the role of organizations in a movement's success is correct, but they often tend to focus on organizations rather narrowly as mobilizing structures. Certainly, the role organizations play in mobilizing the movement's membership is essential. But movement organizations are also—and equally importantly—decision-making structures and preservers of institutional memory. As Marshall Ganz (2000, 2009) has shown, the way an organization is structured to make decisions can result in crucial differences in the quality of the resulting strategy, with deliberative, participatory structures producing far more innovation than top-down structures that operate by fiat. But not all social movement organizations make their decisions through the sort of participatory, deliberative process that the anti-sweatshop movement does. Many individual labor unions, for instance, still make their decisions internally using top-down methods, which, in Ganz's analysis, results in decisions that are less well thought out and more likely to rely on old strategic models than on new ones adapted to changing social conditions. Movement organization is also essential in creating a system of institutional memory, through which knowledge of the movement's ideology, strategic models, and individual strategic practices—tactics, frames, and so on—can be passed on. Without such institutional memory, each new generation of activists would be forced to reinvent strategy from scratch, greatly slowing the rate of progress by which movements can bring about change. Student movements can be particularly vulnerable to this, given that a generation on a college campus is only four years long.

One important point of disagreement among scholars has been how a movement's strategy translates into success—that is, policy changes on the part of its foes. As noted in Chapter 1, most social movement scholars have argued that it is actions that disrupt the smooth flow of social life that produce results by interfering with elites' ability to carry out business as usual, thus threatening their profits or power (Flacks 1988; Gamson [1975] 1990; McAdam 1983; Piven and Cloward 1977; Tarrow 1998). James Jasper (1997), however, argues that movements win their gains by altering the public discourse, forcing new issues onto the public agenda—issues with which policy makers must then deal. What I have found is that, at least in the case of the anti-sweatshop movement, *both* schools of thought are right. It is not an either-or matter. Whether on campus or on the global stage, the anti-sweatshop movement has needed to change the public debate through skillful framing to get its issues onto the agenda and increase its own legitimacy while damaging that of its opponents. When the movement has established such legitimacy, it has found itself in a better position to use disruptive actions to further its goals. In the absence of such legitimacy, for instance, a campus administration could just arrest students who are engaging in a sit-in; when this legitimacy is present, however, the campus administration has a much bigger problem on its hands and faces potential backlash if it handles the sit-in poorly.

In many ways, disruption and discursive change are two sides of the same coin in numerous cases. For instance, in some cases, causing a target to lose some of its legitimacy can be disruptive in and of itself. To the brand-name apparel companies that are so dependent on their image, a loss in legitimacy means a potential loss in sales, and therefore profits, a crisis for any company. When we look at movements that have succeeded in changing public discourse by putting new issues on the public agenda, often they did so by sufficiently disrupting the normal workings of major social institutions that the news media and authorities had to pay attention to them, even if that attention was disapproving. USAS contributed to a larger change in the political discourse in the United States around the issue of sweatshops through the high-profile sit-ins its members conducted on many college campuses to demand codes of conduct. This forced the apparel companies to respond with a counter-framing of corporate social responsibility.

However, what constitutes disruptive action is, to some extent, socially constructed. In his examination of the changing strategies of the Civil Rights Movement, Doug McAdam (1983) notes that one way actions such as sit-ins and freedom rides worked was by creating a "crisis definition of the situation" among all parties in the conflict—the Civil Rights Movement, its segregationist foes, and the Kennedy and Johnson administrations (reluctant allies of the movement)—as well as in bystander publics, who, for instance, refused to shop in areas where sit-ins were happening because they feared the unpredictable nature of the situation. Some of this can be seen in USAS's actions, as well: at large schools, events such as sit-ins did not necessarily disrupt the smooth functioning of the administration so much as they caused a crisis of legitimacy for school officials.

In addition, as Kenneth Andrews (2001) discusses, these tactics of disruption and discursive change help put the anti-sweatshop movement in a position in which it can negotiate with its opponents while avoiding doing so from a position of weakness where it can be co-opted. While the scholars who study them have often defined movements in terms of their use of disruptive protest, certain types of institutional action are consistent with this disruptive profile. In some cases, such as that of SweatFree Communities, a movement may actually have enough institutional power (by being able to marshal key constituencies at the voting booth, for instance) that this can largely substitute for more traditionally disruptive actions such as sit-ins or strikes. In this regard, Doug McAdam, Sidney Tarrow, and Charles Tilly's (2001) concept of "contentious politics"—politics involving conflict over opposing, controversial positions—that includes a spectrum of actions that range from the *contained* (institutional) to the highly *transgressive* (disruptive) is useful. Even as it acts within the realm of local electoral politics and uses associated tactics such as media events, SweatFree Communities is still involved in significant contention with the apparel firms and their allies in city governments. The lines between what is institutional and what is disruptive action may therefore be somewhat blurry in many cases.

Political Opportunity Structures

Using the U.S. anti-sweatshop movement as a case study, I have tried to give the concept of political opportunity structure more specificity, redefining it as a system that includes not only social structures but also cultural factors and non-movement social actors. This model takes account of Jeff Goodwin and James Jasper's ([1999] 2004) critique of political opportunity structure and their proposal for an alternative approach emphasizing strategic interaction by defining the POS as being constituted by, among other factors, both the social arenas within which conflicts take place and the countermeasures (i.e., the strategic choices and actions) a movement's opponents make in interaction with it in these arenas.

It also addresses Elizabeth Armstrong and Mary Bernstein's (2008) call for a multi-institutional approach to political opportunity structure. By doing so, it speaks to the many critiques made by scholars supportive of the political process model that the concept of the POS is poorly defined and deployed in an ad hoc manner. The roots of the ad hoc approach to POS seem to lie in the fact that, when scholars look at a case study, they focus on those elements of the social environment that are most important to the case in question. While in this study I am still looking at only one case—the anti-sweatshop movement—I am examining how its interactions with its opponents play out across multiple social arenas and social institutions: college campuses, city governments, the transnational apparel industry, and sweatshop factories. Because of this, I have had to develop a model that abstracts elements that appear in all of these social arenas—the concept of a social arena itself, leverage, delegitimation, mobilizing opportunities, and countermeasures. For this reason, this model should be robust enough to work across multiple cases with minimal conceptual adjustment, providing consistent elements that scholars can look for in a movement's social environment that can be understood as constituting the movement's political opportunity structure and significantly reducing the ad hoc nature of the resulting models. The exact elements will, of course, always differ from case to case—the means movements have for exercising leverage or delegitimating their opponents, the particular factors that shape their mobilizing opportunities, the choice of countermeasures their opponents take—but these have also differed from arena to arena within this particular case study. As general social patterns, however, they are consistently important in movements' struggles across multiple social institutions.

At first appearance, this model may seem to drop many of the elements McAdam (1996) and other classic theorists of political opportunity structure include in their models. I discussed how the first element, openness, could be understood in terms of my model in Chapter 1. The second and third elements of McAdam's model, elite factionalism and whether any elite factions are willing to ally with the movement, were not actually significant in this case study. For the most part, the anti-sweatshop movement has dealt with a united front of opposition from the apparel industry. A few college administrations were sympathetic to students' demands, and this was important in allowing them to get a foot in the door, but it does not appear to have stimulated any severe conflict among administrators taking different stances on the issue of codes of conduct. But there are doubtless many other cases out there where such conflicts are much more important than in this one. These conflicts can be examined in terms of how different elite actors deal with not only social movements but also one another within the social arenas in which the conflicts play out.

The fourth element of McAdam's model, the capacity for repression, is captured in my model by the broader concept of countermeasures. What this broader concept highlights is that, while repression is certainly important, a range of other options are available to elites. In this study we have seen that they may, for instance, take the tack of appearing to do something without actually doing something, as in college administrations' creation of committees to study the issue and the apparel industry's adoption of serious-sounding but ineffective corporate social responsibility programs. Such measures can, however, prove effective in framing battles, allowing the authorities to cloak themselves in an appearance of taking action and bolstering their legitimacy.

While I have developed these concepts in the context of a movement with a focus primarily on economic and educational institutions, I would argue that they are also useful for understanding movements that focus on challenging nation-states. If the mass media is the master discursive arena in contemporary society—that is, the arena that has the greatest impact on public discourse in other arenas—as Myra Marx Ferree and her colleagues (2002) argue, the nation-state remains the master policy-making arena, even in the age of neoliberal globalization. Not only have states created the neoliberal laws and policies that have facilitated the rise of economic globalization and given corporations freer rein to exploit vulnerable populations; they also continue to carry out the task of repressing those populations when they rebel. Neoliberalism, for all its adherents' talk of a minimal state, could not exist without the repressive violence of the police and military (Harvey 2005). States are not simple organizations; they consist of multiple, interlocking social arenas. The U.S. state, for instance, has multiple levels (local, state, federal) and branches (legislative, executive, judicial), all of which are venues in which movements can seek to influence decision making (Tarrow 1998). In addition, in the age of neoliberal globalization, the policies of not only nation-states but also multilateral organizations that bring together multiple states matter. Bodies such as the Group of Twenty, IMF, World Bank, and WTO all play a crucial role in creating the global architecture of neoliberalism (Robinson 2003).

It is also worth highlighting the role that local media has played as important discursive arenas in the anti-sweatshop movement. When we think about social movements fighting framing battles with their foes, we most commonly do so in connection with the national mass media. Certainly, this has been important in the case of the anti-sweatshop movement—scandals such as the one in which Kathie Lee Gifford's line of clothing was being made by child workers brought the issue of sweatshops to national attention, galvanizing the movement, and much of the conflict around the creation of the FLA and WRC was fought out as framing battles in the national news media. At the same time, though, USAS always made extensive use of student newspapers and other on-campus discursive arenas, such as teach-ins, to fight its framing battles. Indeed, when the arbiters of the national news media decided that sweatshops were old news and coverage declined, USAS could continue to draw attention to the issue through college-based media. Certainly, this is a smaller audience, but it kept the movement from being silenced altogether in the larger public discourse. Similarly, SweatFree Communities made extensive use of local media coverage. And the framing battles fought in these localized discursive arenas ultimately proved critical to the anti-sweatshop movement's ability to have a global impact by giving the movement the legitimacy to win its demands on campus and then use those successes to exert leverage over transnational apparel firms such as Nike and Reebok.

Unanswered Questions

It is, of course, not a given that, simply because the U.S. anti-sweatshop movement develops its strategy in a particular way, other movements do so. This bears further exploration. One issue that is particularly worth considering is that the majority of people I interviewed were conscience constituents: they were involved in the anti-sweatshop movement because of their ideology, not because they had any immediate material outcome at stake. Groups that have specific, material grievances—people such as sweatshop workers, for instance—may strategize somewhat differently. I would argue, however, that how people understand their material interests is, at least in part, socially constructed—that is, defined through their ideology. Nonetheless, such material grievances do exist independently of ideology. No matter how sweatshop workers choose to interpret the causes and meaning of the conditions under which they work, these conditions are brutal, barely allowing workers to scrape by and perhaps support their families—or they may not even be enough to get by, leading to early deaths from malnutrition or illness. Such material grievances doubtless interact with ideology in some complex way in shaping the strategy of activists in such a position. It would be worth exploring in future research how such interactions play out.

Another issue worth examining is how the process of strategizing plays out in movements where there is less agreement on ideology and strategic models than in the anti-sweatshop movement. In conducting my interviews, I was actually surprised by the levels of agreement I found on these issues among activists in different positions. I actively probed for ideological or strategic disagreements between the student and labor wings of the movement, for instance, but found none of significance. The only thing that came up was a critique by some USAS members of unions' overly hierarchical organization and the resulting limits of their internal democracy. While this is an important issue—and certainly shapes the fortunes of the labor movement as such—it does not seem to have a significant impact on the anti-sweatshop movement itself, since union leaders are usually willing to deliberate as equals with other sectors of the anti-sweatshop movement, including student activists. Other movements, however, have surely had much deeper divides around ideology and strategy. This calls to mind the Civil Rights Movement, with the conflicts between the Southern Christian Leadership Conference and the Student Nonviolent Coordinating Committee over whether the organization of the movement should center on charismatic ministers or be broadly egalitarian and participatory, or the disagreements between advocates of nonviolence and groups such as the Black Panther Party, whose members believed in the importance of armed self-defense. One can also look at the contemporary global justice movement, where there are sometimes contentious debates about whether the best path to social transformation is through the capture and transformation of state power or through the carving out of democratic spaces autonomous from the state. Amin Ghaziani (2008) and Holly McCammon (2012) found in their studies of the organization of four gay rights marches on Washington, DC, and the movement to allow women in the United States to serve on juries, respectively, that ideological diversity was beneficial to the movements they studied. A wider range of ideas enriched the process of deliberation over strategy, resulting in better strategic decision making and greater innovation. Ghaziani does caution that this is not true in all circumstances. Rather, it seems to be true when organizations and coalitions actively seek to foster dissent and deliberation. Those that seek to quash such debate in favor of uniformity drive out those with alternative ideologies and lose the benefits of such diversity.

This study also opens up the question of how social actors other than social movements strategize. The transnational apparel corporations that are the movement's main foes certainly acted in a strategic manner, responding to the actions of anti-sweatshop activists with actions of their own meant to defuse the activists' power. Their actions ranged from the brute repression of sweatshop workers using hired guards and the police to sophisticated framing campaigns involving the creation of corporate-controlled monitoring bodies such as the FLA. In *Getting Your Way*, Jasper (2006) assumes that all social actors, individual and collective—social movements, businesses, militaries, and governments—strategize in basically the same way. My research suggests otherwise. While I have not analyzed in depth how apparel corporations formulated their strategy, what I have analyzed leads me to suspect that they strategize in different ways, given the profoundly different nature of corporations from social movements. They command different sorts of resources, are differently positioned within the social structure, have different amounts of legitimacy, and have different sorts of goals.

For instance, Nike's primary goal is to maximize its profits; a secondary goal—as a means to the first goal—is to maintain a certain brand image. It also seeks to maintain the status quo of the social system, although we cannot assume that this is a conscious goal, as opposed to a taken-for-granted, assumed goal that is implicit in all Nike does without ever being spelled out. Nike may have loyal customers, but it is doubtful that it could mobilize them in the way that a movement mobilizes its members. Instead, Nike relies on the vast sums of money it controls to influence policy makers in other social arenas and to promote its frames in the mass media. In doing so, Nike has legitimacy and leverage that a movement can never hope to achieve simply because Nike is a major corporation. In addition, Nike's leverage comes from institutionalized sources: its ability to command vast amounts of resources, workers around the world, and substantial political influence. Unlike USAS, Nike does not have to disrupt the workings of business as usual to exercise leverage; indeed, as long as business as usual is operating, Nike may need to do very little actively to exert leverage, because other social actors (such as its contractors) often react to the implicit threat that such leverage could be exercised without a word ever being spoken. While the way Nike and other corporations strategize may well bear some resemblance to how social movements strategize—and there may indeed be commonalities in how all social actors strategize—it seems unlikely that corporate, government, or military actors strategize in exactly the same way as social movements. This bears further exploration.

Another question that bears a more in-depth look is how the various elements of the political opportunity structure interact with one another. An obvious example is that the lower levels of repression on college campuses than in sweatshop factories mean that there are much greater mobilizing opportunities in the former social arena that the latter. This, in turn, means that student activists have greater potential leverage and ability to delegitimate their opponents. While this is quite specific to college campuses, many of the particularities of how elements of the POS interact will be specific to each social institution. For instance, there will be differences in how authority is organized: the appointed administrations of colleges versus the elected officials of a city government. This, in turn, shapes the potential forms of leverage that activists can use to pressure these authorities, with USAS and SweatFree Communities consequently choosing significantly different strategies. Indeed, USAS's strategy varied from campus to campus. Some campuses relied more on disruption, and some relied more on delegitimation, depending on local factors.

One particular thing worth examining within this context is what impact the structures, norms, and practices of formal democracy have. We can see that the forms of leverage that SweatFree Communities was able to use were much different from those available to USAS, because Sweat-Free Communities was able to use the threat of the loss of key members of electoral coalitions to pressure people in public office. While the emphasis in the study of social movements has been on their use of extra-institutional tactics, how such extra-institutional means interact with institutional ones bears closer examination. SweatFree Communities certainly did not only go through official channels; its public protests and other such actions were calibrated to get the most of the institutional pressure it could potentially exert through elections. However, SweatFree Communities acts at a very localized level. As the scale increases to the level of the nation-state, the degree to which movements can take advantage of formal democracy, especially of elections (as opposed to civil liberties), seems to fall off significantly, to the point that the anti-sweatshop movement has temporarily written off trying to directly influence national governments and is targeting transnational corporations instead. As discussed in Chapter 2, this is a striking choice, given that such corporations pretend to no semblance of democracy, so one would expect them to be much harder for popular movements to affect. But the actual dynamics seem to be considerably more complicated and deserve closer study.

The range of possible actions that fall under what I refer to as "countermeasures" is quite broad. What the concept is meant to capture is that movements' opponents generally have a wide range of responses they can make to movements—of which various forms of repression are an important but by no means exhaustive subset—and that can have a profound impact on how likely movements are to succeed. Comparative studies that map more exactly not only the types of countermeasures that are possible but also which are most readily available to different social actors and the reasons for this variability would be valuable. Take, for instance, the fact that sweatshop factory owners can engage in repression of workers much more readily than college administrators can with student activists. To what extent is this due to the fact that sweatshop workers are more marginal, oppressed social actors than students? To what extent is this due to the larger social context in which these specific arenas are nested, where U.S. colleges, though not themselves democratic, operate in a wider society where democratic norms of freedom of speech and protest are widely upheld and college officials are expected to accord those rights to their students? Could sweatshop factory owners and managers, if they wished, make use of tactics such as committees to tie people up in red tape or social responsibility programs that paper over problems? Or are those limited to other social actors?

What much of this amounts to is that we need a better understanding of the range of options different social actors have, by virtue of their position in the wider social system, to create, prevent, or manipulate social change. This study presents a number of concepts to help us clarify these matters, but these questions could also be examined from many other angles.

Appendix

Methods and Data

My main source of data for this study is thirty in-depth interviews with activists in the U.S. anti-sweatshop movement, conducted between June and October 2007. Because the people I wanted to speak with were scattered across the United States, I conducted the majority of interviews by phone, though I was able to conduct some face-to-face. I noticed no difference in the quality of the interviews—that is, the interviewees' willingness to speak freely, and so on—whether the interview was by phone or in person. My selection of interviewees was guided by the need to create what Robert Weiss (1994) calls a panel of knowledgeable informants: people who have participated in the events in which I am interested and have knowledge that is otherwise difficult to obtain. Part of my purpose was to reconstruct the history of the movement, including such details as the nitty-gritty of strategic decision making, at the local, national, and transnational levels that do not appear in other accounts of the movement, whether journalistic or scholarly. The intent was also ethnographic, since I wanted to understand not only what happened but also how the interviewees understood the social forces they were up against and the strategic reasons for their actions. Although participant observation might seem to be a more appropriate method for capturing these dynamics, given that when such strategic innovation will happen is unpredictable, interviews provided the best method of capturing the events and allowed me to analyze multiple cycles of innovation.

I started with initial contacts in the leadership of the movement and from there engaged in snowball sampling, which ultimately gave me access to a wide range of activists who at one point or another had played leading roles in the anti-sweatshop movement. They included people in formal staff positions such as USAS's national organizer and the WRC's executive director, as well those who were involved in the national movement as volunteers based on college campuses. For the most part, the interviewees allowed me to use their real names. In a few cases, they asked me to use pseudonyms for particular statements, because they were now in positions in which publicly expressing certain opinions could interfere with their work. These pseudonyms are marked with an asterisk the first time they appear. I did a systematic, detailed coding of all interviews with the aid of the computer program HyperResearch, using a number of themes related to movement strategy and the wider social environment.

In various parts of the book, when discussing various phases and aspects of the movement, I rely on various people. The reason for this is that different people were involved at different times and in different parts of the movement, giving the various interviewees insight into particular slices of the whole that I was investigating. For most phases/aspects of the movement, multiple interviewees were involved, and I was able to triangulate among their perspectives (along with written documents in some cases) to gain a deeper understanding of what happened. In addition, triangulating among different points in the history of the movement allowed me to discern patterns in strategizing that occurred multiple times across the history of the development of the movement's strategy.

Some interviewees seemed more broadly knowledgeable about the movement and the apparel industry as a whole, while some were most familiar with the particular niche of the movement within which they were working, such as the campaign to get city and state governments to pass sweat-free purchasing ordinances discussed in Chapter 13. In some ways, I have leaned heavily on the interviewees who were more broadly knowledgeable, but when focusing on specific niches I leaned heavily on the people who had intimate familiarity with that niche. While this may have produced some subtle biases in my findings, I think the impact of how I relied on different interviewees was minimal, if only because almost every interviewee shared the common ideology of worker empowerment discussed in Chapter 6, and their biases therefore all flowed in the same direction.

As a secondary source of data, I used newspaper articles, various groups' reports and websites, and other such material to reconstruct events in detail. The newspapers included not only those that were available in the LexisNexis database but also college newspapers produced by students, which were crucial in reconstructing USAS's campus organizing. These sources helped me fill in the gaps of the historical narratives that my interviewees shared and allowed me to further triangulate among different accounts of what happened.

For practical reasons of time, finances, and linguistic ability, I confined this study to U.S.-based organizations and did not attempt to study the entire global network of the anti-sweatshop movement. As should be clear from my analysis, though, most of the activists I spoke with had spent a considerable amount of time abroad working with allies in the Global South, and many of the actions of the U.S. anti-sweatshop movement were influenced by feedback from these allies.

In doing the interviews, analyzing them afterward, and writing this book, I have treated my interviewees as experts on the topic of anti-sweatshop activism. While as a trained sociologist I bring a particular sort of expertise to these questions that my interviewees lack, as experienced activists who have often thought a good deal about the causes of sweatshops and the strategy of their movement, they have a practical expertise that I lack. In analyzing how the anti-sweatshop movement has strategized, and particularly what makes for successful strategy in the social contexts in which they work, I have found their insights invaluable. The theory of social movement strategy and political opportunity I develop here is my own, but it builds on the practical insights my interviewees shared with me.

References

"Accord, Alliance or Disunity? Clothing Firms in Bangladesh." 2013. *The Economist*, July 13, pp. 57–58. Accessed June 21, 2016. http://www.proquest.com.

Accord on Fire and Building Safety in Bangladesh. 2015. "Signatories." Accessed June 23, 2016. http://bangladeshaccord.org/signatories.

Alimi, Eitan Y. 2007. *Israeli Politics and the First Palestinian Intifada: Political Opportunities, Framing Processes and Contentious Politics*. New York: Routledge.

Alliance for Bangladesh Worker Safety. 2015. "Membership." Accessed June 23, 2016. http://www.bangladeshworkersafety.org/who-we-are/membership.

Andrews, Kenneth T. 2001. "Social Movements and Policy Implementation: The Mississippi Civil Rights Movement and the War on Poverty, 1965 to 1971." *American Sociological Review* 66:71–95.

Anner, Mark. 2011. *Solidarity Transformed: Labor Responses to Globalization and Crisis in Latin America*. Ithaca, NY: Cornell University Press.

Appelbaum, Richard P., and Peter Dreier. 2005. "Students Confront Sweatshops." *The Nation*, November 28, p. 28.

Appelbaum, Richard P., and Gary Gereffi. 1994. "Power and Profits in the Apparel Commodity Chain." In *Global Production: The Apparel Industry in the Pacific Rim*, edited by Edna Bonacich, Lucie Cheng, Norma Chinchilla, Nora Hamilton, and Paul Ong, 42–62. Philadelphia: Temple University Press.

Armbruster-Sandoval, Ralph. 2005. *Globalization and Cross-Border Labor Solidarity in the Americas: The Anti-sweatshop Movement and the Struggle for Social Justice*. New York: Routledge.

Armstrong, Elizabeth A. 2002. "Crisis, Collective Creativity, and the Generation of New Organizational Forms: The Transformation of Lesbian/Gay Organizations in San Francisco." *Research in the Sociology of Organizations* 19:361–395.

Armstrong, Elizabeth A., and Mary Bernstein. 2008. "Culture, Power, and Institutions: A Multi-institutional Politics Approach to Social Movements." *Sociological Theory* 26:74–99.

Aronowitz, Stanley. 2000. *The Knowledge Factory: Dismantling the Corporate University and Creating True Higher Learning.* Boston: Beacon.

Arvidsson, Adam. 2006. *Brands: Meaning and Value in Media Culture.* New York: Routledge.

Asher, Mark, and Josh Barr. 2000. "Nike Cuts Off Funds for 3 Universities: Schools Claim Firm Is Upset at Their Stance on Labor Practices." *Washington Post,* May 4, p. A01. Accessed April 15, 2009. http://www.lexisnexis.com.

Bandy, Joe, and Jackie Smith, ed. 2005. *Coalitions across Borders: Transnational Protest and the Neoliberal Order.* Lanham, MD: Rowman and Littlefield.

Barrientos, Stephanie, and Sally Smith. 2007. "Do Workers Benefit from Ethical Trade? Assessing Codes of Labour Practice in Global Production Systems." *Third World Quarterly* 28:713–729.

Beitsch, Rebecca. 2018. "#MeToo Movement Has Lawmakers Talking about Consent." *Stateline,* January 23. Accessed June 7, 2018. http://www.pewtrusts.org/en/research-and-analysis/blogs/stateline/2018/01/23/metoo-movement-has-lawmakers-talking-about-consent.

Benjamin, Medea. 2000. "Toil and Trouble: Student Activism in the Fight against Sweatshops." In *Campus, Inc.: Corporate Power in the Ivory Tower,* edited by Geoffrey D. White, 237–252. Amherst, NY: Prometheus.

Bernstein, Mary. 2003. "Nothing Ventured, Nothing Gained? Conceptualizing Movement 'Success' in the Lesbian and Gay Movement." *Sociological Perspectives* 46:353–379.

Blaskey, Sarah, and Phil Gasper. 2012. "Campus Struggles against Sweatshops Continue: Indonesian Workers and U.S. Students Fight Back against Adidas." *Dollars and Sense,* September–October, pp. 6–8.

Bob, Clifford. 2001. "Marketing Rebellion: Insurgent Groups, International Media, and NGO Support." *International Politics* 38:311–334.

Bonacich, Edna, Lucie Cheng, Norma Chinchilla, and Paul Ong, ed. 1994. *Global Production: The Apparel Industry in the Pacific Rim.* Philadelphia: Temple University Press.

Bounds, Wendy. 1997. "Labor: Critics Confront a CEO Dedicated to Human Rights." *Wall Street Journal,* February 24, p. B1. Accessed August 27, 2008. http://www.lexisnexis.com.

Brigham, Nancy. 2003. "The Kukdong/Mexmode Victory and Anti-sweatshop Organizing in the Internet Era." *Guild Practitioner,* July 31. Accessed June 29, 2009. http://proquest.umi.com.

Brooks, Ethel C. 2007. *Unraveling the Garment Industry: Transnational Organizing and Women's Work.* Minneapolis: University of Minnesota Press.

Brown, Garrett. 2015. "Bangladesh: Currently the Worst, but Possibly the Future's Best." *New Solutions* 24:469–473.

Brown, Sarah. 2015. "Guns, Prisons, Social Causes: New Fronts Emerge in Campus Fights over Divestment." *Chronicle of Higher Education,* June 30. Accessed June 12, 2018. https://www.chronicle.com/article/Guns-Prisons-Social-Causes-/231243.

Brulé, Elizabeth. 2015. "Voices from the Margins: The Regulation of Student Activism in the New Corporate University." *Studies in Social Justice* 9:159–175.

Bystydzienski, Jill M., and Steven P. Schacht, eds. 2001. *Forging Radical Alliances across Difference: Coalition Politics for the New Millennium.* Lanham, MD: Rowman and Littlefield.

Carty, Victoria. 2006. "Labor Struggles, New Social Movements, and America's Favorite Pastime: New York Workers Take on New Era Cap Company." *Sociological Perspectives* 49:239–259.

Castells, Manuel. 2001. *The Internet Galaxy: Reflections on the Internet, Business, and Society.* New York: Oxford University Press.

Chen, Michelle. 2014. "How Local Governments Are Using Their Purchasing Power to End Sweatshop Labor." *The Nation,* May 30. Accessed June 12, 2016. http://www.thenation.com/article/how-local-governments-are-using-their-purchasing-power-end-sweatshop-labor.

Clean Clothes Campaign. 2007. "Nike Supplier Closes Unionized Factory, Shifts Work to Vietnam." *PeaceWork,* October, p. 17. Accessed February 16, 2010. http://proquest.umi.com.proxy.bc.edu.

Crossley, Nick. 2008. "Social Networks and Student Activism: On the Politicising Effect of Campus Connections." *Sociological Review* 56:18–38.

Dale, John G. 2008. "Burma's Boomerang: Human Rights, Social Movements and Transnational Legal Mechanisms 'from Below.'" *International Journal of Contemporary Sociology* 45:151–184.

della Porta, Donatella. 2005. "Multiple Belongings, Tolerant Identities, and the Construction of 'Another Politics': Between the European Social Forum and the Local Social Fora." In *Transnational Protest and Global Activism,* edited by Donatella della Porta and Sidney Tarrow, 175–202. Lanham, MD: Rowman and Littlefield.

Designated Suppliers Program Working Group. 2006a. "Designated Suppliers Program—Revised." Worker Rights Consortium. Accessed September 14, 2009. http://www.workersrights.org/dsp.

———. 2006b. "Memo from DSP Working Group to Universities." Worker Rights Consortium. Accessed September 31, 2009. http://www.workersrights.org/dsp.

———. 2006c. "Summary of Modifications to the Designated Suppliers Program, September 29, 2006." Worker Rights Consortium. Accessed September 14, 2009. http://www.workersrights.org/dsp.

Diamond, Sara. 1995. *Roads to Dominion: Right-Wing Movements and Political Power in the United States.* New York: Guilford.

Dietrich, David R. 2014. *Rebellious Conservatives: Social Movements in Defense of Privilege.* New York: Palgrave Macmillan.

Dixon, Marc, Andrew W. Martin, and Michael Nau. 2016. "Social Protest and Corporate Change: Brand Visibility, Third-Party Influence, and the Responsiveness of Corporations to Activist Campaigns." *Mobilization* 21:65–82.

Dolan, Catherine S. 2004. "On Farm and Packhouse: Employment at the Bottom of a Global Value Chain." *Rural Sociology* 69:99–126.

Downey, Dennis J., and Deana A. Rohlinger. 2008. "Linking Strategic Choice and Macroorganizational Dynamics: Strategy and Social Movement Articulation." *Research in Social Movements, Conflicts and Change* 28:3–38.

Downey, Gary L. 1986. "Ideology and the Clamshell Identity: Organizational Dilemmas in the Anti–Nuclear Power Movement." *Social Problems* 33:357–373.

Edwards, Jim. 2015. "Inside the 'Conspiracy' That Forced Dov Charney Out of American Apparel." *Business Insider*, August 21. Accessed June 7, 2016. http://www.business insider.com/dov-charney-forced-out-of-american-apparel-2015-8.

Epstein, Barbara. 1991. *Political Protest and Cultural Revolution: Nonviolent Direct Action in the 1970s and 1980s*. Berkeley: University of California Press.

Esbenshade, Jill. 2004a. "Codes of Conduct: Challenges and Opportunities for Workers' Rights." *Social Justice* 31:40–59.

———. 2004b. *Monitoring Sweatshops: Workers, Consumers, and the Global Apparel Industry*. Philadelphia: Temple University Press.

Evans, Peter B. 1995. *Embedded Autonomy: States and Industrial Transformation*. Princeton, NJ: Princeton University Press.

Fair Labor Association. 2008a. "Board of Directors." Accessed April 28, 2009. http://www.fairlabor.org/about_us_board_directors_d1.html.

———. 2008b. "FLA 3.0." Accessed April 28, 2009. http://www.fairlabor.org/what_we_do_fla_3.0_c1.html.

———. 2008c. "Workplace Code of Conduct." Accessed April 28, 2009. http://www.fairlabor.org/about_us_code_conduct_e1.html.

———. 2012a. "Our Methodology." Accessed June 8, 2014. http://www.fairlabor.org/our-work/our-methodology.

———. 2012b. "Sustainable Compliance Methodology." Accessed August 17, 2015. http://www.fairlabor.org/sites/default/files/sci-factsheet_7-23-12.pdf.

———. 2017. "Affiliates: Colleges and Universities." Accessed May 29, 2017. http://www.fairlabor.org/affiliates/colleges-universities.

Fantasia, Rick, and Kim Voss. 2004. *Hard Work: Remaking the American Labor Movement*. Berkeley: University of California Press.

Featherstone, Liza. 2002. *Students against Sweatshops*. New York: Verso.

Ferman, Barbara. 1996. *Challenging the Growth Machine: Neighborhood Politics in Chicago and Pittsburgh*. Lawrence: University Press of Kansas.

Ferree, Myra Marx. 1992. "The Political Context of Rationality: Rational Choice Theory and Resource Mobilization Theory." In *Frontiers in Social Movement Theory*, edited by A. D. Morris and C. M. Mueller, 29–52. New Haven, CT: Yale University Press.

Ferree, Myra Marx, William A. Gamson, Jürgen Gerhards, and Dieter Rucht. 2002. *Shaping Abortion Discourse: Democracy and the Public Sphere in Germany and the United States*. New York: Cambridge University Press.

Ferree, Myra Marx, and David A. Merrill. (2000) 2004. "Hot Movements, Cold Cognition: Thinking about Social Movements in Gendered Frames." In *Rethinking Social Movements: Structure, Meaning, and Emotion*, edited by Jeff Goodwin and James M. Jasper, 247–261. New York: Rowman and Littlefield.

Flacks, Richard. 1988. *Making History: The American Left and the American Mind*. New York: Columbia University Press.

Flaherty, Colleen. 2013a. "Making the Case for Adjuncts." *Inside Higher Ed*, January 9. Accessed June 8, 2018. https://www.insidehighered.com/news/2013/01/09/adjunct-leaders-consider-strategies-force-change.

———. 2013b. "Northeastern Students Participate in Adjunct-Themed 'Thriller'

Flash Mob." *Inside Higher Ed*, November 1. Accessed June 8, 2018. https://www
.insidehighered.com/quicktakes/2013/11/01/northeastern-students-partici pate-
adjunct-themed-thriller-flash-mob.

———. 2017. "Missing the Mark on Consent." *Inside Higher Ed*, August 14. Accessed June
7, 2018. https://www.insidehighered.com/news/2017/08/14/study-suggests-big-
difference-between-how-college-men-describe-affirmative-consent.

FLA Watch. n.d. "FLA's New Approach to Labor Enforcement Lets Corporations Off
the Hook: A New Spin on the Same FLAws." Accessed June 18, 2014. https://web
.archive.org/web/20070812234712/http://www.flawatch.org/newapproach.htm.

Fourcade-Gourinchas, Marion, and Sarah Babb. 2002. "The Rebirth of the Liberal
Creed: Paths to Neoliberalism in Four Countries." *American Journal of Sociology*
108:533–579.

Fox, Jonathan A., and L. David Brown, ed. 1998. *The Struggle for Accountability: The
World Bank, NGOs, and Grassroots Movements*. Cambridge, MA: MIT Press.

Frank, Thomas. 2004. *What's the Matter with Kansas? How Conservatives Won the Heart
of America*. New York: Picador.

Fraser, Nancy. 2017. "The End of Progressive Neoliberalism." *Dissent*, January 2. Accessed June 15, 2018. https://www.dissentmagazine.org/online_articles/progres
sive-neoliberalism-reactionary-populism-nancy-fraser.

Friedman, Thomas. 2000. *The Lexus and the Olive Tree*, rev. ed. New York: Anchor.

Gamson, William A. (1975) 1990. *The Strategy of Social Protest*, 2d ed. Belmont, CA:
Wadsworth.

Gamson, William A., and David S. Meyer. 1996. "Framing Political Opportunity." In
*Comparative Perspectives on Social Movements: Political Opportunities, Mobilizing
Structures, and Cultural Framings*, edited by D. McAdam, J. D. McCarthy, and M. N.
Zald, 275–290. New York: Cambridge University Press.

Ganz, Marshall. 2000. "Resources and Resourcefulness: Strategic Capacity in the
Unionization of California Agriculture, 1959–1966." *American Journal of Sociology* 105:1003–1062.

———. 2009. *Why David Sometimes Wins: Leadership, Organizing, and Strategy in the
California Farm Worker Movement*. New York: Oxford University Press.

Garwood, Shae. 2011. *Advocacy across Borders: NGOs, Anti-sweatshop Activism, and the
Global Garment Industry*. Sterling, VA: Kumarian Press.

Gaus, Mischa. 2006. "Students vs. Sweatshops, Round III: The Designated Suppliers
Program Targets College Clothing Companies." *In These Times*, August, pp. 31–33.

Gearheart, Judy, and Sarah Newell. 2017. "Nike Signs Factory Access Agreement."
Huffington Post, September 1. Accessed June 20, 2019. https://www.huffpost.com/
entry/nike-signs-factory-access-agreement_b_59a9d7c3e4b0c50640cd5f5a?guc
counter=1&guce_referrer=aHR0cHM6Ly93d3cuZ29vZ2xlLmNvbS88&guce_refer
rer_sig=AQAAAM9XRL54lVUS5-jC7mvvQP23K2j8USI4Tm8ALamscLyF3PZW4H
4ghqVbNHP5boALt5QYGBrifgFqYPR8B0U31pd9vhWEe9waUKonCtwoj8SDh
grAuFVVmjsCfv-tS1Lcsijm9r1mZw8Hj32hiXCnFLvwOiGCMpMP1gLB4tiXZp9u.

Gereffi, Gary. 1994. "The Organization of Buyer-Driven Global Commodity Chains:
How U.S. Retailers Shape Overseas Production Networks." In *Commodity Chains
and Global Capitalism*, edited by Gary Gereffi and Miguel Korzeniewicz, 95–122.
Westport, CT: Praeger.

———. 2001. "Shifting Governance Structures in Global Commodity Chains, with Special Reference to the Internet." *American Behavioral Scientist* 44:1616–1637.

Gereffi, Gary, and Mei-Lin Pan. 1994. "The Globalization of Taiwan's Garment Industry." In *Global Production: The Apparel Industry in the Pacific Rim*, edited by Edna Bonacich, Lucie Cheng, Norma Chinchilla, Nora Hamilton, and Paul Ong, 126–146. Philadelphia: Temple University Press.

Ghaziani, Amin. 2008. *The Dividends of Dissent: How Conflict and Culture Work in Lesbian and Gay Marches on Washington*. Chicago: University of Chicago Press.

Gillan, Kevin. 2008. "Understanding Meaning in Movements: A Hermeneutic Approach to Frames and Ideologies." *Social Movement Studies* 7:247–263.

Gitlin, Todd. 1980. *The Whole World Is Watching: Mass Media in the Making and Unmaking of the New Left*. Berkeley: University of California Press.

———. 2016. "Fossil Fuels Off Campus." *Dissent*, Spring, pp. 32–37.

Goodwin, Jeff, and James M. Jasper. (1999) 2004. "Caught in a Winding, Snarling Vine: The Structural Bias of Political Process Theory." In *Rethinking Social Movements: Structure, Meaning, and Emotion*, edited by Jeff Goodwin and James M. Jasper, 3–30. New York: Rowman and Littlefield.

———, ed. 2012. *Contention in Context: Political Opportunities and the Emergence of Protest*. Stanford, CA: Stanford University Press.

Grasgreen, Allie. 2011. "New Round of Protests on Food Service Provider." *Inside Higher Ed*, May 31. Accessed June 8, 2018. https://www.insidehighered.com/news/2011/05/31/new-round-protests-food-service-provider.

Green, Nancy L. 1997. *Ready-to-Wear and Ready-to-Work: A Century of Industry and Immigrants in Paris and New York*. Durham, NC: Duke University Press.

Greenhouse, Steven. 1998a. "Groups Reach Agreement for Curtailing Sweatshops." *New York Times*, November 5, p. A20. Accessed April 15, 2009. http://www.lexisnexis.com.

———. 1998b. "Two More Unions Reject Agreement for Curtailing Sweatshops." *New York Times*, November 6, p. A15. Accessed April 15, 2009. http://www.lexisnexis.com.

———. 1999a. "Activism Surges at Campuses Nationwide, and Labor Is at Issue." *New York Times*, March 29, p. A14. Accessed January 29, 2009. http://www.lexisnexis.com.

———. 1999b. "Student Critics Push Attacks on an Association Meant to Prevent Sweatshops." *New York Times*, April 25, p. 18. Accessed April 15, 2009. http://www.lexisnexis.com.

———. 1999c. "Students Urge Colleges to Join a New Anti-sweatshop Group." *New York Times*, October 20, p. A23. Accessed April 15, 2009. http://www.lexisnexis.com.

———. 1999d. "Union Criticizes Plant Closing in Guatemala." *New York Times*, February 28, p. 14. Accessed August 27, 2008. http://www.lexisnexis.com.

———. 2000a. "Nike's Chief Cancels a Gift over Monitor of Sweatshops." *New York Times*, April 25, p. A16. Accessed April 15, 2009. http://www.lexisnexis.com.

———. 2000b. "Sweatshop Monitor Invites Corporate Input." *New York Times*, April 29, p. A9. Accessed April 15, 2009. http://www.lexisnexis.com.

———. 2009. "Labor Fight Ends in Win for Students." *New York Times*, November 17, 2009. Accessed August 11, 2011. http://www.nytimes.com/2009/11/18/business/18labor.html.

———. 2010. "Pressured, Nike to Help Workers in Honduras." *New York Times*, July 27, p. B1. Accessed June 20, 2016 http://www.lexisnexis.com.

Grigo, Heather. 2000. "HC Joins Worker Rights Consortium." *Bryn Mawr and Haverford Bi-College News*, February 1. Accessed May 14, 2009. http://www.biconews.com/?p=4396.

Hardisty, Jean. 1999. *Mobilizing Resentment: Conservative Resurgence from the John Birch Society to the Promise Keepers*. Boston: Beacon.

Harvey, David. 2005. *A Brief History of Neoliberalism*. New York: Oxford University Press.

Hermanson, Jeff. 2009. "International Solidarity in the Struggle for Justice at Kukdong in Mexico." Writers Guild of America West, Los Angeles. Unpublished ms.

Hochschild, Arlie Russell. 2016a. "The Ecstatic Edge of Politics: Sociology and Donald Trump." *Contemporary Sociology* 45:683–689.

———. 2016b. *Strangers in Their Own Land: Anger and Mourning on the American Right*. New York: New Press.

Horowitz, Adam, and Philip Weiss. 2010. "The Boycott Divestment Sanctions Movement." *The Nation*, June 28, pp. 11–17.

Horwitz, Robert B. 2013. *America's Right: Anti-establishment Conservatism from Goldwater to the Tea Party*. Malden, MA: Polity.

Human Rights Watch. 1997. "Corporations and Human Rights: Freedom of Association in a Maquila in Guatemala." Human Rights Watch, March 1. Accessed June 27, 2019. https://www.hrw.org/report/1997/03/01/freedom-association-maquila-guatemala.

Jamieson, Dave. 2016. "Watchdog Group Kept Out of Nike Supplier's Factory after Worker Strike." Huffington Post, March 3. Accessed June 28, 2016. http://www.huffingtonpost.com/entry/nike-labor-rights-vietnam_us_56d893f2e4b0000de403b7d0.

Jaschik, Scott. 2006. "Codes Don't Work." *Inside Higher Ed*, September 28. Accessed September 31, 2009. http://www.insidehighered.com/news/2006/09/28/wrc.

Jasper, James M. 1997. *The Art of Moral Protest: Culture, Biography, and Creativity in Social Movements*. Chicago: University of Chicago Press.

———. 2004. "A Strategic Approach to Collective Action: Looking for Agency in Social-Movement Choices." *Mobilization* 9:1–16.

———. 2006. *Getting Your Way: Strategic Dilemmas in the Real World*. Chicago: University of Chicago Press.

———. 2012. "Introduction: From Political Opportunity Structures to Strategic Interaction." In *Contention in Context: Political Opportunities and the Emergence of Protest*, edited by Jeff Goodwin and James M. Jasper, 1–33. Stanford, CA: Stanford University Press.

Jasper, James M., and Jane Poulsen. 1993. "Fighting Back: Vulnerabilities, Blunders, and Countermobilization by the Targets in Three Animal Rights Campaigns." *Sociological Forum* 8:639–657.

Jessup, David, and Michael E. Gordon. 2000. "Organizing in Export Processing Zones: The Bibong Experience in the Dominican Republic." In *Transnational Cooperation among Labor Unions*, edited by Michael E. Gordon and :Lowell. Turner, 179–201. Ithaca, NY: Cornell University Press.

June, Audrey Williams. 2006. "8 Colleges Sign onto Anti-sweatshop Plan but Worry over Antitrust Issues." *Chronicle of Higher Education*, March 17, p. A38.

Juravich, Tom, and Kate Bronfenbrenner. 1999. *Ravenswood: The Steelworkers' Victory and the Revival of American Labor*. Ithaca, NY: Cornell University Press.

Katzenstein, Mary Fainsod. 1998. *Faithful and Fearless: Moving Feminist Protest inside the Church and the Military*. Princeton, NJ: Princeton University Press.

Kazin, Michael. 1995. *The Populist Persuasion: An American History*. New York: Basic.

Keck, Margaret E., and Kathryn Sikkink. 1998. *Activists beyond Borders: Advocacy Networks in International Politics*. Ithaca, NY: Cornell University Press.

Kelderman, Eric. 2017. "Sanctuary Campus." *Chronicle of Higher Education*, February 26. Accessed June 8, 2018. https://www.chronicle.com/article/Sanctuary-Campus/239289.

King, Brayden G. 2008. "A Political Mediation Model of Corporate Response to Social Movement Activism." *Administrative Science Quarterly* 53:395–421.

King, Leslie. 2008. "Ideology, Strategy and Conflict in a Social Movement Organization: The Sierra Club Immigration Wars." *Mobilization* 13:45–61.

Kitroeff, Natalie. 2014. "Colleges Cut Ties with Apparel Maker over Worker Safety." October 20. Bloomberg. Accessed June 21, 2016. http://www.bloomberg.com/news/articles/2014-10-20/students-push-cornell-to-end-vf-corp-deals-over-labor-practices.

Klein, Naomi. 1999. *No Logo: Taking Aim at the Brand Bullies*. New York: Picador.

Kniffin, Kevin. 2000a. "Give Me an $: Moonlighting in the Company Boardroom." In *Campus, Inc.: Corporate Power in the Ivory Tower*, edited by Geoffrey D. White, 157–170. Amherst, NY: Prometheus.

———. 2000b. "The Goods at Their Worst: Campus Procurement in the Global Pillage." In *Campus, Inc.: Corporate Power in the Ivory Tower*, edited by Geoffrey D. White, 36–50. Amherst, NY: Prometheus.

Kolowich, Steve. 2018. "The American Campus, under Siege." *Chronicle of Higher Education,* March 4. Accessed June 4, 2018. https://www.chronicle.com/article/Colleges-Are-Under-Fire-They/242635.

Koopmans, Ruud. 2005. "The Missing Link between Structure and Agency: Outline of an Evolutionary Approach to Social Movements." *Mobilization* 10:19–35.

Korzeniewicz, Miguel. 1994. "Commodity Chains and Marketing Strategies: Nike and the Global Athletic Footwear Industry." In *Commodity Chains and Global Capitalism*, edited by Gary Gereffi and Miguel Korzeniewicz, 247–265. Westport, CT: Praeger.

Krupa, Gregg. 1999. "The Battle Cry against Sweatshops Resounds across College Campuses: Activists Score in Campaign Targeting Athletic Retailers." *Boston Globe*, April 18, p. F1. Accessed April 15, 2009. http://www.lexisnexis.com.

Kurwa, Rahim. 2015. "Why Invest in Occupation?" *Inside Higher Ed*, December 22. Accessed June 12, 2018. https://www.insidehighered.com/views/2015/12/22/campus-divestment-activists-arent-secret-haters-who-support-violence-essay.

Levin, Andy. 1996. "Race, Class and Union Summer." *Poverty and Race*, December 31, p. 3. Accessed January 2, 2010. http://proquest.umi.com.

Levin-Waldman, Oren M. 2005. *The Political Economy of the Living Wage: A Study of Four Cities*. Armonk, NY: M. E. Sharpe.

Lewis, Ruth, Susan Marine, and Kathryn Kenney. 2018. "'I Get Together with My Friends and Try to Change It:' Young Feminist Students Resist 'Laddism,' 'Rape Culture' and 'Everyday Sexism.'" *Journal of Gender Studies* 27:56–72.

Locke, Richard M., Matthew Amengual, and Akshay Mangla. 2009. "Virtue out of Necessity? Compliance, Commitment, and the Improvement of Labor Conditions in Global Supply Chains." *Politics and Society* 37:319–351.

Locke, Richard M., Fei Qin, and Alberto Brause. 2007. "Does Monitoring Improve Labor Standards? Lessons from Nike." *Industrial and Labor Relations Review* 61:3–31.

Luce, Stephanie. 2014. *Labor Movements: Global Perspectives*. Malden, MA: Polity.

Luders, Joseph. 2006. "The Economics of Movement Success: Business Responses to Civil Rights Mobilization." *American Journal of Sociology* 111:963–998.

Lukes, Steven. 2005. *Power: A Radical View*, 2d ed. New York: Palgrave Macmillan.

MacLaren, Caitlin. 2013. "Adidas Caves, Pays Garment Workers What They're Owed." Labor Notes, May 2. Accessed May 17, 2018. http://labornotes.org/blogs/2013/05/adidas-caves-pays-garment-workers-what-they-re-owed.

Maney, Gregory M. 2012. "Agreeing for Different Reasons: Ideology, Strategic Differences, and Coalition Dynamics in the Northern Ireland Civil Rights Movement." In *Strategies for Social Change*, edited by Gregory M. Maney, Rachel V. Kutz-Flamenbaum, Deana A. Rohlinger, and Jeff Goodwin, 170–196. Minneapolis: University of Minnesota Press.

Manheim, Jarol B. 2001. *The Death of a Thousand Cuts: Corporate Campaigns and the Attack on the Corporation*. Mahwah, NJ: Lawrence Elbaum.

Marklein, Mary Beth. 1999. "Sweatshop Foes Form Alliance of Universities." *USA Today*, October 20, p. 4D. Accessed April 15, 2009. http://www.lexisnexis.com.

———. 2015. "Universities Worldwide Face Increasing Pressure to Drop Fossil-Fuel Investments." *Chronicle of Higher Education*, April 1. Accessed June 12, 2018. https://www.chronicle.com/article/Universities-Worldwide-Face/229021.May, Patrick. 2000. "University Says No to Nike: And the Company, which Makes Clothing for Oregon School's Teams, Takes Back $30-Million Gift." *Montreal Gazette*, June 4, p. C4. Accessed April 15, 2009. http://www.lexisnexis.com.

McAdam, Doug. (1982) 1999. *Political Process and the Development of Black Insurgency, 1930–1970*, 2d ed. Chicago: University of Chicago Press.

———. 1983. "Tactical Innovation and the Pace of Insurgency." *American Sociological Review* 48:735–754.

———. 1986. "Recruitment to High-Risk Activism: The Case of Freedom Summer." *American Journal of Sociology* 92:64–90.

———. 1996. "Conceptual Origins, Current Problems, Future Directions." In *Comparative Perspectives on Social Movements: Political Opportunities, Mobilizing Structures, and Cultural Framings*, edited by Doug McAdam, John D. McCarthy, and Mayer N. Zald, 23–40. New York: Cambridge University Press.

———. (1999) 2004. "Revisiting the U.S. Civil Rights Movement: Toward a More Synthetic Understanding of the Origins of Contention." In *Rethinking Social Movements: Structure, Meaning, and Emotion*, edited by J. Goodwin and J. M. Jasper, 201–232. New York: Rowman and Littlefield.

McAdam, Doug, John D. McCarthy, and Mayer N. Zald, ed. 1996. *Comparative Perspectives on Social Movements: Political Opportunities, Mobilizing Structures, and Cultural Framings*. New York: Cambridge University Press.

McAdam, Doug, Sidney Tarrow, and Charles Tilly. 2001. *Dynamics of Contention*. New York: Cambridge University Press.

McCammon, Holly J. 2003. "'Out of the Parlors and into the Streets': The Changing Tactical Repertoire of the U.S. Women's Suffrage Movements." *Social Forces* 81:787–818.

———. 2012. *The U.S. Women's Jury Movement and Strategic Adaptation: A More Just Verdict.* New York: Cambridge University Press.

McCammon, Holly, Soma Chaudhuri, Lynda Hewitt, Courtney Sanders Muse, Harmony D. Newman, Carrie Lee Smith, and Teresa M. Terrell. 2008. "Becoming Full Citizens: The U.S. Women's Jury Rights Campaign, the Pace of Reform, and Strategic Adaptation." *American Journal of Sociology* 113:1104–1147.

Meyer, David S. 2004. "Protest and Political Opportunities." *Annual Review of Sociology* 30:125–145.

Micheletti, Michele. 2003. *Political Virtue and Shopping: Individuals, Consumerism, and Collective Action.* New York: Palgrave Macmillan.

Micheletti, Michele, Andreas Follesdal, and Dietland Stolle, ed. 2004. *Politics, Products, and Markets: Exploring Political Consumerism Past and Present.* New Brunswick, NJ: Transaction.

Miller, John. 2014. "After Horror, Change?" *Dollars and Sense*, September–October, pp. 9–11.

Moody, Kim. 1997. *Workers in a Lean World: Unions in the International Economy.* New York: Verso.

Morris, Aldon D. 1984. *The Origins of the Civil Rights Movement: Black Communities Organizing for Change.* New York: Free Press.

———. 1993. "Birmingham Confrontation Reconsidered: An Analysis of the Dynamics and Tactics of Mobilization." *American Sociological Review* 58:621–636.

Najmabadi, Shannon. 2016a. "Could Colleges Become Sanctuaries for Undocumented Immigrants?" *Chronicle of Higher Education*, November 17. Accessed June 8, 2018. https://www.chronicle.com/article/Could-Colleges-Become/238442.

———. 2016b. "How Colleges Are Responding to Demands that They Become 'Sanctuary Campuses.'" *Chronicle of Higher Education*, December 2. Accessed June 8, 2018. https://www.chronicle.com/article/How-Colleges-Are-Responding-to/238553.

Nepstad, Sharon Erickson, and Stellan Vinthagen. 2012. "Strategic Choices in Cross-National Movements: A Comparison of the Swedish and British Plowshares Movements." In *Strategies for Social Change*, edited by Gregory M. Maney, Rachel V. Kutz-Flamenbaum, Deana A. Rohlinger, and Jeff Goodwin, 263–284. Minneapolis: University of Minnesota Press.

New, Jake. 2014. "The 'Yes Means Yes' World." *Inside Higher Ed*, October 17. Accessed June 7, 2018. https://www.insidehighered.com/news/2014/10/17/colleges-across-country-adopting-affirmative-consent-sexual-assault-policies.

Nova, Scott. 2007a. "Designated Suppliers Program—Update." Worker Rights Consortium. Accessed March 3, 2010. http://www.workersrights.org/dsp/012208_DSP_update.html.

———. 2007b. "Severance Agreement at BJ&B (Dominican Republic)." Worker Rights Consortium, May 30. Accessed February 16, 2010. http://www.workersrights.org/freports/bjandb.asp.

———. 2011. "WRC Communication to Universities Concerning DSP Business Review Letter." Worker Rights Consortium, December 16. Accessed September 4, 2015. http://www.workersrights.org/university/memo/121611.html.

———. 2014. "Testimony of Scott Nova, Hearing on 'Prospects for Democratic Reconciliation and Improving Workers' Rights in Bangladesh,' Senate Committee on Foreign Relations." Worker Rights Consortium, February 11. Accessed June 23, 2016. http://www.workersrights.org/university/Nova%20Testimony%202.11.14.pdf.

———. 2015. "WRC Memo: Nike Wants to Keep Independent Monitors Out of Its Factories." Worker Rights Consortium, December 7. Accessed June 28, 2016. http://www.workersrights.org/university/memo/120715.html.

Oberschall, Anthony. 1996. "Opportunities and Framing in the Eastern European Revolts of 1989." In *Comparative Perspectives on Social Movements: Political Opportunities, Mobilizing Structures, and Cultural Framings*, edited by D. McAdam, J. D. McCarthy, and M. N. Zald, 93–121. New York: Cambridge University Press.

Olesen, Thomas. 2005. *International Zapatismo: The Construction of Solidarity in the Age of Globalization*. New York: Zed.

Oliver, Pamela E., and Hank Johnston. 2000. "What a Good Idea! Ideologies and Frames in Social Movement Research." *Mobilization* 5:37–54.

O'Neill, James M. 2000. "Penn Students Are Staying Put to Protest Labor-Group Backing." *Philadelphia Inquirer*, February 12, p. B03. Accessed April 15, 2009. http://www.lexisnexis.com.

O'Rourke, Dara. 2003. "Outsourcing Regulation: Analyzing Nongovernmental Systems of Labor Standards and Monitoring." *Policy Studies Journal* 31:1–29.

Pallas, Christopher L. 2017. "Inverting the Boomerang: Examining the Legitimacy of North-South-North Campaigns in Transnational Advocacy." *Global Networks* 17:281–299.

Pangsapa, Piya. 2007. *Textures of Struggle: The Emergence of Resistance among Garment Workers in Thailand*. Ithaca, NY: Cornell University Press.

Pearson, Ruth, and Gill Seyfang. 2001. "New Hope or False Dawn? Voluntary Codes of Conduct, Labour Regulation and Social Policy in a Globalizing World." *Global Social Policy* 1:49–78.

Piven, Frances Fox, and Richard Cloward. 1977. *Poor People's Movements: Why They Succeed, How They Fail*. New York: Vintage.

Polletta, Francesca. 2002. *Freedom Is an Endless Meeting: Democracy in American Social Movements*. Chicago: University of Chicago Press.

———. 2005. "How Participatory Democracy Became White: Culture and Organizational Choice." *Mobilization* 10:271–288.

Rabach, Eileen, and Eun Mee Kim. 1994. "Where Is the Chain in Commodity Chains? The Service Sector Nexus." In *Commodity Chains and Global Capitalism*, edited by G. Gereffi and M. Korzeniewicz, 123–141. Westport, CT: Praeger.

Rahman, Md Zillur. 2014. "Accord on 'Fire and Building Safety in Bangladesh': A Breakthrough Agreement?" *Nordic Journal of Working Life Studies* 4:69–74.

Redden, Elizabeth. 2016a. "Can a Campus Be a Sanctuary?" *Inside Higher Ed*, November 15. Accessed June 7, 2018. https://www.insidehighered.com/news/2016/11/15/growing-movement-calls-universities-limit-their-cooperation-federal-immigration.

———. 2016b. "What's in a Name?" *Inside Higher Ed*, December 2. Accessed June 7, 2018. https://www.insidehighered.com/news/2016/12/02/outlining-commitments-undocumented-immigrant-students-some-presidents-avoid-term.

———. 2018. "DACA Lives, but for How Long?" *Inside Higher Ed*. March 5. Accessed June 8, 2018. https://www.insidehighered.com/news/2018/03/05/daca-continues-now-colleges-and-students-face-uncertainties.

Rhoades, Gary, and Sheila Slaughter. 1997. "Academic Capitalism, Managed Professionals, and Supply-Side Higher Education." *Social Text* 15:9–38.

Robbins, Allie. 2013. "The Future of the Student Antisweatshop Movement: Providing Access to U.S. Courts for Workers Worldwide." *American University Labor and Employment Law Forum* 3:120–151.

Robinson, William I. 2003. *Transnational Conflicts: Central America, Social Change, and Globalization.* New York: Verso.

Rodríguez-Garavito, César A. 2005. "Global Governance and Labor Rights: Codes of Conduct and Anti-sweatshop Struggles in Global Apparel Factories in Mexico and Guatemala." *Politics and Society* 33:203–233.

Rosen, Ellen Israel. 2002. *Making Sweatshops: The Globalization of the U.S. Apparel Industry.* Berkeley: University of California Press.

Ross, Andrew, ed. 1997. *No Sweat: Fashion, Free Trade, and the Rights of Garment Workers.* New York: Verso.

Ross, Robert J. S. 2004. *Slaves to Fashion: Poverty and Abuse in the New Sweatshops.* Ann Arbor: University of Michigan Press.

———. 2006. "A Tale of Two Factories: Successful Resistance to Sweatshops and the Limits of Firefighting." *Labor Studies Journal* 30:65–85.

Ross, Robert J. S., and Kent C. Trachte. 1990. *Global Capitalism: The New Leviathan.* Albany: State University of New York Press.

Ryan, Charlotte. 1991. *Prime Time Activism: Media Strategies for Grassroots Organizing.* Boston: South End Press.

Ryan, Charlotte, Karen Jeffreys, and Linda Blozie. 2012. "Raising Public Awareness of Domestic Violence: Strategic Communication and Movement Building." In *Strategies for Social Change*, edited by Gregory M. Maney, Rachel V. Kutz-Flamenbaum, Deana A. Rohlinger, and Jeff Goodwin, 61–92. Minneapolis: University of Minnesota Press.

Schmidt, Peter. 2013. "Advocates for Adjunct Instructors Think Broadly in Search for Allies." *Chronicle of Higher Education*, November 18. Accessed June 8, 2018. https://www.chronicle.com/article/Advocates-for-Adjunct/143139.

Schurman, Rachel. 2004. "Fighting 'Frankenfoods': Industry Opportunity Structures and the Efficacy of the Anti-biotech Movement in Western Europe." *Social Problems* 51:243–268.

Sculos, Bryant William, and Sean Noah Walsh. 2016. "The Counterrevolutionary Campus: Herbert Marcuse and the Suppression of Student Protest Movements." *New Political Science* 38:516–532.

Segran, Elizabeth. 2017. "Here's How Georgetown Convinced Nike to Make a Major Concession on Workers' Rights." *Fast Company*, August 30. Accessed June 21, 2019. https://www.fastcompany.com/40460462/heres-how-georgetown-convinced-nike-to-make-a-major-concession-on-workers-rights.

Seidman, Gay W. 2007. *Beyond the Boycott: Labor Rights, Human Rights, and Transnational Activism.* New York: Russell Sage Foundation.

Shriver, Thomas E., and Alison E. Adams. 2010. "Cycles of Repression and Tactical Innovation: The Evolution of Environmental Dissidence in Communist Czechoslovakia." *Sociological Quarterly* 51:329–354.

Sikkink, Kathryn. 2005. "Patterns of Dynamic Multilevel Governance and the Insider-Outsider Coalition." In *Transnational Protest and Global Activism*, edited by

Donatella della Porta and Sidney Tarrow, 151–173. Lanham, MD: Rowman and Littlefield.

Skidmore, Thomas E., and Peter H. Smith. 2005. *Modern Latin America*, 6th ed. New York: Oxford University Press.

Slaughter, Sheila, and Gary Rhoades. 2004. *Academic Capitalism and the New Economy: Markets, States, and Higher Education.* Baltimore, MD: John Hopkins University Press.

Snow, David A., and Robert D. Benford. 1988. "Ideology, Frame Resonance, and Participant Mobilization." *International Social Movements Research* 1:197–217.

Snyder, Susan. 2000. "Penn Agrees to Review Labor Group: Pending a Committee Study, School Will Withdraw from an Association That Students Protested." *Philadelphia Inquirer*, February 16, p. B01. Accessed April 15, 2009. http://www.lexisnexis.com.

Soule, Sarah A. 2009. *Contention and Corporate Social Responsibility.* New York: Cambridge University Press.

Staggenborg, Suzanne. 1989. "Stability and Innovation in the Women's Movement: A Comparison of Two Movement Organizations." *Social Problems* 36:75–92.

Steck, Henry. 2003. "Corporatization of the University: Seeking Conceptual Clarity." *Annals of the American Academy of Political and Social Science* 585:66–83.

Stewart, Julie. 2004. "When Local Troubles Become Transnational: The Transformation of a Guatemalan Indigenous Rights Movement." *Mobilization* 9:259–278.

Stone, Clarence N. 1989. *Regime Politics: Governing Atlanta, 1946–1988.* Lawrence: University Press of Kansas.

Stone, Clarence N., Marion E. Orr, and David Imbroscio. 1991. "The Reshaping of Urban Leadership in U.S. Cities: A Regime Analysis." In *Urban Life in Transition*, vol. 39, *Urban Affairs Annual Reviews*, edited by Mark Gottdiener and Chris G. Pickvance, 222–239. Newbury Park, CA: Sage.

SweatFree Communities. 2007. "Updates 2007." Accessed August 7, 2011. http://www.sweatfree.org/campaign_news07.

———. 2011. "Advisory Board." Accessed August 1, 2011. http://www.sweatfree.org/leadership_board.

SweatFree Purchasing Consortium. 2012. "Santa Fe Joins Sweatfree Purchasing Consortium," August 14. Accessed June 12, 2016. http://buysweatfree.org/member_news#Santa%20Fe%20joins.

———. 2016a. "SweatFree Purchasing Consortium Board of Directors." Accessed June 14, 2016. http://buysweatfree.org/leaders.

———. 2016b. "Uniform Management Program Cooperative Contract." Accessed June 9, 2017. http://buysweatfree.org/uniform_management_program.

———. 2017. "SweatFree Purchasing Consortium Members." Accessed June 6, 2017. http://buysweatfree.org/contact.

Sweat-Free Stanford Campaign. 2007. "FLA 3.0 vs. DSP: Sweat-Free Stanford's Position." Accessed June 18, 2014. https://web.archive.org/web/20140618221345/http://www.stanford.edu/group/sweatfree/report.pdf.

Tarrow, Sidney. 1998. *Power in Movement: Social Movements and Contentious Politics*, 2d ed. New York: Cambridge University Press.

Taylor, Verta, and Nella Van Dyke. 2004. "'Get Up, Stand Up': Tactical Repertoires of Social Movements." In *The Blackwell Companion to Social Movements*, edited by D. A. Snow, S. A. Soule, and H. Kriesi, 262–293. Malden, MA: Blackwell.

Tilly, Charles. 1978. *From Mobilization to Revolution*. New York: McGraw-Hill.

Tsogas, George. 2009. "International Labour Regulation: What Have We Really Learnt So Far?" *Relations Industrielles/Industrial Relations* 64:75–94.

United Students Against Sweatshops. 2000. "Minutes from the Worker Rights Consortium Founding Conference." Worker Rights Consortium. Accessed May 10, 2009. http://www.workersrights.org/about/history.asp.

———. 2009a. "About Campus Community Solidarity." Accessed February 2, 2009. http://www.studentsagainstsweatshops.org/index.php?option=com_content&task=view&id=59&Itemid=69.

———. 2009b. "History and Formation of USAS." Accessed January 31, 2009. http://www.studentsagainstsweatshops.org/index.php?option=com_content&task=view&id=21&Itemid=88888915.

———. 2016. "Campus Worker Justice." Accessed June 19, 2016. http://usas.org/campaigns/campus-worker-justice.

———. n.d.(a). "Campus Worker Justice." Washington, DC: United Students Against Sweatshops. Accessed June 8, 2018. http://usas.org/campaigns/campus-worker-justice.

———. n.d.(b). "Tag Archives: Adjunct Faculty." Washington, DC: United Students Against Sweatshops. Accessed June 8, 2018. http://usas.org/tag/adjunct-faculty.

———. n.d.(c). "Tag Archives: Campus Workers." Washington, DC: United Students Against Sweatshops. Accessed June 8, 2018. http://usas.org/tag/campus-workers.

Van Dyke, Nella, and Marc Dixon. 2013. "Activist Human Capital: Skills Acquisition and the Development of Commitment to Social Movement Activism." *Mobilization* 18:197–212.

Van Dyke, Nella, Marc Dixon, and Helen Carlon. 2007. "Manufacturing Dissent: Labor Revitalization, Union Summer and Student Protest." *Social Forces* 86:193–214.

Wahlström, Mattias, and Abby Peterson. 2006. "Between the State and the Market: Expanding the Concept of 'Political Opportunity Structure.'" *Acta Sociologica* 49:363–377.

Waugh, William L., Jr. 2003. "Issues in University Governance: More 'Professional' and Less Academic." *Annals of the American Academy of Political and Social Science* 585:84–96.

Weiss, Robert S. 1994. *Learning from Strangers: The Art and Method of Qualitative Interview Studies*. New York: Free Press.

Wells, Don. 2007. "Too Weak for the Job: Corporate Codes of Conduct, Non-governmental Organizations and the Regulation of International Labour Standards." *Global Social Policy* 7:51–74.

Westby, David L. 2002. "Strategic Imperative, Ideology and Frame." *Mobilization* 7:287–304.

White, Geoffrey D., ed. 2000. *Campus, Inc.: Corporate Power in the Ivory Tower*. Amherst, NY: Prometheus.

Wilson, Robin. 2016. "'Yes' to Sex? Students Consider What That Looks and Sounds Like." *Chronicle of Higher Education*, May 18. Accessed June 7, 2018. https://www.chronicle.com/article/Yes-to-Sex-Students/236510.

Worker Rights Consortium. 2001a. "WRC Assessment re Complaint against New Era Cap Co., Inc. (Derby, NY, USA): Preliminary Findings and Recommendations." Accessed July 5, 2009. http://www.workersrights.org/Freports/NewEraCap_NY.asp.

———. 2001b. "WRC Investigation re Complaint against Kukdong (Mexico): Prelimi- nary Findings and Recommendations." Accessed June 29, 2009. http://www.work ersrights.org/Freports/Kukdong.asp.

———. 2001c. "WRC Investigation re Complaint against Kukdong (Mexico): Report and Recommendations." Accessed June 29, 2009. http://www.workersrights.org/ Freports/Kukdong.asp.

———. 2002. "WRC Assessment re Complaint against New Era Cap Co., Inc. (Derby, NY, USA): Report and Recommendations." Accessed July 4, 2009. http://www.work ersrights.org/Freports/NewEraCap_NY.asp.

———. 2007a. "Frequently Asked Questions." Accessed June 1, 2009. http://www.work ersrights.org/faq.asp.

———. 2007b. "Governance." Accessed June 1, 2009. http://www.workersrights.org/ about/govern.asp.

———. 2007c. "Model Code of Conduct." Accessed June 1, 2009. http://www.workers rights.org/university/coc.asp.

———. 2007d. "WRC Investigative Protocol." Accessed June 17, 2009. http://www.work ersrights.org/Freports/investigative_protocols.asp.

———. 2014. "WRC Labor Rights Verification." Accessed January 21, 2015. http://www .workersrights.org/verification/index.asp.

———. 2017. "WRC Memo." August 30. Accessed June 20, 2019. http://www.work ersrights.org/university/memo/083017.html.

Zald, Mayer N. 2000. "Ideologically Structured Action: An Enlarged Agenda for Social Movement Research." *Mobilization* 5:1–16.

Zarocostas, John. 2009. "U.N. Expert Expresses Doubt on Monitoring." *Women's Wear Daily*, June 4.

Zernike, Kate. 1999. "College Activism, '90s Style, Unites Two Sides: Students, Admin- istrators Agree on Protests." *Boston Globe*, February 15, p. A1. Accessed January 29, 2009. http://www.lexisnexis.com.

Index

Page numbers followed by *f* refer to figures.

Abad, Carmencita (Chie), 210
Abrams, Ken, 83, 107, 132, 163
Accord on Fire and Building Safety in Bangladesh, 4, 32, 182, 200, 201–202, 216, 224, 225
Adams, Sam, 213
Adidas, 47, 116, 126, 153, 175, 198, 225
affirmative consent, xviii
AFL-CIO (American Federation of Labor–Congress of Industrial Organizations), 61, 101; Agricultural Workers Organizing Committee, 9–10; Solidarity Center, 92, 142, 147, 149, 150, 167, 172, 187
AIP (Apparel Industry Partnership), 100–101
Albuquerque, Rafael, 159
Alimi, Eitan, 8, 11, 13
Alliance for Bangladesh Worker Safety, 202, 224
Alta Gracia, 182, 194, 196, 225
Alvarado, David, 75, 90
Amengual, Matthew, 103n2, 107
American Apparel, 204, 205n1
American Federation of Labor–Congress of Industrial Organizations. *See* AFL-CIO
Andrews, Kenneth, 7–8, 76, 229

Ann Taylor (company), 177
Anoushiravani, Mitra, 104
anti-sweatshop movement: as a black box, 11, 15, 226; contributions to the literature on, 26–29; critique of FLA and CSR by, 104–111, 138; future of, 223–225; globalization implications for, 42–44; origins/rise of, 2–3, 29–30, 57–59; unanswered questions about, 232–236. *See also* student activism; *specific organizations*
antitrust laws, 191, 198–199
apartheid, struggles against, 67
apparel industry: structural change in, 193–195; structure of, 29, 38–42. *See also* Apparel Industry Partnership (AIP); brands; *specific companies*
Apparel Industry Partnership (AIP), 100–101
Appelbaum, Richard, 82
Aramark, 47
Armbruster-Sandoval, Ralph, 27, 168
Armstrong, Elizabeth, 18, 21, 230
Asher, Mark, 126
Atlixco, Puebla (Mexico). *See* Kukdong
Austin, Texas, 220
Australian FairWear, 27

Bangladesh, 147, 153. *See also* Accord on
     Fire and Building Safety in Bangladesh;
     Alliance for Bangladesh Worker Safety
Bard College, 124
Barenberg, Mark, 138
Barnes and Noble, 47
Barr, Josh, 126
Barrientos, Stephanie, 104–105
Bartlett, Andrew Kang, 205–206
Bas, Nikki, 116
Benjamin, Medea, 116
Berkeley, California, 220
Bernstein, Mary, 18, 21, 230
Bibong, 159
biographical availability, xvi
Birmingham civil rights protests, 7
BJ&B, 137, 150–151, 153, 155, 170, 181, 191
Black Lives Matter, xvi
Black Panther Party, 233
Blasi, Jeremy, 133, 136, 169–170
boomerang effect, 167–169, 179, 182
Bonacich, Edna, 82
Bounds, Wendy, 38
boycotts, 19, 24, 25, 48, 62, 64, 82, 148, 174
Brakken, Eric, 51, 60, 63, 86, 106, 115,
     118, 119–121, 177
brand image, 98, 117, 136, 207, 228, 234;
     as major asset, 38–39, 116; solidarity
     campaigns and, 146, 155, 160, 161–164,
     169, 171, 179
brands: countermeasures by, 97–114; use
     of term, 154. *See also* apparel industry;
     brand image; *specific brands*
Brause, Alberto, 98
Bronfenbrenner, Kate, 61
Brooks, Ethel, 27
Brown University, 89, 123–124, 125–126
Budweiser, 62
Bureau Veritas, 108–109
Bush, George W., 198
business unionism, x

Caine, Alyssa, 119, 122, 124, 126
Cambodia, 141–142, 157, 177
Camisas Modernas, 35–38, 39
Campus Reform, xvi
CARI (College Apparel Research Initiative),
     176–177
Caterpillar, xix
Catholic Church, 7, 18, 53
Catholic Register, 99

Central America, 2, 27, 40, 57, 119, 204
certification, 4, 31, 102, 104, 105, 106,
     120, 134, 135, 196, 200, 201
Champagne, Jess, 70–71, 115–116
Champion (company), 47
child labor, 2, 58, 63, 104, 105, 232
China, 40, 104, 108–109, 120, 147, 153,
     159, 161, 177
Church, Sarah, 212, 220
Cintas, 207, 211, 221, 225
city governments, 203, 205, 206–209, 217,
     218, 221. *See also* SweatFree Communities
Civil Rights Movement, 7–8, 25, 200, 229,
     233
Claessen, Bjorn, 204–205, 206, 208, 210,
     213–215, 218, 221, 222
Clean Clothes Campaign, 27, 178, 205
climate change, xvi, xix
Clinton, Hillary, xii
Clinton, William (Bill), xii–xiii, 37, 100, 101
Coates, Stephen, 158, 174
Coca-Cola, 47, 52
codes of conduct, 30–31, 32, 48, 52, 67,
     69, 74, 80, 90, 101, 114, 145, 229, 231;
     Designated Suppliers Program and,
     185, 191–192, 194, 195, 196, 198,
     199; early campaigns for, 63–64; Fair
     Labor Association and, 103, 110, 111;
     solidarity campaigns and, 156, 161, 166,
     170, 172; student, xvi–xvii; SweatFree
     Communities and, 203, 204, 205, 214,
     217; Worker Rights Consortium and,
     116–117, 129, 133, 143
collective bargaining, 104, 105, 107. *See
     also* unions
College Apparel Research Initiative
     (CARI), 176–177
colleges and universities: Accord on Fire and
     Building Safety in Bangladesh and, 201;
     characteristics of as facilitators of activ-
     ism, xvi; committees formed by adminis-
     trations of, 25, 74–75, 93, 231; corporate
     social responsibility programs and, 113;
     and corporatization of education, 45–48,
     49–53, 69, 91; countermeasures by
     administrations of, 73–75; democracy's
     influence on, 236; Designated Suppliers
     Program and, 67, 68, 71, 196–199, 200;
     Fair Labor Association and, 102; fight
     for on-campus labor rights, xvii–xviii;
     governance of, 48–53; Ivy League,

70–71, 124; and outsourcing of campus services, 46; and right-wing backlash on campuses, xvi–xvii; sanctuary campuses, xviii; solidarity campaigns and, 146, 151, 154–155; sports schools, 47–48, 124, 126; United Students Against Sweatshops strategy, 66–76; Worker Rights Consortium and, 121–126, 130, 132–133. *See also* student activism
Colombia, 52
Columbia University, 138
commitment-oriented approach, 103n2
Committee on Investment and Social Responsibility, 67
communication, 85, 91–94
Communication Workers of America (CWA), 152–153, 161, 163, 164–165
Communist Party (China), 109, 159
community unionism, xii
Confederación Revolucionaria de Obreros y Campesinos (CROC), 147–150, 156
confidentiality, worker, 103, 108, 138, 141
conflicts of interest, 97n1, 104, 110, 117, 185, 216, 218
conscience constituents, 90, 232
conservativism, xiii–xv
consumers, 6, 26, 30, 38–39, 43, 48, 60, 64, 69, 81, 82, 105, 106, 113, 164, 190, 215
contentious politics, 229
contractors, 39, 40; Camisas Modernas and, 38; Designated Suppliers Program and, 182–183, 185, 191–192, 195; Fair Labor Association and, 101, 110; solidarity campaigns and, 154, 155, 160–161, 167
Contras, 57
cooperative contracts, 209
corporate campaigns, 61, 62, 63, 64, 65; defined, 29; Designated Suppliers Program and, 182; Fair Labor Association and, 116; solidarity campaigns and, 166; Worker Rights Consortium and, 115, 121, 128
corporate social responsibility (CSR) programs, 16, 25, 59, 100, 103, 125, 140, 156, 185, 216, 231; anti-sweatshop movement critique of, 104–111, 138; benefits for industry, 28, 31; as counter-framing, 111–114, 229; limits of, 97–99. *See also specific programs*
corporatization of higher education, 45–48, 49–53, 69, 91; counterweights to, 49–51; variation in degree of, 52

Coughlin, Ginny, 61, 62, 86, 87
counter-framing, 111–114, 229
countermeasures, 25–26, 230, 231, 236; by brands, 97–114; by college administration, 73–75; to solidarity campaigns, 156–157
CROC (Confederación Revolucionaria de Obreros y Campesinos), 147–150, 156
CSR programs. *See* corporate social responsibility (CSR) programs
cultural opportunity structure (COS), 18
CWA (Communication Workers of America), 152–153, 161, 163, 164–165
Czechoslovakian environmental movement, 9

Dale, John, 168
Dalton, Liana, 68, 79–80, 83, 157, 161, 176, 177, 188, 189–190, 194
death squads, 23, 44, 52
decision making, 5, 14, 227–228; democratic (consensual), 5, 11, 16, 30, 91–93, 175–179; in Designated Suppliers Program, 187–188; hierarchical, 5; in solidarity campaigns, 172–179; in United Students Against Sweatshops, 85, 91–94
delegitimation, 25, 43, 61, 62, 230; of college administration, 72, 75, 76; corporate campaigns and, 116; solidarity campaigns and, 146. *See also* legitimacy
della Porta, Donatella, 79
democracy, 43, 159, 235–236
Democratic Leadership Council, xii
Democratic Party, xii–xiii, xiv
Department of Justice, U.S., 191, 198, 199, 200
Department of Labor, U.S., 58, 101
Derby, New York. *See* New Era Cap
Designated Suppliers Program (DSP), 4, 15, 27, 32, 77, 78, 83, 94, 106, 120, 143, 153, 178, 180, 181–202, 203, 214, 216, 217, 218, 225, 227; antitrust laws and, 191, 198–199; campus campaigns for, 67, 68, 71, 196–199, 200; DSP Working Group, 197, 198, 199; ideological shifts in, 195–196; and long-term commitment stipulation, 189, 191–192; origins of, 183–186; strategic innovation and crafting of, 186–190; structural change in the industry and, 193–195; workings of, 191–193

Diamond, Sara, xiii

Dirnbach, Eric, 3, 58, 60, 82, 112, 134, 162, 164, 168, 170, 184, 214, 219, 220

disclosure: of factory locations, 64–65, 99–100, 101, 107, 116, 142, 189; of wages, 189, 190

discursive arenas, 111–112, 113, 231, 232

discursive change, 76, 228–229

discursive opportunity structure (DOS), 18, 19, 21, 24

Disney, 99

disruptive action, xvi–xvii, 7–8, 11, 19, 24, 43, 72–73, 172, 228–229

Dixon, Marc, 43, 85

Dominican Republic, 137, 159, 163, 170–171. *See also* Alta Gracia; BJ&B

DOS (discursive opportunity structure), 18, 19, 21, 24

DSP. *See* Designated Suppliers Program

Duke University, 42, 48, 52–53, 62, 63, 69, 74, 93, 109, 197

economic opportunity structure (EOS), 18, 19, 21

economic recession of 2008, 90, 221

education (on labor issues), 68–70

elites, xi, xiii, xv, 131; colleges and, 49; neoliberalism and, 42; political opportunity structure and, 17, 20, 21, 24, 26, 231

El Monte, California, 2–3, 58

El Salvador, 57, 58, 99, 159, 177–178, 189–190

embedded autonomy, 130–134, 143–144

enabling rights, 104–105, 107, 108, 119, 120

EOS (economic opportunity structure), 18, 19, 21

Epstein, Barbara, 5, 10, 11

EPZs (export-processing zones), 57, 58, 153, 159

Ernst and Young, 106

Esbenshade, Jill, 27, 102, 105, 110–111, 113; *Monitoring Sweatshops*, 106–107

escalation, 70–73, 123

European Clean Clothes Campaign, 27

experience-ideology dialectic, 11–13, 128, 199, 227

export-processing zones (EPZs), 57, 58, 153, 159

Fair Labor Association (FLA), 15, 16, 28, 31, 73, 97, 97n1, 134, 135, 139, 141, 142, 185, 188, 227, 232, 234; anti-sweatshop movement critique of, 104–111, 138; compliance program of, 103n2, 105–109, 198; as a corporate counter-framing, 111–114; corporate power in, 109–111; creation of, 99–102; Designated Suppliers Program and, 192, 197–198; inspections by, 102–103, 107–108, 117, 136–137; operations of, 102–104; solidarity campaigns and, 151; Worker Rights Consortium and, 103, 109, 115–116, 117, 118, 119–120, 121, 123, 124, 125, 128, 130, 131, 132, 133, 143

fair trade movement, 81, 83, 105, 190

FairWear Australia, 27

Featherstone, Liza, 27

Federación Nacional de Trabajadores de Zonas (FENATRAZONAS), 151

feminism, xiv, 7, 18

FENATRAZONAS (Federación Nacional de Trabajadores de Zonas), 151

Ferree, Myra Marx, 18, 19, 21, 231

Fight for 15, xvii

fire alarm model, 31, 119, 128, 134–140

fires, 201. *See also* Accord on Fire and Building Safety in Bangladesh

FLA. *See* Fair Labor Association

Focus on Globalization, 172–173

Foxvog, Liana, 206, 210, 215, 218, 220, 221

frames/framing, 19, 25, 28, 156, 199, 232; counter-, 111–114, 229; defined, 13–14; solidarity campaigns and, 169–172

freedom of association, xvi, 101, 104, 105, 107, 108, 119, 149, 192, 224

freedom of speech, xvi, 236

Gamson, William, 13, 17

Ganz, Marshall, 9, 10–11, 227–228

Gap, The, 57–58, 69, 84, 112, 113, 167, 177, 202

Garwood, Shae, 27, 168

gay rights, xiv, 233

Gee, E. Gordon, 123

Georgetown University, 62, 63, 72, 73, 75, 88–89, 99, 143, 170–171, 197

Gereffi, Gary, 38

Getting Your Way (Jasper), 234

Ghaziani, Amin, 233–234

Gifford, Kathie Lee, 2–3, 58, 59, 100, 113, 162, 232
Global Exchange, 85, 86, 116, 118, 210, 211
Global Fashions, 58
globalization, 223–224, 231–232; implications for activists, 42–44; worker empowerment and, 81–82
global justice movement, 223, 233
Goodwin, Jeff, 19–21, 230
GOS (government opportunity structure), 21
government, 42–43; city, 203, 205, 206–209, 217, 218, 221; Fair Labor Association and, 102, 103; solidarity campaigns and, 146, 159; state, 203, 206, 214, 217, 218, 221. See also nation-states
government opportunity structure (GOS), 21
grand ideology, 78–79
Green, Ken, 99
Group of Twenty, 232
Guatemala, 57, 159. See also Camisas Modernas
guerrilla theater and art, 59, 60, 226
Guess, 62, 113

Hanes, 163
Harrisburg, Pennsylvania, 221
Haverford College, 67, 124
health and safety standards, 63, 104, 191
Hermanson, Jeff, 37, 147, 155, 156, 159, 166, 172–173, 175–176, 177–179
higher education, 45–53. See also colleges and universities
Honduras, 2, 58, 159
Hong Kong, 83, 161
Howald, Jane, 163, 173, 175
Human Rights Watch, 35, 36n1, 37, 166
hunger strikes, 30, 67, 72, 122, 209, 210

ideology, 12–13, 16, 31, 232–233; defined, 12, 14, 78; of Designated Suppliers Program, 189, 195–196, 199; dialectic between experience and, 11–13, 128, 199, 227; frames distinguished from, 13–14; grand, 78–79; instrumentalist perspective compared with, 8, 81, 167, 226–227; worker empowerment, 77–79
ILRF (International Labor Rights Fund), 103, 155, 170

IMF (International Monetary Fund), 223, 232
immigrants, xii, xiv, xv, xvi, xvii, xviii, 2, 41, 58
Immigration and Customs Enforcement, xviii
independent monitoring, 58, 64, 80, 99, 185, 217–218. See also Fair Labor Association (FLA); Worker Rights Consortium (WRC)
Indiana University, 93, 124, 197
Indonesia, 3, 119, 147, 177
industry economic structure (IOS), 18
influence opportunities, 23–24
innovation. See strategic innovation
inspections: by Fair Labor Association, 102–103, 107–108, 117, 136–137; by Worker Rights Consortium, 117, 125, 136–137, 193
institutional memory, 14, 85, 87, 227, 228
instrumentalist perspective, 8, 81, 167, 226–227
Interfaith Center on Corporate Responsibility, 101, 127
International Labor Rights Fund (ILRF), 103, 155, 170
International Monetary Fund (IMF), 223, 232
Internet, 93, 148, 175, 177
intifada, first, 8–9
Israel, xix, 8–9
Ivy League schools, 70–71, 124

Jansport, 201
Japan, 40, 131
Jasper, James, 19–21, 228, 230; Getting Your Way, 234
Jewish community, 212
Jobs with Justice, 152
Joffe-Block, Miriam, 119
Johnson, Lyndon, 8, 229
Johnston, Hank, 14, 78–79
Juravich, Tom, 61
Just Don't Do It Campaign, 60
Just Garments, 189–190

Karp, Roberta, 125
Katzenstein, Mary Fainsod, 7, 18
Keck, Margaret, 167, 168, 170
Kennedy, John F., 229

Keohane, Nan, 52
Kernaghan, Charles, 2, 58, 116, 127
Killer Coke campaign, 52
Klatsky, Bruce, 37
Klein, Naomi, 99
Knight, Phil, 126
Knorr, Zack, 53, 67–68, 71, 74, 84, 88, 89, 90–91, 94, 164, 198
Kukdong, 117, 138–139, 146–150, 151, 153, 155, 156, 159, 170, 181, 191

Land's End, 190
left-wing populism, xiii
legitimacy, 18, 24, 28, 31, 228, 229, 231, 234; of brands, 98; of college admin-istrations, 49, 50, 51; corporate social responsibility programs and, 59, 100, 103; Fair Labor Association and, 116; solidarity campaigns and, 155, 159–165; of United Students Against Sweatshops, 30, 69, 70, 75, 76; of Worker Rights Consortium, 31, 117, 119, 122, 123, 124. See also delegitimation
leverage, 25, 29, 30, 230, 234; campus campaigns and, 66, 73; corporatization and, 45; defined, 24; Designated Suppli-ers Program and, 194–195; globaliza-tion and, 42, 43; licensing agreements and, 48, 59, 61; solidarity campaigns and, 146, 159–165; SweatFree Com-munities and, 207, 210; Worker Rights Consortium and, 117, 126, 129
Levi Strauss (company), 41–42
libertarianism, xiii–xiv
licensing agreements, xvii, xix, 29–30, 31, 43, 59, 60–61, 62, 63, 101; Des-ignated Suppliers Program and, 32, 182–183, 190, 193–195, 200; solidar-ity campaigns and, 146, 147, 150, 160, 164–165, 172, 175; with sports schools, 47–48, 124, 126; SweatFree Communi-ties and, 204; Worker Rights Consor-tium and, 121, 124, 126, 129
living wage, 64, 101, 219; Designated Suppliers Program and, 182, 184–185, 189, 191, 192, 194, 198; Worker Rights Consortium and, 133
Liz Claiborne (company), 113, 125
Locke, Richard, 98, 103n2, 107
Los Angeles, California, 41, 215
Los Angeles Times, 2

Loyola University, 124
Luders, Joseph, 18, 19, 24
Lukes. Steven, 51

Madison, Wisconsin, 208–209, 214, 216, 222. See also University of Wisconsin, Madison
Majtenyi, Cathy, 99
Manager, Vada, 125
Mandarin International, 58
Mangla, Akshay, 103n2, 107
maquiladoras, 84. See also Kukdong
Maquilapolis (film), 210–211
Martin, Andrew, 43
maternity leave, 2
McAdam, Doug, 9, 12, 17–18, 20, 23, 25, 229, 230–231
McCammon, Holly, 9, 11, 12, 233
McGrath, Molly, 75, 87, 90–92, 148, 154
McSpedon, Laura, 62, 70, 72, 73–75, 79, 80, 86, 87, 88–89, 99–100, 118, 133, 135, 158, 162–163, 165, 170–171
media, 2–3, 18, 19, 21, 57–59, 60, 229, 231, 232; Fair Labor Association and, 111–113; solidarity campaigns and, 146, 155; SweatFree Communities and, 209, 210–211
#MeToo, xviii
Mexico, xiii, 40, 41, 117, 147, 210. See also Kukdong
Mexmode, 150, 153, 156, 181, 191
Meyer, David, 13, 17, 23
minimum wage, xvii, 63, 101, 133
missionaries, 107
Mississippi, 7–8
mobilizing opportunities, 23–24, 154–159, 230
monitoring. See independent monitoring
Monitoring Sweatshops (Esbenshade), 106–107
moral traditionalism, xiii–xiv
Morris, Aldon, 7
Muñoz, Marcela, 148

naming and shaming, 61, 160
National Association of College Stores, 197
National Labor Committee (NLC), 2–3, 57–58, 85, 86, 116, 118, 127
nation-states, 17–18, 23, 43, 231–232. See also government
Nau, Michael, 43

Nebel, Gregg, 198

negotiation, 76

neoliberalism, xii, xiv–xv, 41–43, 223–224, 225; in higher education, 45, 46; nation-state role in, 23, 231–232

New Democrats, xii, xiv

New Era Cap, 145, 150, 151–153, 161, 163, 164–165, 169, 170, 173, 175

New Faculty Majority, xvii

New York City, 2, 37, 40–41, 58, 61, 63, 88

New York State, 212, 222. See also New Era Cap

New York Times, 155

NGOs (nongovernmental organizations), 31, 81, 97, 97n1, 101, 102, 103, 106, 118, 120, 166, 187

Nicaragua, 57

Nien Hsing, 172

Nike, 3, 4, 29, 30, 40, 47, 48, 69, 82, 207, 225, 232, 234–235; brand image of, 116, 234; corporate social responsibility programs and, 98, 99, 113; Fair Labor Association and, 101, 111; Just Don't Do It Campaign, 60; solidarity campaigns and, 147, 148–150, 151, 153, 155, 162, 164, 167, 171, 175; Worker Rights Consortium and, 117, 122, 125–126, 139, 143

NLC (National Labor Committee), 2–3, 57–58, 85, 86, 116, 118, 127

nongovernmental organizations (NGOs), 31, 81, 97, 97n1, 101, 102, 103, 106, 118, 120, 166, 187

nonviolent tactics, 8–9, 10

norms, 12, 14, 78, 83–84

North American Free Trade Agreement, xii–xiii

Nova, Scott, 128, 138–139, 184, 189, 202

Obama, Barack, xii, 199

Oberschall, Anthony, 18

Occupied Territories (Palestine), xvi, xix, 8–9

O'Donovan, Leo, 72

Ohio State University, 165

Oliver, Pamela, 14, 78–79

openness/closure (of political system), 17, 23, 231

organization, 9–10; of solidarity campaigns, 172–179; of United Students Against Sweatshops, 85–94

Orth, Valerie, 211, 216

O'Shaughnessy, Brian, 212

outcome standards, 104. See also protective rights

outsourcing, 4, 39–42, 223; Camisas Modernas and, 37–38; on college campuses, 46, 91; Designated Suppliers Program and, 193, 195

overtime, 2, 63, 104

Palestine (Occupied Territories), xvi, xix, 8–9

Palmer, David, 153, 161, 164–165

Partido Revolucionario Institucional (PRI), 147

paternalism, 16, 60, 78, 81, 83, 105

Peace Corps, 107

Peace through Inter-American Community Action (PICA), 204

Pearson, Ruth, 105, 196, 224

people of color. See race and racism

People of Faith Network, 127

Pepsi, 47

Peterson, Abby, 18

Pfordresher, Kate, 127

Philippines, 157

Phillips–Van Heusen (PVH), 35–38, 166

PICA (Peace through Inter-American Community Action), 204

piggyback contracts, 209

Pitzer College, 148

Pizza Hut, 47

Plumb, Amanda, 52, 62–63, 69, 80, 84, 89–90

political opportunity structure (POS), 10, 13, 16–26, 31, 226; in city governments, 206–209; critics in current literature, 17–18, 19–21; defined, 1; Designated Suppliers Program and, 196, 200; elements of, 22f; four aspects of, 17, 20; higher education as, 45–53; problems with current model of, 5–6; revised model of, 21–26, 230–232; solidarity campaigns and, 146, 157–158, 167, 179; supporters in current literature, 16–19; SweatFree Communities and, 203, 206–209; unanswered questions about, 235

Polletta, Francesca, 8, 81, 92, 167, 226

populism, ix, xi, xii–xiv, xvi–xvii, xix

Portland, Oregon, 210–211, 212, 213

POS. *See* political opportunity structure
Presbyterian Church Hunger Program, 205
PRI (Partido Revolucionario Institucional), 147
process rights. *See* enabling rights
Progressive Jewish Alliance, 212
progressive student activism. *See* student activism
protective rights, 104–105, 108, 119, 120
PVH (Phillips–Van Heusen), 35–38, 166

Qin, Fei, 98

race and racism, xii, xiii, xiv, xv, 2
Rana Plaza, 201
Ravenswood Aluminum Corporation, 61–62
Reagan, Ronald, 57
Reebok, 4, 29, 47, 48, 60, 207, 232; Fair Labor Association and, 111; solidarity campaigns and, 147, 148–149, 155, 171; Worker Rights Consortium and, 122, 125, 139
Reich, Robert, 100
religious groups, xii, 53, 57, 204
repression, 17, 20, 23, 24, 25, 26, 44, 97, 146, 156, 157, 231, 234, 236
Retail, Wholesale and Department Store Union, 101
Reville, Nick, 70, 89, 118, 123–124, 134
Reyes, Roselio, 151, 170–171
Rich, Marc, 61–62
right-wing populism, ix, xi, xii–xiv, xvi–xvii, xix
Rodriguez, Kenia, 151, 170–171
Rodriguez-Garavito, César, 104–105
Roeper, Maria, 121, 124–125, 126–127, 134, 140, 142
Ross, Andrew, 27
Ross, Robert J. S., 50n1, 82
Ruggie, John, 98
Russell Athletics, 47, 175
Rutter, Jessica, 42, 48, 50, 81, 82, 83, 158–159, 164, 178, 183–184, 186–187

SAI (Social Accountability International), 97n1, 132n1
Sandinista government, 57
San Francisco, California, 211, 212, 213–214, 216, 219–220
Santa Clara University, 197

Santa Fe, New Mexico, 222
Schilling, David, 127
Schmaedick, Agatha, 107, 110, 119, 135, 137, 139, 140, 142
Schurman, Rachel, 18
Schwartz, Deborah, 211–212, 213, 215
Seidman, Gay, 106, 112
sexual harassment and assault, xvi, xvii, xviii, 2, 104, 151
Seyfang, Gill, 105, 196, 224
Sikkink, Kathryn, 167, 168, 170
Sindicato de Trabajadores de Camisas Modernas (STECAMOSA), 36–37
Sindicato de Trabajadores de la Empresa BJ&B S.A., 151
Sindicato Independiente de Trabajadores de la Empresa Mexmode (SITEMEX), 150
sit-ins, 30, 59, 63, 67, 69, 70, 71, 72–73, 75, 93, 122, 123, 124, 172, 198, 209, 210, 228, 229
Smith, Sally, 104–105
Smith College, 197
snowball sampling, 237–238
Social Accountability International (SAI), 97n1, 132n1
social actors, 21, 22–23, 25, 26, 29, 76, 192, 234
social analysis: of Designated Suppliers Program, 195–196, 199; of worker empowerment, 81–82
social arenas, 19, 20, 21–23, 26, 230, 231; colleges and universities as, 50; globalization and, 42, 43; metaphorical aspect of, 25; solidarity campaigns and, 154–159; SweatFree Communities and, 203, 206, 226; worker empowerment and, 82
social compliance departments, 31, 97, 107
social movement theory, 225–236
social movement unionism, xii, xv
social policy enclaves, 196, 224
social responsibility departments, 132
Sodexho Marriott (Sodexo), xvii, 47
solidarity campaigns, 57, 78, 80, 83–84, 181, 183; boomerang effect and, 167–169, 179; common threads in, 145–146; examples of, 146–154; and fighting framing battles, 169–172; legitimacy and, 155, 159–165; leverage and, 146, 159–165; organization of, 172–179;

social arenas and mobilizing opportunities for, 154–159; strategic model for, 146, 165–172, 179; transnational, 14, 31–32, 145–180; workers' tours and, 170–171

Solidarity Center. *See under* AFL-CIO

Soule, Sarah, 18

Southern Christian Leadership Conference, 233

South Korea, 39, 40, 131, 147, 151

speech, freedom of, xvi, 236

sports schools, 47–48, 124, 126

Staggenborg, Suzanne, 11

Starbucks, 47

state governments, 203, 206, 214, 217, 218, 221. *See also* SweatFree Communities

STECAMOSA (Sindicato de Trabajadores de Camisas Modernas), 36–37

Steffan, Nancy, 133, 135, 137, 141–142, 143, 184–185, 186, 190, 192

Stewart, Julie, 168

STITCH, 27, 119

Stoppard, Caroline, 93–94, 108–109, 122, 171, 195, 197

strategic blunders, 20–21

strategic innovation, 9–10, 11–16, 30–31, 226; cycles of, 4, 15–16, 15f, 32; in Designated Suppliers Program creation, 186–190; in SweatFree Communities, 214–218; in Worker Rights Consortium creation, 115–121

strategic interaction, 20, 25, 230

strategic models, 11–16, 226, 233; defined, 12; for solidarity campaigns, 146, 165–172, 179; for SweatFree Communities, 209

strategizing, 11, 226, 233–235

strategy: current literature on, 6–11; defined, 6–7; elements of, 12f; tactics distinguished from, 6–7, 226; theory of, 225–229; unanswered questions about, 233–235

strikes, 24, 146, 160, 179, 229; Kukdong, 148–150; New Era Cap, 152–153, 161; Tainan Enterprises, 177–178

Stroh's, 62

structural problems and change: Designated Suppliers Program and, 193–195; worker empowerment and, 80, 81–82

student activism, ix, xii, xiii, xv–xix, 236; campus governance and, 48–53; for

Designated Suppliers Program, 198; hunger strikes, 30, 67, 72, 122, 209, 210; sit-ins, 30, 59, 63, 67, 69, 70, 71, 72–73, 75, 93, 122, 123, 124, 172, 198, 209, 210, 228, 229; start of, 59–65; for Worker Rights Consortium, 121–126. *See also* colleges and universities; *specific student organizations*

Student Labor Action Coalition, 60

Student Nonviolent Coordinating Committee, 233

Students for a Democratic Society, 50n1

Sustainable Compliance Initiative, 103n2, 198

SweatFree Communities, ix, xii, 1, 4, 15, 27, 32, 78, 203–222, 224, 226, 229, 232, 235; overview of, 204–206; purchasing campaigns and, 209–214; purchasing implementation and, 218–222; strategic innovation in, 214–218

SweatFree Purchasing Consortium, 4, 203, 205, 207, 210, 215, 216, 218–222, 227

sweatshops: history of, 1–2; tours of, 86–87. *See also* anti-sweatshop movement; apparel industry

Sweatshop Watch, 86, 116, 118

Taco Bell, 47

tactics, 6–10, 59, 226

Tainan Enterprises, 177

Taiwan, 39, 40, 131, 172–173, 177

Tarrow, Sidney, 229

Tazreen Fashion, 201

telecommunications technology, 93, 175–176

Thai immigrants in sweatshop, 2, 58

Thailand, 119

Tijuana, Mexico, 210

Tilly, Charles, 229

Tocco, Trina, 64, 155, 174

tolerant identities, 79

trade secrets, 64, 100

Traub-Werner, Marion, 64–65, 80, 119, 193

Travis County, Texas, 220

Trump, Donald, xi, xv

Turning Point USA, xvi

UFW (United Farm Workers), 9–10

uniform companies and purchasing departments, 207–209, 219–220, 221 unions, x–xii, xiv, xix, 16, 25, 30, 31, 57, 60, 61, 64, 78, 79, 111, 145, 223, 233; attempts to revitalize, xi–xii; business closures and, 32, 181; Camisas Modernas and, 36, 38; China and, 40, 153, 159; corporate social responsibility programs and, 107; decline of, x–xi; Designated Suppliers Program and, 180, 182, 184, 188, 190, 191, 192, 196, 199, 200; Fair Labor Association and, 101, 104; neoliberalism and, 42; on-campus, xvii, 46; retaliation against leaders of, 23, 44, 52; solidarity campaigns and, 83–84, 145, 146, 153, 156, 158, 159, 161, 179, 181; SweatFree Communities and, 204, 214, 217; Vietnam and, 40, 104, 153, 159; Worker Rights Consortium and, 117, 133, 134; "yellow," 156. *See also individual unions*

Union Summer, 61, 62

UNITE, 2–3, 29–30, 58, 59–60, 61–62, 77, 80, 81, 84, 86, 87, 100; and American Apparel, 204–205; crucial role in rise in student activism, 61; Fair Labor Association and, 101, 133; solidarity campaigns and, 151, 171; Worker Rights Consortium and, 118, 127. *See also* UNITE HERE

United Farm Workers (UFW), 9–10

United States Student Association (USSA), 14, 87

United Steelworkers, 61–62

United Students Against Sweatshops (USAS), ix, xii, xv, xvi, xvii–xix, 1, 3–4, 5, 6, 11, 13, 16, 29–31, 44, 45, 49, 57–94, 100, 106, 140, 207, 223, 224, 225, 229, 232, 233, 234, 235; Accord on Fire and Building Safety in Bangladesh and, 201; campus administration countermeasures against, 73–75; campus-level strategy of, 66–76; CARI program of, 176–177; chapter size of, 88–89; conferences of, 87–88; corporate social responsibility programs and, 113; decision making and communication in, 85, 91–94; Designated Suppliers Program and, 183, 184, 185, 187, 188, 189, 190, 191, 193–194, 195, 197–200; education phase of, 68–70; escalation phase of, 70–73, 123; Fair Labor Association and,

102, 116, 121, 128, 141; goal of, 4; lack of literature on, 27; on-campus labor rights and, xvii–xviii; organization of, 85–94; origins of, 57–65; political opportunity structure and, 22, 23; and research methods used by the author, 238; solidarity campaigns and, 145, 146, 147, 148–149, 150, 151, 152, 153, 154, 158, 160, 161, 164–165, 166, 167, 169, 171–172, 173, 174–175, 176–177; SweatFree Communities and, 203, 204, 205, 206, 209, 210, 215–216, 217, 222; training by, 87–88, 90–91; two-level approach of, 27–28; worker empowerment and (*see* worker empowerment); Worker Rights Consortium and, 28–29, 115, 116, 117, 118–119, 121, 122, 124, 125, 126–127, 129, 130, 132, 133–134, 136, 139, 142, 143

UNITE HERE, 14, 58, 70, 82, 85, 112, 162, 184; solidarity campaigns and, 170, 176; SweatFree Communities and, 205, 212, 214; Worker Rights Consortium and, 134. *See also* UNITE

University of Arizona, 63

University of California (UC), 68, 71, 94, 125; at Berkeley, 60, 83

University of Connecticut, 197

University of Maine, Farmington, 197

University of Massachusetts (UMass), 52, 90

University of Michigan, 3, 60, 124, 126

University of North Carolina (UNC), Chapel Hill, 60, 63, 64, 80

University of Oregon, 104, 126

University of Wisconsin (UW), Madison, 51, 60, 63, 72, 73, 75, 79, 87, 89, 90, 92, 124, 197

USAS. *See* United Students Against Sweatshops

U.S./Guatemala Labor Education Project (US/GLEP), 36, 37

U.S. Labor Education in the Americas Project (USLEAP), 36, 37, 57, 86, 158

USSA (United States Student Association), 14, 87

values, 12, 14, 78, 79–81

Van Dyke, Nella, 85

van Heerden, Auret, 143, 197

Verité, 106, 142, 149
VF Corporation, 201
Vietnam, 40, 104, 153, 159

wages, 2, 104, 151; at Camisas Modernas, 35–36; of college campus staff, 46; disclosure of, 189, 190; at Kukdong, 147; living (*see* living wage); minimum, xvii, 63, 101, 133
Wahlström, Mattias, 18
Wall Street Journal, 38
Walmart, 58, 162, 170, 202
Ward, David, 51
War on Poverty, 8
Waugh, William, 49
Weiss, Robert, 237
Western Michigan University, 64
Wheatley, Thomas, 51, 72, 73, 88, 92–93, 116, 121, 127, 132
white middle class, xiv, xv
white working class, ix, x, xi, xii–xv
Wilkerson, Jim, 52, 109–110, 111, 197
women, xii, 2, 147, 151
women's suffrage movement, 233
Wood, Brent, 52, 99, 162, 163, 185–186, 194
worker empowerment, 30, 60, 66, 77–84, 86, 227; as core value, 79–81; corporate social responsibility programs versus, 105; Designated Suppliers Program and, 183, 189, 190, 199; enabling rights and, 105; ideology of, 77–79; norms of action in support of, 83–84; social analysis of, 81–82; solidarity campaigns and, 164, 167, 179; SweatFree Communities and, 203, 204, 215; Worker Rights Consortium and, 120
Worker Rights Consortium (WRC), ix, xii, 1, 4, 5, 15, 16, 27, 28–29, 31, 32, 77, 83, 89, 90, 91, 94, 102, 105, 106, 111, 130–144, 145, 146, 147, 186, 199, 224, 226,

227, 232; Accord on Fire and Building Safety in Bangladesh and, 201; budget of, 132–133; campus campaigns for, 67, 73, 75, 121–126; creation of, 28, 30, 59, 115–129; Designated Suppliers Program and, 182–183, 184, 185, 187, 188, 191, 192–193, 195, 196, 197, 198; embedded autonomy of, 130–134, 143–144; Fair Labor Association and, 103, 109, 115–116, 117, 118, 119–120, 121, 123, 124, 125, 128, 130, 131, 132, 133, 143; and fire alarm model of independent monitoring, 31, 119, 128, 134–140; foundation of, 126–129; inspections by, 117, 125, 136–137, 193; issuing reports and working with companies as part of monitoring strategy of, 140–144; and research methods used by the author, 238; solidarity campaigns and, 149–150, 151, 153, 155, 166, 169–170, 171, 174, 176; strategic innovation in creation of, 115–121; SweatFree Communities and, 203, 205, 214, 215, 216, 217, 218, 220, 221, 222; white paper, 121, 123
working to rule, 152, 152n1
World Bank, 232
World Trade Organization (WTO), 223, 232
Worldwide Responsible Apparel Production (WRAP), 97n1, 132n1
WRC. *See* Worker Rights Consortium
WTO (World Trade Organization), 223, 232

Yale University, 70–71
"yellow" unions, 156
Yupoong company, 151, 153

Zepeda, Evelyn, 148, 151, 175–176
Zoned for Slavery: The Children behind the Label (film), 58

Matthew S. Williams is a lecturer in the Department of Sociology and the Global and International Studies Program at Loyola University Chicago.